Ethics *in the* Professions

Edited by
Rick McDonald
& David Yells

Proceedings of the 8th Annual
Utah Valley State College
Conference by the Faculty

EDITED BY Rick McDonald & David Yells

WE GRATEFULLY ACKNOWLEDGE the support of the Bastian Foundation, the Office of the Vice President for Academic Affairs, and the Office of the Vice President for institutional Advancement. Without their admiration of the work of the faculty at Utah Valley State College, this publication would not be possible.

UTAH VALLEY STATE COLLEGE
Center for the Study of Ethics
Mailstop 243
800 West University Parkway
Orem, UT 84058
www.ethicscenter.info

ISBN: 0-9744261-3-X, 978-0-9744261-3-6
Orem, UT: Utah Valley State College, 2006

DESIGN BY: Don LaVange
PHOTOGRAPHY BY: Don LaVange
PRINTED in the U.S.

Table of Contents

≋ Foreword

David R. Keller
Director, Center for the Study of Ethics

W hen the first Conference by the Faculty was planned, there was no expectation whatsoever that it would blossom into an annual event. The intention at the time was to provide Utah Valley State College faculty a forum to discuss research interests which normally would not be taken up in conservation during classroom discussion, as well as to showcase campus talent which might otherwise go unnoticed. As it turned out, there is so much interesting and worthwhile faculty scholarship going on at UVSC that the conference continued unabated for seven additional years.

As the conference has provided fertile ground for public discussion surrounding faculty scholarship, each year the Center for the Study of Ethics chooses a timely, multidisciplinary topic which can be approached from a wide variety of disciplines. The inaugural Social Construction of Gender conference of 1999 led to Biology in the Twenty-First Century: New Horizons for the Sciences, Humanities, and Business, American Studies, What is Postmodernism?, Sustainability in Theory and Practice, Law, Justice, and Citizenship, Spheres of Globalization, and most recently, on January 19 2006, the Eighth Annual Conference by Faculty, Ethics in the Professions, organized by UVSC faculty Rick McDonald and David P. Yells.

The Eight Annual Conference by Faculty was an outgrowth of the Center's annual Ethics Across the Curriculum Faculty Summer Seminar held May 8-12, 2006, facilitated by Michael S. Pritchard, Professor of Philosophy and Director of the Center for the Study of Ethics in Society at Western Michigan University. Titled Professional Ethics, the seminar addressed the unique ethical challenges professionals face in specific vocational roles in given social frameworks.

Attendees of Eighth Annual Conference by the Faulty were so impressed by the quality of the presentations that Drs. McDonald and Yells have compiled a conference proceedings for future reference. I'm sure that you will be as impressed by the breadth and depth of the papers as I have been.

Experimentation
& The Social Sciences

Dr. Anton Tolman

Historical Review of Unethical Experimentation in Humans

By
Olga Kopp

The use of human beings to understand a particular mechanism of disease or the mode of transmission of such disease(s) has played an important role in medical science. Clinical trials are necessary for the advancement of medical treatments. Throughout history, human subjects have been used to test particular drugs or treatments before they become common use in the medical community. However, questionable uses of human subjects have been documented. In order to protect human subjects, Institutional Review Boards have been designed with strict regulations and guidelines; furthermore, the World Medical Association declaration of Helsinki gives guidelines for the ethical principles for medical research involving humans. The application of these guidelines in different countries varies. In this paper I will discuss examples of unethical conduct in human experimentation, with emphasis in United States history. The paper will also discuss the use of vulnerable individuals in clinical trials, unable to properly understand the actual risks of the trial and the resulting mistrust of the public, leading to the low participation of individuals in clinical trials.

After Robert Koch discovered the bacillus that causes tuberculosis and more and more bacteria were found to be the cause of infections in humans, techniques for bacteriological research were developed. Once the microorganism was isolated, a living organism was necessary to produce the disease and study its course. Since model organisms suitable for this experimentation were not available, physicians studied patients. In many cases, physicians experimented on themselves, especially when they did not believe that microscopic organisms could cause disease. More than forty reports in the transmission of syphilis and gonorrhea in humans were done before it was discovered that monkeys could be used for this purpose, since they could get infected with these diseases. Individuals with genetic and/or mental defects were most commonly used. For example, in 1895 Henry Heiman described successful gonorrheal infections of a 4 and a 16 year old boy (considered idiots) and the additional infection of a 26 year old man who suffered from tuberculosis and was in the late stages of the disease (Heiman, 1895).

At the end of the nineteenth century, in some cases when patients entered a hospital, experimental treatments were performed. Some of those experiments caused damage to the patient. For example, in 1874, a 30 year old woman, Mary Rafferty, entered the Good Samaritan Hospital in Cincinnati. She was suffering from what was diagnosed as a cancerous ulcer in her scalp. Since she was terminally ill, experiments using electrodes were performed on her. The treatments caused pain and suffering to the patient, as described by the doctor who performed the experiments: Roberts Bartholow (Bartholow, 1874). The American

Medical Association condemned Bartholow's experiments because of the suffering inflicted on the patient. Mary Rafferty was feeble-minded and therefore, by our present standards not able to give consent for the experiments. However, Dr. Bartholow insisted that informed consent was given by the patient and therefore the experimental procedure was within the ethical boundaries. Informed consent in the late nineteenth century was an ambiguous concept that doctors sometimes applied when convenient to a particular procedure. Doctors were obliged to require informed consent when the research could involve pain and discomfort or when it did not have a therapeutic benefit. Under other circumstances, the doctor could just ask the patient to participate "as a favor", or the experimental treatments were given to the patient when the doctor considered it was of some benefit for the patient. A physician from Boston: Charles Francis Withington published an essay indicating the possible conflict between medical science and the right and interests of the patient (Withington, 1886). In many cases patients did not refuse to participate in experimental treatments because they wanted to keep good relations with the doctor who was treating them, or because the patient was too ill to be able to give proper informed consent.

The Tuskegee Syphilis Study

Perhaps one of the most infamous experiments conducted throughout a long period of time where the subjects involved were not well informed about the consequences of participation was the Tuskegee syphilis study. During forty years the Public Health Service (PHS) studied the effects of untreated syphilis in Macon County, Alabama, among African American poor and mostly illiterate men. In return for their participation, they were given free rides to and from the clinic, free food the day of the exams, free physical examinations and a $50.00 payment to the survivors after the death of the participant. This study started in 1932 and even though it was widely discussed among the scientific community, it was not known to the public until around 1972 when the Associated Press published the story.

The cause of the disease was well known by the time the experiment began. Early diagnosis was possible by 1907 using the Wassermann test. Treatment using a preparation of mercury and organic arsenic was developed in 1910; an often painful treatment that sometimes lead to death, but in some cases it was effective against the disease. The individuals involved in the Tuskegee experiment had advanced cases of syphilis and they may have not benefited from the treatment, but this could not be an argument for denying an individual the basic treatment for a known disease. In the 1940s, when penicillin was discovered, it was known that this antibiotic could be used as a reliable cure for syphilis, but still the people involved in the Tuskegee experiment were denied such a treatment.

Malaria Therapy

Neurosyphilis is the late stage of syphilis, characterized by damage to the peripheral neurological system, resulting in insanity and dementia. From the 1920s, physicians started experimenting with the use of "fever therapy" to kill the syphilis spirochete without killing the patient. These studies included infecting patients with malaria parasites (malariatherapy), injections of typhoid vaccine, streptococci and staphylococci (Bierman, 1942).

Malariatherapy was widely used in the 1920s and 1930s in the U.S. and Europe. In 1931, the Rockefeller Foundation in cooperation with the Florida State Board of Health initiated a study in Malariatherapy. The person in charge of this research was Mark Boyd, an expert on malaria, who was more interested in knowing about malaria and learning to treat it than in syphilis. Boyd devised a system to grow the mosquitoes to be malaria transmitters of the Plasmodium vivax parasite. Boyd was assigned patients by the psychiatrists who were studying neurosyphilis. In some cases, those patients became very ill and Boyd applied a quinine treatment against malaria even before he had finished the programmed experiments on that individual. In one case an 18 year old boy was brought to Talahassee (Florida) to be treated with malariatherapy. According to Boyd, it was an ideal subject for experimentation because he had not taken quinine before. However, the boy was very sick and every time he had a malaria fever, a new outbreak of fever blisters appeared on his face. Even though the doctors at the hospital where the experiments were carried out told Boyd to continue with his experimental treatment, Boyd decided to interrupt the last experimental treatment of feeding mosquitoes on the boy's blood and give him quinine because he couldn't bear to see the boy suffering from malaria without helping him.

As a result of this work, Boyd and Stratman-Thomas published several papers describing the knowledge gained from this human experimentation. They were the first researchers to be able to show that different strains of malaria elicit different immune responses. They found that if patients were inoculated with one strain of malaria and later on they were re-inoculated with the same strain, little or no symptoms were shown after the re-inoculation. However, when patients were re-inoculated with a different strain from the one they already had, the patients developed full symptoms as if they had never been exposed to the disease (Boyd and Stratman-Thomas, 1933). The use of malariatherapy has not been totally abandoned by some doctors. In 1989, a Mexican clinic offered malariatherapy for late-stage Lyme disease (Mertz and Spitalny, 1990; Heimlich et al., 1997).

In the experiments of malariatheraphy, individuals or their families "consented" to the treatment. Boyd seemed to have retained his role as a caring physician with the subjects of his experiments. In some cases it was the psychiatrists that insisted that an additional malaria infection be induced to the patient in order to kill the syphilis-causing bacteria with the high temperature produced by the malaria fevers. It took Boyd some restraint and care to see beyond his experiments and try to help those patients who were very ill with the malaria symptoms. In some cases however, patients died just after the malaria infections and Boyd attributed their death to other causes than the malaria infection.

Human Radiation Experiments

From the earliest times of radioactivity studies, scientists found the deleterious effects of radiation. Soon after the discovery of the X-rays in 1895, it was observed that radiation caused burns and skin ulceration. However, it was not well understood how humans responded to radiation. Studies in animals were non-conclusive since some animals excrete radioactive isotopes at different rates. This led to human experimentation to understand radioactive effects and therefore protect individuals working and exposed to radioactivity. These experiments included injecting radioactive plutonium into 18 patients without their knowledge. The injections were given between 1945 to 1947 at the University of Rochester (Chicago) and the University of California San Francisco (UCSF). The purpose of the experiment was to develop a diagnostic tool to determine the uptake of plutonium in the body by measuring its excretion in feces and urine (Moss and Eckhardt, 1995). When terminally ill patients were used, a higher amount of plutonium was injected in the initial doses; however, since they had short survival times after injections, they did not receive the highest total doses in the experiment. The results were going to be used to protect the workers involved in the production and purification of uranium and plutonium. In experiments with animals, it was shown that the rate of elimination of plutonium in excreta was different for different species. This variation made it difficult to extrapolate the values to those of human. The first experiments showed that in humans, compared to animals, a lower amount of plutonium was excreted in fecal matter, up to six times lower. The skeleton and the liver were the tissues that accounted for 90% or more of the total plutonium. Since the level of plutonium in blood fell rapidly after 10 days, it was not possible to use blood analysis to determine the degree of exposure of personnel (Moss and Eckhardt, 1995).

Other studies on the effect of radiation on kidney damage were done by injecting patients with uranium. These studies were done with 13 terminal cancer patients, some of them comatose or semi-comatose at the beginning of the experiment (Lussenhop et al., 1958). Studies on the effect of X-ray exposure to testicular damage were done by irradiating "volunteer" inmates from the Oregon State Prison. These individuals were paid one hundred dollars for their participation (Markey report, 1986). In 1947 and 1951, the Atomic Energy Commission set up some rules for this type of experimentation including the requirement that all radiation experiments have the hope of being therapeutic. A year before, the American Medical Association and the War Crimes Tribunal at Nuremberg had established required consent of research subjects. Despite this, some researchers continue their experimentation violating the premises indicated above. These researchers classified their experiments as secret and continued their research. It is debatable whether a jail inmate could give voluntary consent for an experiment since he/she is under conditions that require subordination to the jailers and other authorities. It is possible that some inmates participated in these experiments because of fear of negative action taken against them by the jailers.

A study in seven women who had just delivered babies was done in 1943 to study the absorption of radioactive sodium by the vagina. The study attempted to understand the absorption by the vagina with recommendations about the use of toxic ingredients that could be included in a douche (Pommerenke and Hahn, 1943). There is no mention as to whether the women were willing participants in the study. These experiments caused some discomfort to the subjects involved and it is doubtful they 'benefited' from participating in such experiments.

Between 1945 and 1949 at Vanderbilt University in Tennessee, more than 800 pregnant women were fed single doses the radioactive isotope Fe59. The objective of the research was to understand the iron absorption process in pregnant women and to calculate the amount of iron needed (Hahn et al.,1951). The women involved in the research report were told that the dose was a "vitamin cocktail". Vanderbilt University claimed that in the 1945-1949 it was not necessary to obtain informed consent for research. However, this topic had been discussed before in the medical field, including a publication of the Introduction to the Study of Experimental Medicine by Claude Bernard in 1865 indicating that "experiments should never be performed on men if they are harmful to him to any extent" (Bernard, 1927, Osler, 1907).

Radiation Experiments In The Military

Joseph Hamilton, a chemist with medical training focused his efforts on military research, producing a report that explained the potential use of fission products for military applications. He indicated how microgram doses of radioactive materials could be used as weapons because they caused tissue damage with chronic effects. Hamilton described in his report the potential use of the weapons to contaminate specific areas such as mountain passes or beachheads; additionally his report included the effects of dispersion of these materials on large areas on civilian populations (ACHRE, 1995). Concern for the effect of radioactivity on soldiers led to experiments where military personnel were exposed to atomic blasts in Nevada. As an example, a study of the effect on vision of atomic detonations used volunteers either with red goggles or no protection who watched a blast and reported the time it took for them to be able to see their instruments after the blast. Some volunteers developed eye lesions that later healed (ACHRE, 1994). To study the effect of being at ground zero during an explosion, volunteer officers were positioned only 2000 yards from ground zero where a 40-kiloton blast was detonated. One officer described in good detail the effect of the blast on nearby trees and sheep and how the trenches protected soldiers from immediate damage (Goodman et al. 2003).

Guidelines for these experiments were provided by the Armed Forces Medical Policy council that indicated that human subjects should be used only as a mean to develop mechanisms of defense against atomic, biological or chemical agents. Some consulting physicians advised against some of these experiments, including stationing troops within seven miles of ground zero. The military however, in some cases ignored the advice and continued tests with personnel within 2000 yards of the blasts (Goodman et al., 2003).

Use Of Subjects "Unable" Or "Coerced" To Give Informed Consent

The use of individuals who should be considered unable to give informed consent includes feeble-minded individuals, with a low mental capacity, prisoners, children from orphanages, poor and needy individuals looking for medical care, terminal patients or patients in comma. These individuals, given their circumstances are unable to give consent to a treatment that they either don't understand or that they feel somewhat coerced to participate in because of their rank in the social structure(e.g. prisoners may feel the need to please the guards to avoid punishment). Several examples of the use of mental patients are included in the literature. To mention a few, in 1897, Henry J. Berkley from Johns Hopkins University studied the toxicity of a commercial preparation of thyroid extract in patients at Bay View Insane Asylum in Baltimore. The treatment produced irritability, mental excitement, motor distress and other symptoms.

The symptoms remained after the treatment was suspended and one patient died, and the conclusion of the experiment was that even the purest commercially available thyroid tablets could harm the health and life of a patient (Berkley, 1897). The patients, being mentally ill, were not able to give proper consent and understand the risks of the treatments in question.

Studies on diagnostics tests for tuberculosis involved more than one hundred and sixty children, twenty six of them from the St. Vincent's Home for Orphans. The tests involved tuberculin testing using different tests including the either injection of tuberculin solution in the eye (Calmette test), the muscle (Moro Test) or the skin (von Pirquet test). Children subjected to the Calmette test developed serious lesions and inflammations in the eye and suffered a great deal from the treatment (Lederer, 1992, 1995). Some of their caregivers protested about the pain and suffering of these children, but the experiments continued.

In 1911, Hideyo Noguchi at the Rockefeller Institute of Medical Research used a luetin test (injection of an inactive solution of Trepanoma pallidum, the agent that causes syphilis) into some orphans and hospital patients (Lederer, 1995). Noguchi produced the luetin by heating ascitic fluid cultures and mixing them with phenol (Lederer, 1985). The test results were not as expected and the reliability of the test was not good after it was commercially manufactured.

In some cases physicians used their own children for experimentation: two pediatricians, Hugh and E.J. MacDonald used their four sons to evaluate the safety of the whooping cough vaccine. They vaccinated two of their children with pertussis vaccine and then sprayed their noses with whooping cough microbes. The two children who were vaccinated remained free of the disease, whereas the other two children (6 year old twins) develop the symptoms corresponding to the disease (McDonald and McDonald, 1933). However, the most vulnerable population of children used for experimentation was children who lived in orphanages. In 1914, at the home of Hebrew Infants, a New York City Orphan asylum, experiments were conducted to study the development of scurvy by pediatrician Alfred F. Hess and doctors Mildred Fish and Lester Unger. In this experiment, orange juice was withheld from infants until the babies developed symptoms of the disease. To evaluate whether children could develop the disease again, a second scurvy treatment was done. They also did tests to diagnose scurvy that involved puncturing the abdomen (Hess and Fish, 1914). In some cases the publications describe the children as "volunteers". Given the age of the children, it is clear their inability to be able to give an informed consent. In other cases, when parents "volunteered" their children for the experiments, it is not clear whether they really understood the risks involved in the process.

The use of prisoners for research also proved to be controversial since the participation could be coercive. In 1915 a study of pellagra was done at a Mississippi prison. The objective of the research was to investigate the causes of pellagra. Healthy prisoners were put on a pellagra diet that included meat, meal and molasses for six months. In order to encourage the participation of the inmates, the governor offered pardons for male prisoners willing to follow this diet for six months. Twelve men were selected and developed symptoms of the disease. After their release, even though they were offered free medical service to facilitate their recovery, none of them took advantage of it (Etheridge, 1972). Perhaps these 'volunteers' did not understand the need to follow up the effect of the experiments on their health and the risks involved. Experiments in testicular transplantation in 1920 by L.L. Stanley included the implantation of human testes from executed convicts into eleven male prisoners and the implantation of ram testicles into 23 prison inmates (Stanley, 1920). The ethics of using prisoners for research was highly debated. Prisoners don't have the 'freedom' to consent to an experiment given the possibility for coercion in a highly regulated environment.

Slaves were also used for experimentation, as illustrated by the experiments conducted by Marion Sims, considered the 'father' of gynecological surgery. Sims experimented on slave women who had vesico-vaginal fistulas and were unable to control their bladders because of a hole in the vaginal wall. These women were not able to work and were given to Sims for experimentation. Sims promised to return the slaves to their owners if the experiments were successful. The surgeries were performed before the use of anesthetic and Sims described the heroism and bravery of some of these women during the surgery treatments (Lederer, 1995). These women were unable to consent because they were slaves; they were at the mercy of their owners.

The use of military personal in research was very controversial since some of the soldiers were under threat of court-martial if they did not participate in the experiments. For example when soldiers were identified as carriers of typhoid fever during War World II, physicians recommended the removal of the gall bladder. The treatment was risky and even though some soldiers gave their "consent" for the surgery, some of the ones that didn't were threatened to be subject to court martial (Johnson, 1953). Given this evidence, nobody could argue that military personnel could give informed consent when the participation in an experimental trial was 'suggested' by superiors. There are examples that show some coercion to participate as described by Keiffer (1905) in which he had to insure the compliance of several privates and a sergeant in an experiment involving the use of smokeless powders. This type of 'coercion' makes these experiments unethical according to our current regulations.

Germ Warfare Tests In The United States

Only one example will be described even though there are records of wide research in this area. Since 1950, several trials were conducted in the U.S. in parallel tests that were conducted in the United Kingdom to test the use of fluorescent tracer particles such as zinc cadmium sulfide as a simulation of a biological agent cloud. Zinc cadmium was chosen because of its glow that allowed researchers to observe the spread of a particular cloud and because of the particle size that was regarded as the most effective for lung penetration. According to a later report from the National Research Council, this molecule was not toxic to humans, animals and plants (NRC, 1997). Conclusions from the studies in the United Kingdom and the U.S. indicated that the release of 300 pounds of particles could affect 28 million people with a dose of one hundred particles, enough to be effective for infecting these individuals with tularemia (Pasturella tularensis) and Q fever disease, non lethal diseases (Balmer, 2003). In these types of experiment many individuals involved perhaps were never aware of their unwilling participation. Decisions were made by physicians and personnel with authority to 'treat' big areas that include human activity.

Medical Research Self-Experimentation

The use of oneself or one's family for experimentation was viewed as a way to ellicit the trust of other patients. Some physicians even advocated self-experimentation as a way to demonstrate how safe a procedure will be. One of the most well known examples of self-experimentation includes the discovery of the transmission of yellow fever by mosquitoes. James Reed, James Carroll, Jesse Lazear and Aristides Agramonte belonged to the Yellow Fever board and proposed to expose healthy human beings to the disease. Carrol and Lazear tested the mosquito hypothesis on themselves. Reed was at that time in Washington and did not participate in the experiment. Carroll developed a severe attack of fever after exposure to "infected mosquitoes". Lazear died in 1900 after becoming infected. Giving this evidence, Reed decided against self-experimentation but several American soldiers offered themselves as research subjects. Reed accepted only individuals over twenty four who could consent and required that subjects were not older than forty. One hundred dollars in gold with free medical care plus an additional one hundred dollars if the subject became infected were offered to participants (Bean, 1977).

Joseph W. Strickler in 1887 infected himself and two young children with foot and mouth disease under the assumption that this would protect children from scarlet fever. The children were exposed to scarlet fever patients and their infected bed linens (Stickler, 1887). The children did not get sick and the experiment was not considered unethical by some of the same people that condemned other types of experiments in humans because the researcher also used himself as the subject of experimentation.

Conclusion:

There has been at least some degree of concern for the ethical ramifications of human experimentation throughout history. For example, antivivisectionist societies were created that tried to stop animal experimentation at medical colleges. Many of the members argued a link between the protection of children and the humane treatment of animals. This antivivisectionist movement led to the creation of bills that restricted animal research. Strong opposition for the use of dying individuals, prisoners, children, feeble-minded and patients at insane asylums led to changes in how physicians carry out their experiments. Some questionable experimentation has been done all throughout the world using these individuals or people without proper consent.

This paper addressed some cases of questionable human experimentation in the United States. History helps us to recognize our mistakes and to avoid repeating them. New strict regulations are in place to allow experimentation with humans and other animals. Scientific progress cannot be hindered by the lack of regulation and understanding of the necessity of animal and human experimentation for the advance of medicine. We are learning how to do things right, but we still have more things to learn. The creation of Internal Review Boards (IRB) oversees that research complies with the proper regulations. Continuing the scrutiny of medical experimentation is vital to the development of new techniques for treating human diseases. The acquisition of knowledge in medicine is vital for our survival and we need to make sure the research is properly done. We owe it to those individuals who participate in clinical trials: the risks they take could make a difference for the development of live-saving procedures.

Literature Cited

ACHRE 1994. Human Experimentation in connection with atomic bomb tests. September 8, 1994.

ACHRE, final report (Washington, D.C.) 1995. Included also in The Human Radiation Experiments: Final Report of the President's Advisory Committee. 1996.

Balmer, B. Using the population body to protect the national body. 2003. In: *Useful bodies: Humans in the service of medical science in the twentieth century.* Goodman, J., McElligott, A. and Marks, L. (Editors). The John Hopkins University Press. Baltimore. 217 p.

Bartholow, R. 1874. Experimental investigations into the functions of the human brain. *Am. J. Med. Sci.* 67: 305-313.

Bean, W.B. 1977. The Fielding H. Garrison lecture: Walter Reed and the ordeal of human experiments. *Bull. Hist. Med.* 51(1): 75-92

Berkley, H. 1897. Studies on the lesions induced by the action of certain poisons on the cortical nerve cell. Study VII: Poisoning with preparations of the thyroid gland. *Bull. Johns Hopkins Hosp.* 8: 137-140/

Bernard, C. 1927. An introduction to the study of experimental medicine. McMillan Eds. N.Y.

Bierman, W. 1942. The history of fever therapy in the treatment of disease. *Bulletin of the New York Academy of Medicine* 18: 65-75

Boyd, M.F. and Stratman-Thomas, W.K. 1933. Studies on benign tertian malaria. On the occurrence of acquired tolerance to Plasmodium vivax. *American Journal of Hygiene*: 55-59.

Etheridge, E. 1972. *The Butterfly Caste: a social history of pellagra*. Westport, Conn.: Greenwood. 93-96

Goodman, J., A. McElligott and L.Marks. (Eds) 2003. *Useful bodies: Humans in the service of medical science in the twentieth century*. The John Hopkins University Press. Baltimore. 217 p.

Hahn, P.F., Carothers, E.L. et al. 1951. Iron metabolism in human pregnancy as studied with the radioactive isotope Fe59. *Amer. J. Obstet. & Gyn.* 61(3): 477-486.

Heiman, H. 1895. A clinical and bacteriological study of the Gonococcus Neisser in the male urethra and in the vulvovaginal tract of children. *J. Cut. Genito-Urinary Diseases.* 13: 384-387

Heimlich, H et al., 1997. Malariotherapy for HIV patients. *Mechanisms of Aging and Development* 93: 79-85.

Hess, A.F. and Fish, M. 1914. Infantile Scurvy: The glood, the blood-vessels and the diet. *Am. J. Dis. Child.* 8: 386-405.

Johnson, W.H. 1953. Civil rights of military personnel regarding medical care and experimental procedures. *Science* 117: 212-215.

Kieffer, C.F. 1905.Smokeless Powders. *JAMA* 44: 1359-1365

Lederer, S. 1985. *Hideyo Noguchi's Luetin experiment and the antivivisectionists*. 76(1): 31-48

Lederer, S.E. 1992. *Orphans as Guinea Pigs: American children and medical experimenters*, 1890-1940. Roger Cooter Ed. 96-123.

Lederer, S. E. 1995. *Subjected to science: Human experimentation in America before the Second World War*. The Johns Hopkins University Press. Baltimore. 193 p.

Lusenhop, A.J., J.C. Galfimore, W.H. Sweet, E.G. Struxness and J. Robinson. 1958. The toxicity in man of hexavalent uranium following intravenous administration. *American Journal of Roentgenoloy* 79: 83-100.

Markey Report. U.S. Congress, House of Representatives, Committee on Energy and Commerce. 1986. American Nuclear Guinea pigs: Three decades of radiation experiments on U.S. citizens. Washington D.C. p. 15

McDonald, H. and E.J.MacDonald. 1933 Experimental Pertussis. *J. Inf. Dis.* 53:328-330.

Mertz, K. and K.C. Spitalny. 1990. Imported Malaria associated with malariotherapy of Lyme disease. *Morbidiy and Mortality Weekly report*. New Jersey. 873-875.

Moss, W. and Eckhardt, R. 1995. The human plutonium injection experiments. *Los Alamos Science.* 23: 177-233

National Research Council. 1997. *Toxicological assessment of the Army's Zinc Cadmiun Sulfide dispersion tests*. Washington D.C.: 177.

Pommerenke, W. T. and Hahn, P.F. 1943. Absorption of radioactive sodium instilled into the vagina. *Amer. J. Obstet. & Gyn*. 46: 853-855.

Osler, W. 1907. The evolution of the idea of experiment in medicine. *Trans. Cong. Amer. Physicians & surg*. 7: 1-8.

Stanley, L.L. 1920. Experiences in testicle transplantation. *Calif. St. J. Med*. 18: 251-253.

Stickler, J.W. 1887. *Foot and Mouth disease as it affects man and animals*. NY 1887. 32: 725-732.

Withington, C.F. 1886. *The relation of hospitals to medical education*. Boston: Cupples, Upham.

Organ Sale and Theft: A Reality Check with an Ethical Perspective

by
Ted Butterfield & Ruhul Kuddus

Introduction

Organ transplantation is a highly effective method of treating end-stage organ failure. In other words, organ transplantation offers a new lease on life to a dying person. Like any other discipline, organ transplantation has its problems. Paradoxically, the major problem of transplantation medicine is not the sciences or technologies that support the processes but a shortage of organs. The supply of human donor organs has plateaued while demand has been steadily increasing. When demand and supply make such a curve, illegal and unethical activities such as cheating, stealing, hoarding, robbing and profiteering may ensue. There are many ethical concerns in essentially every aspect of organ transplantation. This article only examines the ethical issues of organ theft and sale.

The concept of organ theft predates the science of organ transplantation. We have all been influenced, since childhood, by tales of blood stealing vampires, body snatching, or flat out organ theft for religious rituals, black magic or untraditional medicinal usage. Many of us can readily recall scenes from the movie Indiana Jones and the Temple of Doom, where the priest removes a beating heart from the chest of a man in a grisly ritualistic fashion. These images have a profound effect on our fears and emotions. With the advent of blood transfusion and organ transplantation technologies, rumors of a new kind of organ and tissue theft have swept the nations of the globe and engendered a certain degree of generalized fear and skepticism with regards to the ethics of organ procurement. Whether these fears are the unfounded product of generations of folklore and urban legend or the result of actual, discreetly organized organ merchant profiteers are questions we seek to answer in this investigational study. We also seek to know whether such fear has negative impact on organ donation. A goal of this study is to help propagate awareness in an effort to increase the organ donor pool. For that reason we seek to advocate appropriate fund allocations to xenotransplantation and stem cell research. We conclude by highlighting the implications of ethics in the practice of organ transplantation conducive to widespread enlisting as organ donors.

Alleged Organ Theft in Mexico

We initially took interest in organ theft after finding an article in the Internet news source *Skeptical Inquirer*, reporting a string of killings in Mexico, in the state of Chihuahua, in the desert outside of Ciudad Juarez (Radford 2003). This city is just across the Mexican-American border from El Paso, Texas. Apparently, the several-year-long spree of killings has been investigated as a series of rape-murders, and very little headway has been made in solving the cases, or even in slowing the killings. At a conference in Chihuahua, on April 30, 2003, Mexican Assistant Attorney General Carlos Javier Vega Memije made the shocking announcement that fourteen of the nearly ninety victims appear to have been kidnapped and killed for their organs. The implication is that the women were killed, their organs extracted and then transported across the border and transplanted into wealthy US Citizens in the affluent hospitals of neighboring United States cities. In a statement, the Mexican Justice Department said that, "several details support the idea that these women were killed to extract their organs and sell them" (Radford 2003). The article gives no specifics as to what these details might be. It only adds that Vega Memije did not explicitly state that the killings were definitely organ theft-related, but that it was probable (Radford 2003). It is of importance to note that Vega Memije and the Justice Department gave no explanation why the victims were only women. Nor did they give any means by which it was determined that organs were removed, since, for the most part, the bodies were extremely decomposed at the time of their recovery. Furthermore, three forensics examiners in Juarez, two of whom had examined the majority of the bodies in question, state that they had observed no evidence of organ theft (Radford 2003).

Having the cryptic evidence presented by the above article, we decided to see if the Mexican Justice Department and Vega Memije would comment on the debate. After many phone calls to local and state agencies affiliated with Mexico, we procured the phone number to the Mexican Embassy in Washington D.C. In a conversation with the officials, we were informed that Vega Memije no longer worked in the Attorney General's Office and that they were unable, or not allowed, to give us any contact information that we might use to call him or write to him. With this set-back we turned to a more direct approach and finally found a number directly to the Mexican Attorney General's Office (Procuraduría General de la República) in Mexico City. Upon contacting them we found that they too informed us of his transfer to another post and were unwilling, or unable to give us any information by which we might contact him. They did, however, inform us that we were welcome to write a letter to which they would respond or forward the letter to Vega Memije so that he might verify the accuracy of the *Skeptical Inquirer's* report on his conference statements. We mailed the letter using a reliable mailing service (FedEx Trade Network, USA), and as of three months after the mailing have yet to receive any reply. At this time we do not expect any reply.

The lack of any attainable supporting evidence for Vega Memije's statement suggests that we encountered an urban legend based on an attempted explanation of the unexplainable cause of these fourteen purportedly organ-theft related homicides. According to Scheper-Hughes (1996), these types of rumors often arise in groups experiencing unequal wealth-power distribution with others, as is the case with many Mexican nationals in comparison to their neighbors north of the border. The author (Scheper-Hughes 1996) states that "Blood sucking rumors in Africa and organ theft and fat stealing rumors in South America are cogent metaphors expressing the often grotesque nature of colonialist and neo-colonialist economic, social relations and labor practices. The root metaphor concerns the radical commodification of the body and of body parts in work and in new medical practices". The above statement perhaps presents a potential explanation for the root of the allegation that the killings were transplantation related. However, it must be considered that while this statement may have had influence from the oppressed, poverty-stricken lower class, it was nonetheless a comment made by an individual and an organization representing those who are in power; therefore we felt that there might be something more to the answer about whether or not organ theft occurs.

Organ Importation and Organ Theft in the United States

The next apparent question, we were forced to ask ourselves is whether or not there has ever been a verifiable case of organ theft within the United States. To find the answer to this question we turned to Dr. Todd Cameron Grey, of the Utah State Medical Examiner's Office. He is a board certified forensic and anatomic specialist who began working in forensic pathology in New Mexico in 1983 (coincidentally, New Mexico shares borders with Ciudad Juarez and the Mexican-American region in question of organ theft). Grey has been Chief Medical Examiner in the State of Utah since 1988 and estimates that he has personally performed autopsies on 300-400 homicides during the course of his career.

In our recorded interview with him, Grey stated that in no case, homicide or otherwise, has he performed an autopsy on an individual who appeared to have organs missing without justification. At times, the organ recovery group has received consent from next of kin to recover tissue and organs, thus, with the forensic pathologist's consent, organs are occasionally removed prior to an autopsy's being performed. This, of course, is a perfectly legal pursuit and has the best interests of the mourning family and those in need of donated tissue at heart. Over the years Grey regularly attended two national conferences: The American Academy of Forensic Sciences (Pathology/Biology Section) and The National Association of Medical Examiners. Never in any of these conferences, has he seen any case involving possible organ theft; neither has he heard rumor of such a case. We also found not a single peer-reviewed publication reporting such an event. We present this as fairly concrete evidence against the possibility of homicidal organ theft having occurred within the United States in the past two decades. Such a case would undoubtedly be noteworthy and worth presentation at any national conference of forensic personnel. As it has not, and we cannot find evidence that it may have, then we accept that the likelihood of its occurrence is negligible.

To further substantiate this conclusion, we next conducted an unofficial interview with Mr. Scott McDonald RN, who is the Director of Tissue Recovery Services and an Organ Procurement Coordinator for Intermountain Donor Services (IDS), a regional group that participates in the procurement and distribution of donated organs throughout the intermountain west. Our main objective in that interview was to delineate the time constraints of organ procurement and transplantation so that we might better understand the intricate organizational requirements necessary for successful long-term retention of transplanted solid organs such as heart, kidneys, liver and pancreas. He has kindly given us permission to repeat any portion of that conversation (most or the entire information can be found at www.idslife.org or www.unos.org at any rate).

McDonald presented us with explanations of the logistical difficulties of transporting organs to the United States for transplantation. These difficulties apply to the concept of randomly killing any individual, anywhere in the world with the intent to harvest and distribute their organs. One of the big issues is time. Organ and tissue recovery can take 1-4 hours to complete, depending on the number of organs being recovered. In addition to time requirements for recovery, the amount of time needed for transportation and transplantation of organs must be considered. The main components here are:

A. The organ must be harvested, preserved and transported properly: Harvesting the organs properly (so that they may be transplanted), preserving the organ in specially formulated nutrient-preservative solution at controlled temperature and transporting to hospitals within 4-36 hours of recovery. It is to be noted that optimum organ preservation time for different organs are, heart 4-6 hours, lung 4-6 hours, liver 8-16 hours, pancreas 8-16 hours, kidney 24-36 hours (IDS 2006). Improperly harvested and preserved organs may rapidly loose transplantation quality.

B. The organ must be well-matched with the recipient's tissue: Ensuring proper compatibility of the donated organ to the recipient's ABO blood group, Rh blood group and several Human Leukocyte Antigen types (mismatched organs may be rapidly rejected by the immune system of the recipient).

C. The recipient must obtain adequate post-procedural medical care: The care includes physician-supervised check-ups and the necessary prescribed medications in proper dosage. Recipients of organs of questionable sources may not receive such specialized services without someone noticing.

There are obvious time constraints inherent in the procedural recovery and subsequent transplantation of a living, viable human organ. Given the facts about the small window of opportunity in which an organ can be procured and successfully transplanted, the logistical difficulties involved in stealing an organ in Mexico or anywhere else and transplanting that organ in the United States will plainly manifest itself as impossible. McDonald's conclusion is that all these requirements could never be circumvented with any chance at a successful, long-term functioning organ transplant and without anyone noticing. He was very firm in his statement that illegal procurement and transplantation of organs cannot occur within the system currently in place in the United States. He further stated that these circulating rumors tend to create superstitions about organ donation in general and can have a negative impact on people's willingness to donate. In performing our research, we have found this information to be accurate.

Kidneys as a Commodity for Sale and Trade

Based on information available at The Organ Procurement and Transplantation Network (OPTN 2007), there are 95,223 individuals on the organ donation waiting list in the United States as of February 28, 2007 (Fig 1A). From January to November of 2006, there were a total of 26,690 transplants performed in the United States (using organ from 13,582 donors). While these numbers for donation and transplantation represent a wonderful success story of modern medicine, the ratio of organs available versus those needed is staggering. What's more, the deficit is continuously on the rise; therefore the problem only becomes more desperate with the passing of time (Fig. 1B). Fig. 1A also indicates that ~74% of the individuals waiting for (any) organs are waiting for a kidney, indicating that renal failure is the predominant category of organ failures and that kidney is the most sought-after organ in transplantation medicine. Interestingly, kidneys are the only vital organs that an individual has in duplicate and a living person may donate one of the two kidneys (other duplicate organs such as testes, ovary, eyes, and ears are not essential for survival). After surgical removal of one kidney, the other kidney increases in size to compensate for the donated kidney. Data indicate that kidney donation does not decrease life expectancy or quality of life, nor does it appear to increase the risk of future renal failure (Johnson et al. 1999); although kidney donation may increase the risk of developing stress (Johnson et al. 1999, Lima et al. 2006) and hypertension (IALOD 2007) in some donors. Hypertension is a relatively controllable side affect. It can be noted that donation of a kidney by mere 0.04% of the 175, 000,000 potential organ donor (18-64 years old) population of the United States would wipe out the kidney waiting list from this country.

This knowledge may make one wonder why there is still such a large and growing waiting list for kidneys. There are many answers to the question. According to McDonald, most people have a difficult time with the notion of freely giving away a kidney when there is a chance (however slight) that they might need that kidney in the future. Fear of pain and complications (including infection), uncertainty, family pressure, religious or cultural norms, ignorance (lack of awareness) and possible mistrust of the organ procurement and distribution system may also contribute to the lack of widespread kidney donation. Notably, procurement of a kidney (or any organ) from dead and dying persons also face many restrictions. This later topic is not addressed in this article but it underscores the need of informing the public of this important issue.

The Bathtub Rumor on Kidney Theft

Since a kidney (or blood) can be harvested from an unwilling person without committing a homicide, kidney (and blood) stealing legends abound. We have come to call it the Bathtub Rumor since that is usually the place where the storied victim ultimately finds himself. The following is a legend we have found repeatedly and throughout many cultures in one form or another. The garden variety of the legend is as follows:

My aunt's friend works with this guy whose nephew was on a business trip to Chicago. One night he went out to a bar and met this amazingly stunning woman. She started flirting with him and asked if she could buy him a drink. Shortly after that she invited him over to her apartment. The next thing he knows he wakes up in a bathtub filled with ice, and the last thing he can remember is getting into a car with the girl from the bar. He looks around to try to figure out where he is and what had happened. That's when he feels the pain in his back and looks down to see a note written in red lipstick on his chest that says 'call 911'. Upon calling 911 he is informed to stay where he is in the ice-filled tub; his kidneys have been stolen (also see Scheper-Hughes 1996, Adams 2007, Emery 2007).

In 1997 a variant of this rumor hit New Orleans just as the city geared up for Mardi Gras. It was circulated via word-of-mouth, fax, and E-mail. Essentially the message being passed around was that an organized group of organ thieves in New Orleans planned to drug people at Mardi Gras, steal their organs and sell them on the black market. The rumor caused such concern that the New Orleans Police Department had to publish a statement denying any truth to the allegations in order to quell public fears (Emery, 2007).

The United States government has established an official website (USINFO, 2007) to aid in the identification and clarification of common misinformation. On the subject of organ theft it states,

> Health and organ transplant officials in the United States and other countries have stated emphatically that it would be impossible to successfully conceal any clandestine organ trafficking ring. In addition to the legal and moral deterrents to organ trafficking, the technical requirements that would be involved in arranging and operating an alleged murder-for-organ-transplantation scheme are so formidable that such clandestine activities are a practical impossibility.

Accepting this comment to be wholly the truth, we should then prepare to understand why such rumors as the bathtub rumor are so widely distributed and believed by those who perpetrate their survival.

The International Donor Kidney Trade and Human Trafficking

As a Scheper-Hughes (1996) believes that these fables on organ theft are, at the very least, metaphorically true. The business of organ trade and transplant takes place at an international level. Often, like most capitalistic business ventures, at the expense of the poor for the benefit of the wealthy. Elements of legal and illegal procurement and transplantation exist in certain regions in the world (Scheper-Hughes 1996). In India for example, poor people place advertisements in local newspapers soliciting a buyer for one of their kidneys. Often, wealthy patients in need of a kidney place advertisements offering to pay for a donor. This happens despite the prohibition of the sale of organs by the Indian Organ Transplantation Act 1994 (BBC News 2006). From 1983-1988, 131 patients from Oman and the United- Arab Emirates traveled to Bombay, India where they purchased kidneys from local brokers. The kidney sellers (donors!) were from local shantytowns and the price was $2000-3000/kidney. Scheper-Hughes opined that where a legal market for the sale of blood and organs exists, there is ample opportunity for an illegal black-market trade for the same (Scheper-Hughes 1996).

One striking case paints the picture for the whole of what is going on in the desperate search for spare kidneys. In August 2003, Alberty Alfonso da Silva was trafficked from Recife, Brazil to Durban, South Africa where his kidney was sold, removed, and donated to an American from New York City (Maclay 2004). Trafficking of live humans as organ donors is increasingly common in a world where cadaveric organs are extremely scarce and desperately poverty-stricken live individuals are easily "available". If an individual needing a donor organ is willing to break laws, travel to distant lands, and has the right amount of financial resources and connections; then a fresh kidney can be made available from a stranger, local or trafficked. Anthropologist Scheper-Hughes refers to this as transplant tourism (Maclay 2004).

Organ Harvesting from Persons of Questionable Death Status

To be effectively transplanted, organs must be harvested as soon as a person is legally (brain) dead. The legal definition of death is not the subject of this article. It is reported that public awareness on this issue is very scanty (Younger et al. 2004). There is a fear (unfounded) that people listed as organ donor are more likely to be prematurely considered "legally dead" for organ harvesting. "If you enlist yourself as a donor, they will not try to wake you up from coma", the some are alleged of saying to the potential young donors. This unfounded fear is perhaps one of the most serious obstacles to widespread donor enlisting. For that reason, the matter warrants systemic examination. The legal death related organ harvest dilemma, however, is not simply a rumor. BBC news (BBC News 2000) reported the arrest of two surgeons and an administrator of Vajiraprakarn Hospital of Bangkok, Thailand accused of selling organs harvested from patient of questionable death status to a wealthy recipient. The report cited government prosecutor Anuchart Kongmalai of saying that the doctors allegedly murdered the patients in 1997, harvested their organs and faked paperwork to cover up the crime. The police investigators investigating the case reported the doctors were paid almost one million baht ($25,000) in each case by patients needing organ transplants.

Let us return, then, to the original question -whether or not organ theft has occurred or is it merely an urban legend? The internet dictionary, Wikipedia defines organ theft as " the practice of stealing people's organs (presumably while they are under the influence of drugs or alcohol) via amateur surgery, and then selling them on a supposed black market for use in organ transplants' (Wikipedia 2007). This definition is quite descriptive of all the horror stories being circulated in the Internet world, as though the definition were pulled directly from the urban legend rumor-mill. If this definition is the accepted one, then it is quite an extremely far-fetched notion indeed to think that organ theft for the purpose of transplantation has occurred or will ever occur. If, however, the question of organ theft is posed in a different light, the answer might become a little less elusive. How would an average, middle-class US citizen feel if the only way to pay for a daughter's wedding was to sell a kidney for $2000? Would the feeling change if selling a kidney $2,000 was the only way to ensure food on the table for a time? Does answering these questions make the situation seem a little more like theft and a little less like a business agreement between two consenting adults?

Organs from Prisons: Harvesting in China

The Chinese government's practice of harvesting organs from executed prisoners has recently become a hot issue on unethical organ procurement. After a long denial by the authorities, China's Ministry of Health spokesman Mao Qunan finally admitted to the practice, in a BBC interview, in mid-January of 2007 (Han 2007). Deputy Health Minister Huang Jiefu acknowledged that, "Apart from a small portion of traffic victims, most of the organs from cadavers are from executed prisoners" (Matas 2007). This may not seem so offensive to a United States citizen, who might think that a serial killer deserves to be put to death, and at least some good may come of it by donating his organs, with or without the permission of the killer. When seen in the proper light, that the Chinese laws on death penalty are extensive, it becomes a different, more complicated matter. According to an Amnesty Watch International report, China executes more people than all other countries combined and for violent and non-violent crimes (Matas 2007). The big debate, lately, has focused on alleged harvesting of organs, by Chinese officials, from practitioners of Falun Gong, a group that is actively involved as nonviolent, conscientious political objectors of the Chinese regime's policies of oppression toward the group's beliefs (Han 2007).

Unlike fellow inmates, Practitioners of Falun Gong are reported to be systematically blood tested and have their organs examined. Those tested are not told the reasons for the testing. In the conclusion to their report, David Matas and David Kilgour stated explicitly that their research has led them to accept the allegations that Falun Gong practitioners are being detained and imprisoned on a large scale by national and local Chinese government officials. They have been used as live organ donors, with their vital organs being seized and sold at high prices, sometimes to foreigners who would otherwise face long waits for voluntary organs to be donated in their home countries (Matas 2007).

Concluding remarks

We found no substantiating evidence whatsoever with regards to Mexican rumors of murder and organ theft for the purpose of transplantation in the United States. That the deaths have occurred is probable, but their being related to organ transplantation in any way, shape or form is quite unlikely. The current system of laws and necessary record keeping in the United States makes illegal organ procurement and transplantation within its borders an almost certain impossibility. The procedure is of such a nature, requiring a cooperative effort from a large number of professionals and several different organizations in tandem, that an undercover operation simply could not be successful. This includes procuring organs from outside U.S. borders and transplanting them within the USA. If for no other reason, the procedure would be a failure due to time constraints for acquired donor organ survival.

Donor organ shortage, particularly donor kidney shortage, is severe and the condition is worsening. Kidneys are being procured abroad by wealthy individuals from US and other wealthy countries and are being transplanted in foreign hospitals under the auspice of corrupt or inept governments. Wealthy nations are supporting this trade in illegal organs through national political inactivity and through direct involvement on the part of the individual citizen and their healthcare providers.

There is a desperate, current and ongoing situation in China where human rights are being violated. Ethical lines need to be drawn, and individuals and countries in positions of power need to take an active role in defining and enforcing legal limits on types of approaches which can and cannot be taken in an effort to procure needed organs for transplantation.

There is a great need and demand for increased funding for research activities that would lead to increase donor organ supply. Educating the public and making the activities of the organ transplantation industry transparent to the public would increase the donor pool. However, it will not solve the shortage problem. Research in the areas of bioengineering may lead to new break through such as developing improved biomaterials and devices that would be helpful in developing artificial organs. Research on xenotransplantation (use of animal organs for transplantation) may lead to genetically altered animals for organ harvest. Artificial (mechanical) and genetically manipulated animal organs may be used as bridging mechanisms for dying patients waiting for a donated human organ. Moreover, the moratorium on clinical xenotransplantation research imposed on the possibility of transmission of animal disease to human should be reexamined.

Stem cell research is the most promising avenue of developing human organs on demand. The blockade on stem cell research funding is fading but not yet totally removed. There are many breakthroughs in stem cell research . Test-tube made real and transplantable human skin and ear are stories of the past decade (Nerem 1992). Recent advancements on stem cell research include test-tube kidney (BBC News 2002), regeneration of infracted heart (Lanza et al. 2004) and urinary bladder (Oottamasathien et al. 2006). Progress in stem cell research commands attention and demands increased funding.

Organ sale creates some difficult ethical dilemmas. Should we compensate willing live donors or the families of cadaver donors? Why shouldn't a starving, poor person be allowed to donate one kidney and receive fair compensation? Should rich (and even middle-class) Americans be able to buy kidneys from donors in impoverished countries? These are important medical ethics questions of our day, and they underscore the importance of ethics in every sphere of life.

Finally, professional ethics should be taught, debated, improved, practiced and enforced in all disciplines including transplantation medicine. A single ethically-motivated person among the group of people involved in organ procurement, transportation, preservation, transplantation and post-transplantation care-giving would prevent any irregular activity regarding organ theft, purchase or import. Transparency and high ethical standard would remove the fear from organ donor enlistment and increase the donor pool.

Acknowledgements: Supported in part by a Presidential Research Award to RK. This article is part of an investigative research project conducted by TB under the supervision of RK. Correspondence: kuddusru@uvsc.edu.

Work Cited

Adams, C. "Have guys awakened after a party to find their kidneys stolen"? (Feb 10, 2007). http://www.straightdope.com

BBC News. "Impoverished Indians advertise kidneys". (Dec 15, 2006). http://news.bbc.co.uk

BBC News. "Surgeons face kidney theft charges". (Aug 31, 2000). http://news.bbc.co.uk/2/hi/asia-pacific/904595.stm

BBC News. "Test tube kidney created". (Jan 24, 2002). http://news.bbc.co.uk/1/hi/health/1788552.stm

Emery D. "The Kidney Thieves–An Urban Legend". (Nov 12, 2006). http://www.urbanlegends.about.com

Han, X. "Chinese regime admits to organ harvesting from prisoners". The Epoch Times (Jan 24, 2007), also available at http://en.epochtimes.com/news/7-1-24/50806.html

IDS (Intermountain Donor Services). (Oct 24, 2006). http://www.idslife.org

IALOD (International Association of Living Organ Donors, Inc.). "Have questions about living kidney donation?" (Mar 2007), http://www.livingdonorsonline.org/kidney/kidneyfaq.htm

Johnson EM, Anderson JK, Jacobs C, Suh G, Humar A, Suhr BD, Kerr SR, Matas AJ. "Long-term follow-up of living kidney donors: quality of life after donation". Transplantation (1999); 67: 717-721

Lanza R, Moore MAS, Wakayama T, Perry ACF, Shieh J-H, Hendrikx J, Leri A, Chimenti S, Monsen A, Nurzynska D, West MD, Kajstura J, Anversa P. "Regeneration of the infarcted heart with stem cells derived by nuclear transplantation". Circulation Research (2004); 94: 820-807

Lima DX, Petroianu A, Hauter HL. "Quality of life and surgical complications of kidney donors in the late post-operative period in Brazil". *Nephrology Dialysis and Transplantation* (2006); 21(11):3238-3242

Maclay, K. "UC Berkeley anthropology professor working on organs trafficking". UC Berkeley News (Apr 30, 2004). http://www.berkeley.edu/news/media/releases/2004/04/30_organs.shtml

Matas D, Kilgour D. "Bloody Harvest: "Revised report into allegations of organ harvesting of falun gong practitioners in China". (Jan 31, 2007). Http://organharvestinvestigation.net/report200701/report 20070131.pdf

Nerem RM. "*Tissue engineering in the USA*". *Medical and Biological Engineering and Computing* (1992); 30: 8-12

Oottamasathien S, Williams K, Franco OE, Thomas JC, Saba K, Bhowmick NA, Staack A, Demarco RT, Brock JW 3rd, Hayward SW, Pope JC 4th. "Bladder tissue formation from cultured bladder urothelium". *Developmental Dynamics* (2006); 235:2795-801

Radford, B. "Organ theft legend resurfaces in Mexico border slayings – News and Comment. Skeptical Enquirer". (July-August 2003). http://www.findarticles.com/p/articles/mi_m2843/is_4_27/ai_104733225

Scheper-Hughes N. "Theft of Life: the Globalization of Organ Stealing Rumors". *Anthropology Today* (1996); 12:3-11

The National Kidney Foundation (Feb 28, 2007). http://www.kidney.org

UNOS (The United Network for Organ Sharing). (Feb 28, 2007). http://www.unos.org

USINFO. "Resource Tools Identifying Misinformation". (Feb 20, 2007). http://usinfo.state.gov

Wikipedia. Organ Theft (Feb 7, 2007). http://en.wikipedia.org

Youngner SJ, Schapiro R, Siminoff LA (eds). Death and Organ Procurement: Public Beliefs and Attitudes. *Kennedy Institute of Ethics Journal* (2004); Volume 14 (special issue), available at http://muse.jhu.edu/journals/kennedy_institute_of_ethics_journal/toc/ken14.3.html

Fig. 1. Waiting list for organs grew faster than the number of organs transplanted. A. Patients waiting for various solid organs as of March 2007 (T- all organs, K-kidney, L- liver, H- heart, Ln- lung, O- other organs including intestine and doubles such as kidney-panaceas and heart-lung). Note that ~75% of the waiting list is for a kidney. B. Number of kidney transplanted and the number of patients waiting for a kidney from 1992-2007. The Y-axis shows waiting list or organs transplanted (in thousands). Data (modified) from OPTN 2006. For more information, please see databases maintained by UNOS (2007) and National Kidney Foundation (2007).

UVSC Students during a Dance Performance for
"Ethics and The Performance Arts"

Ethical Concerns Regarding Pharmaceutical Trials

by
David P. Yells

Abstract

This paper identifies several methodological and ethical concerns with pharmaceutical research. These concerns include lack of random selection, withdrawal of medication, publication bias, and off-label prescribing. Each concern can disadvantage, in some cases in an extreme manner, patients. Several suggestions are offered to reduce these problems.

Ethical Concerns Regarding Pharmaceutical Trials

In January, 2007 The New England Journal of Medicine published two reports on the drugs pergolide and cabergoline (Schade, Andersohn, Suissa, Haverkamp, & Garbe, 2007; Zanettine et al. 2007). These drugs have a long history of use in treating Parkinson's Disease and a somewhat shorter history of treating Restless Leg Syndrome. Both of these reports revealed a significantly increased risk of heart valve damage in patients being treated with these drugs. I am surprised that I have not yet seen a commercial from a law firm soliciting clients for the inevitable class action lawsuit that is bound to be filed.

The process by which drugs are researched and ultimately approved for human use has come under considerable scrutiny in the last few years. Fen-Phen, Vioxx, and Prozac are a few examples of drugs that received approval from the FDA and subsequently became the targets of legal action due to alleged adverse effects. This paper will address concerns about the methods by which drugs are evaluated for approval and use focusing on basic methodological issues as well as related ethical concerns.

I do want to start with a disclaimer: I am a drug study child. My graduate education (I actually crammed 5 years of graduate school into 7) was funded by Eli Lilly. My advisor worked as a consultant for a psychopharmacology research lab at a university medical center which had a very lucrative relationship with the drug company for research on the first Selective Serotonin Reuptake Inhibitor anti-depressant, Prozac.

The traditional gold standard for pharmaceutical trials is the completely randomized double-blind placebo-controlled study. In its simplest form, this involves two groups. Participants are randomly assigned to receive either the experimental compound or an inactive (placebo) compound. The requirement for the placebo controlled condition derives from the high rate of placebo effect-a response to the inactive compound-observed in such studies. Examples of the placebo effect include rates of between 32% and 65% for treatment of lower urinary tract infections (Van Leeuwen et al. 2006), between 30% and 40% in treatment of dyspepsia (Talley et al. 2006), and nearly 50% in treating depression (Arroll et al. 2005).

The goal of a clinical trial, then, is to determine whether the proposed medication has effects above and beyond the placebo effect. In order to eliminate possible expectation effects, neither the participants nor the researchers are aware of which participants receive which compound. Although concerns of the placebo effect are important, the double blind procedure also protects against experimenter bias. Of course, researchers pride themselves on objectivity. However, outcome measures used in evaluating psychiatric drug effectiveness can be subjective in nature. Drug companies themselves cannot conduct the research due to obvious conflict of interest concerns. However, if the research is contracted out to a Medical Center or hospital is there really any less conflict of interest? Clearly, it is equally important to keep the investigators blind to treatment conditions until all analysis is complete. Once the trial period is over and all evaluations are complete, the blind is broken to reveal the treatment conditions.

The first methodological problem relates to the recruitment of the participants. If the issue being investigated is depression, there is a population of people who suffer from depression. Methodologically, the participants in a study should reflect a random sample of the entire population of interest. This is the principle of random selection; each member of the population of interest has an equal chance of being included in the study. This is clearly not the case in drug research. For example, participants are often referred to clinical trials by their physician. However, a substantial percentage, perhaps as high as 50% (Kessler et al., 2003), of individuals suffering from depression do not seek or receive treatment and are therefore out of the loop as far as physician-referred clinical trials are concerned. Another approach to recruiting participants is to run advertisements in newspapers. Again, this excludes people who do not read newspapers or who are understandably reluctant to participate in a drug study on the basis of a newspaper advertisement. Another factor influencing participation is that participants may be compensated monetarily or with free medical services which adds a motivational question to the mix. As a result, participants in clinical trials may not appropriately represent the population of interest. This clearly represents a limitation on the generalizability of the results.

A second methodological issue, with serious ethical implications, is the mechanics of being involved in a study. Generally, participants are already taking a medication to treat their condition. This is especially true for those participants referred by a physician. It is common to discontinue the current medication for some period before the clinical trial begins. Then, following this wash-out period, a participant may be assigned to the placebo condition and be deprived of medication for an even longer time. In the example of anti-depressants, this is a serious concern because of the relapse rate following the termination of pharmacotherapy and the increased suicide rate associated with untreated depression.

Researchers sometimes deflect this criticism by alluding to the idea of informed consent. The participants are aware of what will occur, including the possibility that they may be assigned to the placebo condition, and they freely choose to participate. Well, it is not uncommon for the current medication to be treating the condition, but not as effectively as desired. Alternatively, the treatment may be effective at treating the condition, but with unpleasant side effects. Dangling the possibility of a better treatment in front of someone in this situation may be a subtle form of coercion. Ethical guidelines are very explicit in forbidding the use of coercion for the purposes of research.

The means by which results of clinical trials are made public is also a concern. If a well-designed trial demonstrates that a drug is effective, it is relatively easy to get the results published. However, if the drug does not prove effective, publication is a much more difficult task. This bias toward statistically significant differences between treatment conditions results in a skewed representation of a drug's effectiveness. A drug may have 8 or 10 positive trials and an equal number of negative trials, but the information represented in published literature would most likely not reflect that.

One analysis (Ionnidis, 1998) found that positive trials were submitted for publication significantly more rapidly and were published significantly more rapidly than negative trials. Other researchers (Krzyzanowska, Pintilie, & Tannock, 2003) evaluated the publication pattern of clinical trials that had been initially presented at a professional conference. Significantly more positive trials (81%) than negative trials (68%) were eventually published. Another approach to the issue is to monitor the fate of trials following initial protocol approval (Chan, Hrobjartsson, Haahr, Gotzsche, & Altman, 2004). It was found that ½ of the efficacy outcomes and 2/3 of the harm outcomes per trial were incompletely reported. In both cases, statistically significant results were 2.4 times more likely to be published than non significant results. Among all published trials, 62% changed, introduced, or omitted at least one primary outcome when compared to the original approved protocol. Perhaps most alarmingly, 86% of authors surveyed denied the existence of unreported outcomes despite explicit evidence to the contrary. Finally, in a recent examination of clinical trials for treating acute stroke (Liebeskind, Kidwell, Sayre, & Saver, 2006), it was found that those trials including harmful outcomes were less likely to be published than those without harmful outcomes. There was also underreporting of trials that showed no effects of treatment.

In some cases the decision to not publish is made by the scientific journal as an editorial decision. More ethically questionable is a pharmaceutical company who elects to not even attempt to publish the results of a clinical trial that does not demonstrate the drug's effectiveness. As a result, prescribers and patients may be deprived of information relevant to a treatment plan.

Another issue related to the publication process concerns trials that do not go to completion. In many cases this is because adverse effects occur. In some cases, the participants suffering the adverse reactions are discarded as "outlyers" and the study is completed. In other cases the trial is terminated and does not see the light of day. In either case, prescribers and patients are again deprived of critical information.

Another related concern is how a compound is used once it receives FDA approval. Essentially, at that point a prescriber can prescribe the medication to any patient for any condition and is not limited to only the conditions that were originally researched. This is referred to as off-label use. For example, Prozac was initially investigated and approved for treating Major Depressive Disorder (MDD) in adults. It was not long before it was being prescribed to treat MDD in adolescents and, ultimately, children. It was also used for treating post-luteal phase dysphoric disorder (PMS), eating disorders, and several anxiety disorders. A recent national survey (Radley, Finkelstein, & Stafford, 2006) found that in 2001, there were an estimated 150 million off-label prescriptions. Amazingly, it was estimated that 73% of these off-label uses reflected little or no scientific support. Another recent survey (Cuzzolin, Atzei, & Fanos, 2006) reported that off-label prescriptions had an adverse drug reaction rate of between 23 and 60%. To illustrate that this is not a uniquely American problem, consider that ninety percent of a modest sample of Scottish pediatricians reported having engaged in off-label prescribing (Mc-Clay, Tanaka, Ekins-Daukes, & Helms, 2006). Fifty-five percent of responders indicated that such children are disadvantaged by the use of off label prescribing. Most troubling, perhaps, is that 69% failed to obtain informed consent or inform parents of the situation.

Now that I have introduced the nature of the problems with the pharmaceutical research process, I feel obligated to offer some solutions.

Regarding recruitment of participants, the medical community needs to engage in more aggressive outreach. Disorder screening clinics are an excellent way to tap into population that may be excluded from clinical trials. Mental health days at schools and businesses should be pursued.

The withdrawal of medication for a placebo controlled-condition should not be an absolute requirement for a clinical trial. If a person receiving a drug improves, it may not be necessary to know how much of the response should be attributed to the placebo effect and how much to the drug itself. The goal is to improve the patient. Understanding the source of the improvement is not essential.

Regarding the publication bias, relevant journals and researchers should negotiate prior to the onset of research. Editorial decisions should be made based on the rationale of the experiment and the appropriateness of the design. Well-justified and well-designed research should be accepted for publication a priori. The outcome of a trial should not be a concern.

Off-label prescribing needs to be monitored more closely and there needs to be an outlet to consolidate information from these trials. Researchers and prescribers need to work more closely together.

The current model of pharmaceutical drug trials is broken and in need of repair. The approval of helpful drugs is often delayed unnecessarily. Unsafe drugs are allowed on the marked. The Food and Drug administration, along with the academic community and practitioners, need to develop a system that does a better job of getting useful drugs into the hands of those who need them and keeping dangerous drugs off the market.

References
Arroll, B., Macgillivray, S., Ogston, S., Reid, I., Sullivan, F., Williams, B., & Crombie, I. (2005). "Efficacy And Tolerability Of Tricyclic Antidepressant And Ssris Compared With Placebo For Treatment Of Depression In Primary Care: A Meta-Analysis". *Annals of Family Medicine*, 3, 449-456.

Chan, A. W., Hrobjartsson, A., Haahr, M. T., Gotzsche, P. C., & Altman, D. G. (2004). "Empirical Evidence For Selective Reporting Of Outcomes In Randomized Trials: Comparison Of Protocols To Published Articles". *Journal of the American Medical Association*, 291, 2457-2465.

Cuzzolin, L., Atzei, A., & Fanos, V. (2006). "Off-Label And Unlicensed Prescribing For Newborns And Children In Different Settings: A Review Of The Literature And A Consideration About Drug Safety." *Expert Opinions on Drug Safety*, 5, 703-718.

Ioannidis, J. P. (1998). "Effect Of The Statistical Significance Of Results On The Time To Completion And Publication Of Randomized Efficacy Trials". *Journal of the American Medical Association*, 279, 281-286.

Kessler, R. C., et al. (2003). "The Epidemiology Of Major Depressive Disorder: Results From The National Comorbidity Survey Replication" (NCS-R). *Journal of the American Medical Association*, 289, 3095-3105.

Krzyzanowska, M. K., Pintilie, M., & Tannock, I. F. (2003). "Factors Associated With Failure To Publish Large Randomized Trials Presented At An Oncology Meeting". *Journal of the American Medical Association*, 290, 495-501.

Liebeskind, D. S., Kidwell, C. S., Sayre, J. W., & Saver, J. L. (2006). "Evidence Of Publication Bias In Reporting Acute Stroke Clinical Trials". *Neurology*, 67, 973-979.

McClay, J. S., Tanaka, M., Ekins-Daukes, S., & Helms, P. J. (2006). "A Prospective Questionnaire Assessment Of Attitudes And Experiences Of Off Label Prescribing Among Hospital Based Paediatricians". *Archives of Disorders of Childhood*, 91, 550-551.

Radley, D. C., Finkelstein, S. N., & Stafford, R. S. (2006). "Off-Label Prescribing Among Office-Based Physicians". *Archives of Internal Medicine*, 166, 1021-1026.

Schade, R., Andersohn, F., Suissa, S., Haverkamp, W., & Garbe, E. (2007). "Dopamine Agonists And The Risk Of Cardiac-Valve Regurgitation". *New England Journal of Medicine*,

Talley, N. J., Locke, G. R., Lahr, B. D., Zinsmeister, A. R., Cohard-Radice, M., D'Elia, T. V., Tack, J., & Earnest, D. L. (2006). "Predictors Of Placebo Response In Functional Dyspepsia". *Alimentare Pharmacological Therapeutics*, 23, 923-936.

Van Leeuwen, J. H., Castro, R., Busse, M., & Bemelmans, B. L. (2006). "The Placebo Effect In The Pharmacologic Treatment Of Patients With Lower Urinary Tract Infections". *European Urology,* 50, 440-453.

Zanettine, R., Antonini, A., Gatta, G., Gentile, R., Tesei, S., & Pezzoli, G. (2007). "Valvular Heart Disease And The Use Of Dopamine Agonists For Parkinson's Disease". *New England Journal of Medicine,*

Dr. Sam Rushforth, President WIlliam Sederberg, and Dr. Jans Wager speaking during the panel discussion: "On the Corporate University".

Informed Consent and Ethnography: Dissent, Consent, and Nonsense

By
David Clark Knowlton

Aform, sometimes two pages in length, must be filled out increasingly by research subjects. It details the formal expectations of the subject, their right to refuse participation in the study, and often the specialized theoretical issues of the study and how it might contribute to knowledge. As a tangible manifestation of the ideal of "informed consent" this form is argued to guarantee the ethical treatment of research subjects and, as a result, is required increasingly for expanding areas of research with human subjects.

As such it connects many social domains, not the least of which is the idea of ethical treatment of the people scholars work with to produce knowledge. Others of these domains include the legal protection of institutions where scholars work, such as universities, the needs of committees who perform oversight to carry out their function, and the methodological and professional demands of a scholar's discipline. As you can see, while the first is a norm, indicated by the trope of ethics, the latter are more organizational and institutional areas. In these latter areas ethics are claimed and mobilized as part of the exercise of power. This organizational separation, where ideas have their own existence but must be mobilized in organizational structures that have organizational needs which are not isomorphic with those of the goal of ethics, opens the door for contradictions. Ethics are animated in organizations, therefore, in ways that are not necessarily consonant with ethics understood in a strict sense.

Another potential break opens since scholars have interests that are not the same as those of the organization, as do the people they work with to carry out research. These separate sets of interests open the door for complex contradictions to emerge, under the guise of ethics, that may have little to do with the actual ethics of giving people the necessary information to agree or refuse the role of research subjects and to prevent harm from coming their way as a result of the research. Ethics moves, in this case, from a concern about people to a legitimating and challengeable trope.

Ethics per se argue about the relationship between people and provide principles to guide the relationships. Mobilization of ethics as trope, as part of the exercise of organizational practice, brings another dimension to the issue. Here ethics shift from a practice between people to a symbol and an authorizing set of discourses connected with that symbol. While ethics as trope focuses on portions of interactions among subjects under scrutiny, they also connect these concerns with the justification, operation, and continuity of the organization. Ethics as trope mobilized in institutional spaces carries, therefore, a dimension of theatricality.

Theatres of ethics are constructed for inspection of ethical practice. Audiences for the theatre are also constructed. And, the theatre itself has the function of reproducing things that may not indeed be the primary point of ethics strictly constructed. In this case ethics may come to have more to do with the needs of the theatre itself as well as of other domains than those of the ethical principle. Analytically we ought to perhaps reserve the domain of ethics for the relationship among people and claim another term, perhaps meta ethics, or tropical ethics, for its use in legitimating ideologies, and theatrical ethics for the performance of tropical ethics for formal inspection.

Social Anthropology and Formalization

As a discipline, social anthropology presents some peculiarities that will help us make some sense of this issue. Social and cultural anthropology in the twentieth century emphasized a method known as participant observation, or ethnography—since the written, sustained presentation of data gathered is known as an ethnography (Bernard 2005, Pelto and Pelto 1978, Schensul and Le Compte 1999). In its codified form this method focuses on going to the place where the people studied live and living with them, in their society, as participants. Ethnography in this sense is typified by the detailed keeping of notes and the kinds of questions, theoretical frames, and expectations of writing that these students of human societies carry. These notes and writings constitute data and some analysis. The relationship among the investigator, the social settings that produce the notes, and the questions with which the investigator approaches field work constitute the concerns of methodology.

At a time when the other social sciences have formalized methods and increasingly rely on method as a guarantee of the scientific validity of their work, most anthropologists have resisted both formalization and method as guarantee of science, although they have discussed the field experience at length (Robben and Sluka 2006, Shaffir and Stebbins 2002). Instead validity and rigor are weighed by critique from peers who work in the same area or among similar peoples and, increasingly, in the engagement between anthropologists and the communities where they study.

One could argue that the resistance to formalization of method among anthropologists is less about rigor or science, therefore, than a resistance to method as authorizing and legitimating trope, with its respective theatres of inspection. It seems more a concern for field work itself as the authorizing and legitimating experience, as a process of sustained engagement with other people, rather than the presentation, i.e. performance, of a formally stipulated and surveiled statement which rigidly details and justifies the specific interaction between researcher and subjects as well as their boundaries, using a language of ethics, consent, and rights. Method, ethics, consent, and rights are very important to anthropologists, as is manifested in almost every textbook and in the governing ethics statement on the American Anthropological Association web page (www.aaanet.org). Nevertheless they occupy a different social space in anthropology than in other sciences, such as those characterized by laboratories, or even limited, closed question surveys.

The term "formalization" therefore refers less to a thoughtfulness about research and an explicitness of method than to different legitimating ideas and social practices. The one insists on a natural science approach to observing naturally occurring life and behavior as the trope of authority, while the other attempts to limit interaction between researchers and subjects to narrow, carefully constructed frames, governed by explicit and much evaluated method as governing trope.

Nevertheless, anthropologists, especially those who work interdisciplinarily or who seek funding from interdisciplinary sources are finding themselves required to develop more specificity and justification for their methods in formal ways that are unusual for them. Anthropologists typically leave things somewhat vague, not just because of a different guiding trope, but because of the unpredictability of the field site, the obligation to recognize and amend your project as you go according to the situation and needs of the people with whom you work, and a general reluctance to over specify. This does not mean people go into the field without a sense of rigorous method. They generally are trained in method, as witnessed by the substantial texts produced on method in anthropology. Rather the reluctance is to over specify, and to make unchangeable or rigid the method, before going to the field.

Fieldworkers know they need to justify themselves to an external group of peers. Saying, "I went there and saw," is no longer sufficient. However anthropologists also recognize that field circumstances are unpredictable, as are the specific questions a person may find relevant and possible to study. Generally it is felt that researchers must demonstrate good, solid training and a command of method but they, and they alone, can best determine the actual questions, and hence method, when they are on site, living with the people according to what they find on the ground while there. As anthropologists have formalized, their theatre of review then is guided by the notion of demonstration of competence, in order to allow for competent improvisation as conditions demand, rather than a judgment on an explicit script which is to be performed with almost no modification.

The traditional anthropological stance is difficult to accept in the theatre of ethics of formal Institutional Review. Instead of formally looking at a general plan and approving it, and therefore the credentials of an investigator as well as faith in their ability to carry out an ethically, methodological, and theoretically relevant project, the Review Boards expect to exercise judgment on the explicit, actual practices that a researcher will do. Anthropologists often find this impossible, since there is no way they can absolutely know what they will find once they have traveled, often across continents and oceans, to their field site. But anthropological practice raises problems for the formal expectations of the theatre and its own institutional importance as defined by its mission governed by federal law and university governance policies and practice.

This move in anthropology towards formality and external justification, although not without substantial resistance, is further pushed by changes in the federal system of research review, which mandates that universities that receive federal funds require research to obtain prior approval from Institutional Review Boards (United States Department of Health and Human Services 2005). Ethnography used to be considered an exempt method by Internal Review Board legislation. Recently it has changed from exempt to generally expedited. This change has led to tensions, complaints, and problems from an anthropological position as anthropologists have to submit to a theatre of ethical review, as well as, by implication, methodological review, that requires increasing formality as well as engagement by anthropologists with methodological standards of research developed in other fields, such as those of medical research, that may or may not be applicable to anthropology (Annas 2006, Boster 2006, Bradburd 2006, Brenneis 2006, Fassin 2006, Fitzgerald 2006, Katz 2006, Kjeldgard 2006, Lederman 2006a, 2006b, 2006c, 2006d, Lins Ribeiro 2006, Plattner 2006, Schweder 2006, Strathern 2006, Sundar 2006, Winslow 2006)

But there is another wrinkle. Ethnography has been taken up as a method by many other disciplines, whether qualitative sociology, business studies, nursing, etc. What typifies these other uses is that they generally are much more formalized than ethnography as practiced by anthropologists, and they tend to maintain a clearer distinction between the life of the researcher and that of the ethnographer. They are generally performed fairly close to the institutions where scholars work instead of half a world away. It is not just an issue of distance, however. Anthropology expects researchers' lives to be entwined with those they study, often over many years and perhaps a lifetime, as part of the process of capturing naturally occurring behavior. Within anthropology this social relationship is argued to be a control on ethics and a means of guaranteeing epistemological validity. Nevertheless the claiming of ethnography by other disciplines weakens the disciplinary preference in anthropology for leaving ethnographic methods unformalized. It means anthropologists have to argue strongly for their methods and ethics in theatres where the arguments may not be accepted, less because of relevance for anthropology and the ethical protection of the people with whom anthropologists work, than because of the needs of organizational justification and theatricality of Review Boards.

Anthropological Debates on Research with People

Anthropology has critically and forcefully examined its methods, over the last thirty years, in terms of the power and ethics involved in the interactions between researchers and the communities with which they work (Clifford 1986, Crapanzano 1992, Rosaldo 1993, Scheper Hughes 1993). The concern has been strongly focused on the relative power of the people versus ethnographers in the construction of knowledge and the impact the ethnographic writings might have on the people studied. Anthropologists are very concerned about how their work might damage or benefit the lives of people they study and on how to build people's rights and interests into not just the study, but its publication in scholarly venues. This brings ethics, in terms of a consideration of power relationship between scholars and their research interlocutors, into a completely new level and arena. The people they work with have a voice in this arena as interlocutors and not simply as subjects whose only agency in the project, other than as objects of the research method, is to sign a form agreeing to participate or refusing to sign the form.

Anthropologists are generally reluctant these days to speak of "subjects" of research, with the implied limits on interaction and humanity in that label. They are similarly reluctant to use their old word of "informants". Anthropologists strive instead to find language that can address the co-creation of research, for varied ends and interests, over time between the scholar and the people with whom they work. As a result anthropologists prefer language like consultants or friends or co-researchers even to speak about the people with whom they work, rather than reducing them to the subject position and the researcher, and his/her discipline, to the position of knower. The emphasis is on engagement.

Absent in this discussion are the general considerations that serve as methodological guarantees of more ordinary human research such as the clarity of distinction between researcher and subjects of research by time and place, including the idea of a research subject, and the limited nature of method. Anthropology expects the lives of researchers and people researched to be deeply entwined in time and space although it interrogates that entwining from the standpoint of method, theory, and ethics. Nevertheless the entwining is seen as a methodological necessity for participant observation.

Anthropology and Ethics

As a result anthropology has developed a strong discussion of ethics. The general concern is first for the well being of the people with whom we work, i.e. to cause them no harm, and only secondarily for the well being of the discipline (American Anthropological Association 1998). But anthropology has resisted making rigid statements and procedures to formalize and simplify the ethics. Anthropology has preferred a messier, and perhaps more honest, strategy of making a strong ethics statement, creating a strong discussion in the discipline on ethics, and recognizing that scholars must apply those principles in the field in messy, ongoing and changing situations which, by nature, are not formalizable like those of laboratory or survey research. Anthropologists focus on ethics in practice in the field, and not on the formality of ethics as trope in institutional settings where they can be drawn into other functions, and not on formal theatricality of ethical review.

This is not to say anthropology has not had problems with ethics. The field has been riled recently over allegations against the famous students of the Yanomamo, Napoleon Chagnon and Jacques Lizot, of ethical violations in their increasing engagement with Venezuelan and Brazilian national societies. Although the journalist Patrick Tierney (2002), in his book Darkness in El Dorado, brought this to public attention, it was anthropologists who worked in the same area, such as Alcides Ramos and Terence Turner who first brought the concerns to light. The conflict between defenders of Chagnon and those of Turner and Tierney fought a vigorous battle in anthropology. To be sure, many other epistemological and ontological concerns that divide the field became part of the conversation. As a result it became difficult to take action. But the ethical concerns were strongly ventilated. At the end, anthropology comes out with stronger and better articulated ethical standards than before, even though there was no sanction (American Anthropological Association 2002). The theatre of after the fact judgment and review took a different form than that of a court of law which can weigh behavior according to standards of proper and improper behavior. Anthropological ethics were shown to be guidelines and not rules. The two belong to different notions of what the nature of ethics is, how ethics should be implemented, and how they should be disciplined, involving different arrangements of institutions, tropes, and theatres.

Furthermore the ethical concern in anthropology has arisen because of anthropologist's historical involvement in espionage, government policies of advancement against a given population, and colonialist administration of indigenous peoples. All of these created an enormous crisis and discussion in the last half of the twentieth century and lead to strong concerns in contemporary anthropology about the issues and about ethics. As a result, anthropologists today generally prefer not to have these entanglements that might make their ethical interaction with the people they live with contradictory and problematic. Narrowing the ethics to a small set of rules undoubtedly would make that easier, although it would also change and limit the relationships between anthropologists and their friends-consultants.

Anthropologists are concerned that our employers, especially since about half of all anthropologists are employed outside the university, and our funders not determine the ethical standards of research. Rather they should be focused, if anthropologists are to be involved, with the well being of the people with whom they work. This well being is seen as a negotiated process, rather than a paternalistic one. The latter emphasizes experts and outsiders deciding what is best for you, while the former insists the scholar be engaged with people and in conversation learn their determinations of well being and mutually develop the research to enhance well being. These are very different approaches to ethics.

Informed Consent

As a result anthropologists often worry about the difference between ideals of informed consent and signed forms that claim informed consent. The two, the notion of consent versus forms making consent tangible, serve as a place where the more complex concerns adduced above can be matters of struggle. As a means of explaining the difference between signed forms as a means of making tangible and consent as that which seems to need a more concrete and limited existence, I shall relate two anecdotes of my encounters with medicine. This is particularly germane since medicine and particularly ethical concerns with medical research drive the development and advance of institutional review boards. Medical practice and medical science are directly related.

The last time I went to the Salt Lake Clinic, I was handed a form to sign as I checked in, well before I spoke with anyone other than a busy clerk at a window. In an impish mood, I decided to read the small print on the form. It said that I was signing that I had been informed about the risks of the procedure I was to undergo. When I mentioned to the woman who was checking my insurance card and taking the co-pay that they asked me to sign but had given me no information, she responded in an irritated fashion, asking what information. I showed her the form. She then gave me a pamphlet which had little to do with the service I was to receive. Laughing to myself I signed. I had now participated in a fiction ostensibly meant to show my informed consent, but there was no "informed" about the consent, despite the legal document.

My experience in medical arenas leads me to believe that the signing of "informed consent" forms is a theatre that has more to do with potential lawsuits and with lawyers attempting to build in protections than it actually has to do with informed consent. They are interested in the patient's signature, not whether she or he has actually received relevant information and has the knowledge or capacity to provide consent. When a patient is given material, it is seldom written in any form that is intelligible easily to someone without a college education. Even then it leaves many questions unanswered and unanswerable, since the only person you can interrogate is the form and pamphlet, not someone who actually knows the information and can respond to patient concerns. Informed is a misnomer in this case. It is a legal fiction that protects powerful institutions and powerful people, rather than patients.

This matter of "informed" and the provision of information responds to a priori and formal decisions about what information is necessary. It also presumes how people think, make decisions and process information. It further pre-decides how people should think about risk and the weighing of risk. As such this information is more a practice of power over "subjects" than an empowering of them to make meaningful decisions.

Furthermore, as a gate-keeping mechanism in something the patient has interest in, the form is coerced. As a result consent is a further legal fiction. My clearest example of this happened when I was scheduled for an endoscopy. Under medical instruction, I had changed into the hospital gown, was laying on the gurney, had been wheeled into the room where they would perform the procedure, an intravenous feed had been put in me to administer anesthetic, and then I was given a clipboard with a form to sign. Again it said that I was signing that I had been given information about risks and benefits from the procedure and that I was not only acknowledging its receipt but giving permission for the procedure. I mentioned to the aide with the form that I had not been given the information. She stuttered, not knowing what to do. After hesitating a bit, I decided it was better to sign, so as to receive service, instead of not signing, interrupting the procedure, and labeling myself as a quarrelsome patient as well as not getting the endoscopy. Not only was the informed part a fiction, the consent was coerced.

Although situations like this are not identical to research, there is a lot of commonality. The primary one is that the forms with their notions of "informed", "consent", and signature use the trope of ethics to engage in acts of power which create participants in research as limited subjects, dependent on experts. As a result they are often fictions. From the beginning they do not take into account the different subjectivities of real people and the different ways risk and information are constructed and evaluated in their life worlds. In other words they fail in the first principle of communication. They do not ask how the message must be constructed in order to fit into the languages, cultures, and psychologies of diverse subjects. They engage in a one size fits all universalization of a presumed person, like the "rational man" of law, even though such universalizations are demonstrably false.

Theaters of Review

Institutional Review Boards, like hospitals, have multiple interests when they examine in a theatre of ethics the forms researchers give—or don't give—their subjects detailing risk and benefits in order to obtain "informed consent". They are interested in the legal protection of the university and its funding sources, as well as the committee itself, should a subject ever challenge a piece of research in court with allegations of preventable harm. Arguably the signature on the form, as well as the information the form contains, exercises a primary function of legal protection of these agencies. Only through that theatre, and the small window of formal consideration of subjects' interests, does the ethical treatment of subjects take place. While valuable, still it is easy for form to take precedence over substance, particularly given the overriding interest in protection of the institution. The theatre of ethical review is performed as forms are weighed, discussed, and approved or disproved. But there is no feed back mechanism to know whether it is only a theatre of tropical ethics, or whether it also protects the substantive ethical interests of the subjects as well.

In these theatres of ethics, like courts of law, there is little space to actually consider how the interest of the research subject might take place. The investigator, and the committee attempt to place themselves in the situation of some idealized subject, deciding their interests and needs, and then create logic to meet those presumptions. This approach is a classic tautology of self-reflexive thinking, with little opening to the real, lived and experienced needs of subjects. Max Weber, the founder of sociology, argued a difference between formal rationality and substantive rationality (Weber 1978: 85-86). Formal rationality is characterized by external decisions of means ends relationships, or in his classic example of double entry accounting, of formal criteria requiring enumeration, separate entries, and balancing of accounts at the days end. In contrast Weber held substantive rationality to not be external, but to be embedded within the flow of life of people. It was the logic they generally referred to, rather than formal, externalized logic where formal syllogistic relations could be observed.

Formal rationality generally works to the benefit of elites who can dominate its arcane functionings and methods; it empowers them. Although it may provide some benefit to the general public, by definition it does not represent their forms of thinking, weighing, and assessing risk and benefit. As a result, it stands over them rather than empowering them and enabling them to take control of their own lives and their own risk management.

As anthropologists have pointed out, being presented with a document, formally expressed, and being asked to provide the theatre of a signature, is a difficult task when scholars work with illiterate or marginally literate populations. Literacy here can be taken not to mean simply the ability to read and write, but the ability to read and write—and understand—the formal language of their societies. Not infrequently the act of having to read a document and sign it removes the research from the space of ordinary interactions, although interactions with someone you know to be a researcher, to equivalent acts of signing forms in formal society, where generally something is at risk. As a result, the act itself generates suspicion and distrust. Instead of generating informed consent it can generate outright hostility, fear of loss, and suspicion about the broader concerns of the researcher. It changes the nature of relationships and interactions, not infrequently in ways that can make research impossible.

This is not to say that anthropologists are not concerned with informed consent. They are. But their experience in other societies and with people on the margins leads them to be skeptical of formal consent, and to demand substantive ethical treatment of the people with whom they work Substantive here means not just the meeting of the ends of ethics qua ethics, but the forming of information and consent in ways that are intelligible within the lives, cultures, and interests of anthropologists' interlocutors. It means not a simple opening of a small theatre where consent can be weighed and where the primary function is the legal protection of the researcher and his institution, rather it requires a sustained conversation and engagement with people, such that they can have some control over the nature of the research, the researcher, and the research product. "Consent" and "informed" then are not a singular act witnessed on a signed form, they become part of sustained, ongoing interactions between the researcher and the people with whom s/he works in which the entire project can be reopened and rediscussed at any moment.

Lower Ethical Standards

As a result, many anthropologists are concerned that the imposition of norms of informed consent and consent forms requires them, in order to obtain approval to carry out their research, to accept lower standards of informed consent than those embedded in the standard ethics of their discipline. They feel their ethical code is more demanding and rigorous. But they find themselves having a difficult time explaining that to Institutional Review Boards.

In anthropology, there have been sustained conversations between anthropologists and native communities (e.g. Buckley 2002, Rappaport 1990). Not infrequently we are challenged by the communities in terms of our ethics, our approaches, the purpose of the end results, who they empower and so on. We, as a field, have been chastened and increasingly recognize the importance of reworking the power relationships between us and the people with whom we work. Yet Institutional Review Boards and norms of formal informed consent, seem to force us into a position of greater distance and power vis a vis those people with whom we work. They lose peoplehood, with all its complexity and irregularity, and become subjects. The broader question is one of the relationship of science and research to the communities and individuals who they have traditionally made into subjects. Maybe the questions from anthropology should be translated into a concern about other domains of research with human subjects. Maybe a concern for substantive informed consent, rather than theatrical, tropical, or formal, should be the norm. Maybe there needs to be a sustain rethinking of power relationships between researchers and the subjects of their research.

Conclusion

We anthropologists will find a way to live with Institutional Review Boards and to continue doing ethnography. The questions we pose will inevitably transform portions of the process and have an impact in other areas of human research. The Institutional Review process develops from medical research and medical practice. These domains have already been the subject of much anthropological study. In them the inequality of power has become evident as a force that creates the authority of medicine and medical research (e.g. Farmer 2004, Baer 2001, Scheper Hughes 1993, Locke 2001, Rapp 2000). Many anthropologists find themselves now engaging in critical medical anthropology as a form of critically engaging medicine as a powerful social form that requires, in order to adequately meet the health needs of poorer and marginal populations, to undergo a transformation of power relationships. It must come to an awareness that inequality, including their inequality with their patients, is part of the process of creation of disease and ill health in today's world. Medicine, which proposes to heal, becomes part of the problem in the creation of disease.

Ethics, particularly the relationship between researchers and the people they work with, are very important. The necessity of good ethics is amply demonstrated by abuses we see when we look at the history of scientific advance. The open question, however, is how do we limit abuse. If we are not very careful, the very systems implemented to formally regulate ethics, with their attendant epistemologies and ontologies, may become abusive in their own right. They can create problems that weaken and hurt people who happen to engage in interaction with researchers. They may make the very notion of ethics an empirical impossibility at the same time they argue loudly they are guaranteeing good ethics. It is in the spirit of avoiding that scenario that this essay, with its distinctions between ethics, tropical ethics, and theatres of ethics is offered. Without an awareness of distinctions of this nature we have no hope of avoiding ethics becoming a signifier that has lost its referent, as people become increasingly subject with little other than pottage for rights.

References

American Anthropological Association

1998   Code of Ethics. www.aaanet.org/committees/ethics/ethcode.htm (Consulted April 20, 2007

American Anthropological Association

2002   Final report of the AAA El Dorado Task Force. www.aaanet.org/edtf/index.htm (Consulted April 20, 2007).

Annas, George J.

2006   Anthropology, IRBs, and Human Rights. *American Ethnologist*. 33:4:551-544.

Baer, Hans

2001   *Biomedicine and Alternative Healing Systems in America: Issues of Race, Class, Ethnicity, and Gender*. Madison: University of Wisconsin Press.

Bernard, H. Russell

2005   *Research Methods in Anthropology: Qualitative and Quantitative Approaches*. Lanham, Md.: Altamira Press.

Boster, James

2006   Towards IRB Reform. *Anthropology News*, 47:5:20-21.

Bourgois, Philippe

2002   *In Search of Respect: Selling Crack in El Barrio*. Cambridge: Cambridge University Press.

Bradburd, Daniel

2006   Fuzzy Boundaries and Hard Rules: Unfunded Research and the IRB. *American Ethnologist*, 33:4:492-498.

Brenneism Don

2006   Partial Measures. *American Ethnologist*, 33:4: 538-540.

Buckley, Thomas

2002   *Standing Ground: Yurok Indian Spirituality*, 1850-1990. Berkeley: University of California Press.

Clifford, James

1986   *Writing Culture: The Poetics and Politics of Ethnography*. Berkeley: University of California Press.

Crapanzano, Vincent

1992   *Hermes' Dilemma and Hamlet's Desire: On the Epistemology of Interpretation*. Cambridge: Harvard University Press.

Farmer, Paul

2004   *Pathologies of Power: Health, Human Rights, and the New War on the Poor*. Berkeley: University of California Press.

Fassin, Didier

2006   The End of Ethography as Collateral Damage of Ethical Regulation? *American Ethnologist*, 33:4: 522-524.

Fitzgerald, Maureen H.

2006   The Ethics Review Process. *Anthropology News* 46:6:10-11.

Katz, Jack
2006   Ethical Escape Routes for Underground Ethnographers. *American Ethologist* 33:4:499-506.

Kjeldgaard, Erik
2006   Anthropology and IRBs: A Response to James Boster. *Anthropology News*, 47:6:5-5.

Lederman, Rena
2006a   IRB Consent Form Dilemmas and the Importance of Local Knowledge. *Anthropology News*, 47:5:22-23.

2006b   Introduction: Anxiouis Borders between Work and Life in a Time of Bureaucratic Ethics regulation. *American Ethnologist*, 33:4:477-481

2006c   The Perils of Working at HomeL IRB "Mission Creep" as Context and Content for an Ethnography of Disciplinary Knowledges. *American Ethnologist* 33:4: 482-491.

2006d   The Ethical is Political. *American Ethnologist* 33:4:545-548.

Lins Ribeiro, Gustavo,
2006   IRBs Are the Tip of the Iceberg: State Regulation, Academic Freedom, and Methodological Issues. *American Ethnologist*, 33:4: 529-531,

Locke, Margaret
2007   *Twice Dead: Organ Translplants and the Reinvention of Death.* Berkeley: University of California Press.

Pelto, Pertti J. and Gretel H. Pelto
1978   *Anthropological Research: The Structure of Inquiry.* Cambridge: Cambridge University Press.

Plattner, Stuart
2006   Comment on IRB Regulation of Ethnographic Research. *American Ethnologist.* 33:4:525-528

Rapp, Rayna
2000   *Testing Women, Testing the Fetus: The Social Impact of Amniocentesis in America.* New York: Routlege.

Rappaport, Joanne
1990   T*he Politics of Memory: Native Historical Interpretation in the Colombian Andes.* Cambridge, Cambridge University Press.

Robben, Antonius C.G. M. and Jeffrey A. Sluka
2006   *Ethnographic Fieldwork: An Anthropological Reader.* Oxford: Blackwell Publishing.

Rosaldo, Renato
1993   *Culture and Truth: The Remaking of Social Analysis.* Boston: Beacon Press.

Schensul, Jean J., Margaret D. Le Compte,
1999   *Essential Ethnographic Methods.* Lanham, Md.: Altamira Press

Shaffir, William and Robert A. Stebbins,
2002   *Experiencing Fieldwork: An Inside View of Qualitative Research.* Newbury Park, California: Sage Publications.

Scheper Huges, Nancy
1993   *Death Without Weeping: The Violence of Everyday Life in Brazil.* Berkeley, University of California Press.

Schweder, Richard A.
2006   Protecting Human Subjects and Preserving Academic Freedom: Prospects at the University of Chicago. *American Ethnologist*, 33:4:507-518.

Strathern, Marilyn
2006   Don't Eat Unwashed Lettuce. *American Ethnologist*, 22:4: 532-534.

Sundar, Nandini
2006   Missing the Ethical Wood for the Bureaucratic Trees. *American Ethnologist*, 33:4:535-537.

Tierney, Patrick
2002   *Darkness in El Dorado: How Scientists and Journalists Devastated the Amazon*. New York: W.W. Norton and Company.

United States Department of Health and Human Services
2005   Title 45 Public Welfare, Part 46 Protection of Human Subjects. www.hhs/gov/ohrp/humansubjects/guidance/45cfr46.htm (last consulted April 19, 2007).

Weber, Max
1978   *Economy and Society*. Berkeley, University of California Press.

Winslow, Deborah
2006   NSF Supports Ethnographic Research. *American Ethnologist* 33:4: 519-521.

Dr. Susan Madsen

Conducting Risk Evaluations for Future Violence: Ethical Practice is Possible

By
Anton O' Tolman & Andrea L. Rotzien

This article first appeared in Professional Psychology, Research and Practice, 38(1) 71-79.

In civil and criminal court, judges and juries routinely face the task of considering an individual's risk for future violence, often relying on psychological experts to help them. For example, civil cases might involve consideration of a restraining order to prevent harm to a potential victim, evaluation of a mentally ill individual's danger to others, and deliberation regarding an ex-spouse's potential harm to his children in a custody determination. Criminal cases involve consideration of future risk throughout the adjudication process, including setting bail, jail classification and housing, potential juvenile transfers, sentencing decisions involving violent offenders, management of violence risk on probation or parole, and, in some jurisdictions, opinions regarding a person's status as a "sexually violent predator."

However, early research on the effectiveness of clinical predictions of violence decreased confidence in clinical evaluations of risk and therefore in testimony by psychologists. These early risk evaluations mostly used clinical "intuition," nonstandardized clinical techniques and lore, and psychological instruments not specifically developed to assess future risk. The seminal review of this type of risk evaluation (Monahan, 1981) concluded that these methods were weak in predicting future violence. Monahan (1984) later called for a "second generation" of research to guide practice and policy development.

This second generation of risk research continues, focusing on identified risk factors associated with various forms of violence (e.g., physical, sexual, domestic) and on the development of actuarial and guided clinical instruments to assist clinicians in improving their ability to assess the level of risk posed by a given individual. Evaluations of the reliability, validity, and utility of these instruments generally reach favorable conclusions and indicate that these methods represent a significant advance over unguided clinical inference. For example, regarding one of these second-generation instruments, the Historical, Clinical, Risk Management—20 (HCR–20; Webster, Douglas, Eaves, & Hart, 1997), a recent report concluded, "Research on the HCR–20 generally supports claims that... its items can be scored reliably and are related to violence... interrater reliability coefficients have been found to be acceptable and encouraging for the responsible use of the HCR–20" (Webster & Douglas, 2001, p. 3). Hanson (2005) stated, "The validation research has typically found that all these measures [second-generation instruments] show moderate accuracy in predicting violent recidivism" (p. 214). In addition, in a review of recidivism among adolescent serious offenders, Benda, Corwin, and Toombs

(2005) noted that "combining dynamic needs, criminal history and static factors... maximizes accuracy of prediction in recidivism and... provides targets for intervention" (p. 591). They further stated that recent meta-analyses indicate "that dynamic risk factors predict recidivism as well or better than static or historical variables" (pp. 591–592). A meta-analysis by Hanson and Morton-Bourgon (2005) found that for sexual violence, sexual deviancy and antisocial orientation were strong predictors of recidivism for both adult and adolescent offenders. Violent recidivism, sexual and nonsexual in nature, was related to antisocial personality and psychopathy. In addition, smaller effects were found for intimacy deficits, conflicts in intimate relationships, and emotional identification with children—all dynamic factors that may be amenable to treatment. While not all reports on risk factors are this promising, we see this as progress in the field of risk management.

Despite these significant advances in the understanding of risk factors related to violence and the creation of specific risk-related instruments, some have criticized risk evaluations as part of professional practice. Several past authors evaluated published concerns about statistical base rates and other considerations (e.g., Grisso & Appelbaum, 1992; Saks & Kidd, 1986), universally concluding that the techniques were not perfect but had value in conducting evaluations for legal decision makers. More recently, additional critics have claimed that it is unethical to perform risk evaluations and that the evidentiary basis for these techniques is insufficient to permit their use in court (Berlin, Galbreath, Geary, & McGlone, 2003; Campbell, 2000, 2003). From the perspective of an expert witness to the courts, psychologists conducting risk evaluations should be aware of these criticisms in order to respond to them effectively. This article examines these recent criticisms, not through the lens of theory or conjecture but through the functional perspective of ethical practice and the tasks facing the legal system.

Recent Criticisms of Risk Evaluations

Opposition to the general practice of risk assessment is typically based on three main arguments. The first argument is that risk evaluations do not meet the criteria for admissibility as outlined in Daubert v. Merrell Dow Pharmaceuticals (1993; see Campbell, 2000, 2003, 2004). In this landmark decision, the Supreme Court placed the role of "gatekeeper" on trial judges to consider the reliability or scientific validity of proffered testimony. In describing their rationale, the justices suggested four guidelines for judges to consider: whether the technique in question is falsifiable, whether the method has a known error rate, whether the method or technique has been peer reviewed by other experts, and whether the method has found "general acceptance" in the relevant scientific community. Critics claim (e.g., Campbell, 2003) that existing methods used in risk evaluation, such as the Psychopathy Checklist—Revised (PCL–R; Hare, 2003) and other actuarial instruments, do not meet these criteria.

The second argument (e.g., Campbell, 2003) is that risk evaluations, particularly involving sexual offenders, are unethical because actuarial data will "mislead" decision makers and create the impression that the data are more scientific and clear-cut than is the case. In particular, Campbell (2000, 2003, 2004) criticized what he called the "questionable classification accuracy" particularly of actuarial measures (e.g., Static–99, Harris, Phenix, Hanson, & Thornton, 2003; Violence Risk Appraisal Guide [VRAG], Quinsey, Harris, Rice, & Cormier, 1998; PCL–R, Hare, 2003). Campbell (2003, 2004) and others (e.g., Berlin et al., 2003) maintained, despite reasonable rates of classification accuracy reported in the literature, that these instruments miss too many offenders who will commit future crimes. For example, Berlin and colleagues contended that only half of the potential sexually violent predators assessed with the Static–99 as being in the highest risk group for sexual recidivism will commit a future known sex offense over a 15-year follow-up period.

Campbell (2000, 2003) illustrated the last argument against risk evaluations with a series of "Thou Shalt Not" points. In particular, he reasoned that psychologists performing risk evaluations should not express opinions about risk using predictor variables without significant meta-analytic support. For example, Campbell noted that one of the few meta-analytic studies completed on variables that predict sexual offending (Hanson & Bussiere, 1998) found limited support for the predictive validity of response to treatment, offender's history of sexual victimization, stability of employment, and the fact that an offender is single. Therefore, a mental health practitioner considering these characteristics would be in error. Campbell (2003) argued that psychologists should not rely on unaided clinical judgment in risk evaluations because they are notoriously inaccurate, while simultaneously asserting that they should not rely on actuarial or guided clinical risk assessment tools because their use does not meet the profession's ethical standards. Campbell suggested that psychologists also should avoid "adjusted" actuarial predictions of risk (see Quinsey et al., 1998) because these techniques are nonstandardized and therefore not accurate. He acknowledged that so-called dynamic risk variables, those that may change over time or as a result of treatment (see Rogers, 2000), may be valuable in understanding an individual's risk for violence, but he asserted that they should not be used because there is no published or clearly defined way to combine these variables into a prediction.

Given these arguments that psychologists should not use unaided clinical judgment, should not use actuarial instruments, and should not use guided clinical assessment techniques, it seems clear that critics believe that these evaluations should not be conducted at all. Although we agree that sole use of unaided clinical judgment is unsound practice, we propose that a combination of modern techniques to inform the court of risk, rather than making specific predictions regarding recidivism, is a realistic and ethical form of legal and clinical practice. More specifically, the use of actuarial methods can ensure practitioners review known risk factors and also give consideration to dynamic factors (e.g., Benda et al., 2005; Douglas & Skeem, 2005), protective factors (e.g., Barbaree, Seto, & Langton, 2001; Rogers, 2000), relevant personality traits (Hare, 2003; Mills, Kroner, & Hemmati, 2004), and contextual factors (Edens, 2006).

Risk Evaluations : Addressing the Concerns

With regard to admissibility, first it is worth noting that not all states follow Daubert, so some of the issues raised by critics may not apply in many courts. Regardless, the fact that courts find expert testimony related to violence risk useful has been made abundantly clear. The Supreme Court made a statement about the necessity for expert testimony in evaluating an individual's violence potential in Addison v. Texas (1979), a case that dealt with the issue of civil commitment of persons who might be dangerous to others. The Court stated:

> There may be factual issues in a commitment proceeding, but the factual aspects represent only the beginning of the inquiry. Whether the individual is mentally ill and dangerous to either himself or others and is in need of confined therapy turns on the meaning of the facts which must be interpreted by expert

psychiatrists and psychologists. (Addison v. Texas, 1979, at 429)

It is clear that the court recognized the compelling need for expert input in order for a proper legal decision to be made in these cases, and by extension, to other cases involving psycholegal issues.

In reviewing the role of science in the courtroom, Justice Stephen Breyer of the Supreme Court indicated that "there is an increasingly important need for the law to reflect sound science" (Breyer, 2000, p. 5). He specifically mentioned the issue of "expert predictions of defendants' 'future dangerousness'" as an example of how scientific issues pervade legal decision making and that issues of the potential threat posed by violent individuals to society implicate science, medicine, and the law. Further, a review of federal and state appellate decisions involving the use of actuarial measures such as the Static–99 (Harris et al., 2003) and PCL–R (Hare, 2003) found that over 90% of the time, judges found actuarial data to be admissible (Tolman & Rhodes, 2005). DeMatteo and Edens (2006) found that the use of the PCL–R in court cases has increased steadily since 1991.

Thus, the courts as well as individual judges acknowledge the critical need for scientific information to assist judicial decision makers in this area and find that information relevant and admissible. The fact that Justice Breyer used the term expert predictions indicates a need for our profession to educate the courts, not withdraw from them.

As aforementioned, the implication in previous critiques of risk assessment is that it represents unethical practice. Arguments against risk evaluations center mostly on content—what an expert witness should or should not say in court, what measures should be included, and even whether or not such evaluations should be performed. However, we believe that sound ethical practice is more about how one practices—the process of an evaluation. An article on practicing ethically stated, "There is no single, definitive way of thinking about what it means to be an ethical psychologist" (Behnke, 2005, p. 115). Behnke also noted that ethics is reasoning about situations that are often mired in competing values. In risk evaluations, there are two potentially conflicting values: public safety versus potential negative outcomes that may affect primarily one party (e.g., increased sentence, custody decision). We believe the best balance of these two ethical values is to conduct objective risk evaluations according to the best standards available. Such practice balances public safety with personal rights; an objective evaluation may not only indicate which evaluees pose a higher risk to the public but also describe those persons who may actually be at lower risk for causing future harm (e.g., Monahan et al., 2001). In contrast, decisions made without such input may be based on emotion, cognitive bias, and/or public pressure without regard to actual issues of public safety and risk. Our fear is that, in some ways, these earlier criticisms have led to the perception that practicing ethically is somehow simple, a one-time decision to avoid certain situations, instruments, clients, settings, and so on. In reality, ethical practice is an evolving process based on the changes in the field, the demands of society, and the growing qualifications of the mental health practitioner. Ethics is about balance, and in this case the struggle is between a burgeoning science and the demands or needs of the legal system. Although challenging, ethical practice in the field of risk management is possible.

The crux of the antirisk assessment position revolves around the prediction ability (or lack thereof) of mental health practitioners, as well as the questionable predictive accuracy of the various measures used in the field. One pitfall here is the tendency to see the role of the expert as a forecaster rather than an advisor. Mental health professionals are not psychic. The science of psychological measurement is imperfect and probably always will be because of the difficulties in predicting human behavior in the context of the individual and societal systems. Nevertheless, we postulate one can advise the court and do so ethically. Grisso and Appelbaum (1992) indicated that there are several types of predictive testimony that vary along at least "three ethically relevant dimensions: the nature, foundation, and consequences of the prediction" (p. 632). They concluded that it may be unethical to offer dichotomous predictions of a given individual's potential for future violence (due to relatively low base rates of violent recidivism), but there appears to be sufficient scientific evidence to support the use of probabilistic or comparative risk statements. It is worth noting that their article was published only 1 year after the publication of the PCL–R (Hare, 1991), an instrument that measures one of the more intensely examined constructs related to future violence (e.g., Hemphill, Hare, & Wong, 1998). If the scientific basis to support a conclusion of ethical testimony using probabilistic risk statements was present in 1992, then such a conclusion is obviously stronger today.

A key process issue in conducting risk evaluations is to distinguish between a prediction focus and a management/prevention focus (Douglas & Skeem, 2005). The bulk of the first generation of risk assessment research efforts (see Monahan, 1981) focused on evaluating how well clinicians could predict a specific episode of future violence. The conclusions, as noted earlier, were discouraging, but that situation has changed. In particular, the continued identification of empirical risk factors for future violence and the development of both actuarial and guided clinical risk instruments represent significant advances in the field's ability to customize an evaluation of the degree of risk posed by an evaluee. For example, offenders high in psychopathic personality traits and sexually deviant patterns of arousal commit a significantly greater number of both violent and sexual offenses than other groups of sexual offenders (Becker, Stinson, Tromp, & Messer, 2003; Rice & Harris, 1997; Seto & Barbaree, 1999), at least among adults. Similarly, the personality features of psychopathy have been found to be significantly related to future violence potential in both criminal (e.g., Hanson & Morton-Bourgon, 2005; Hare, 2003; Hemphill et al., 1998) and civil psychiatric populations (e.g., Monahan et al., 2001; Skeem, Miller, Mulvey, Tiemann, & Monahan, 2005). Further advances include the iterative classification tree model of Monahan and colleagues (Banks et al., 2004; Monahan et al., 2001, 2005; Skeem et al., 2004) that not only identifies psychiatric patients at high risk for engaging in community violence but also identifies a group of individuals at low risk for the same behaviors. On the basis of this research, Monahan and his colleagues have developed classification of violence risk (COVR) software to aid in assessment. These innovations in the field have improved the ability of practitioners to identify the specific risk factors present with a given individual, improving the consistency of estimates that a given individual may engage in violence in the future. Such information is certainly relevant and of value to the courts.

Although progress has been made, more advancement is needed, a factor that critics of risk assessment spend much time discussing (e.g., Campbell, 2004). In particular, Campbell (2003, 2004) demonstrated a heightened concern about prediction rather than management and prevention of violence and repeatedly expressed concerns with the classification accuracy of current instruments. In this, the critics are missing the point.

As noted by Grisso and Appelbaum (1992), given the state of the science and the base rates of violent behavior, it is probably unethical to offer dichotomous decisions regarding future dangerousness. Additionally, there is more to risk assessment than simple prediction of a specific behavior. Heilbrun (1997) described two distinct approaches to risk assessment that could be triggered by the different legal contexts in which the evaluations were requested. The first approach was a prediction approach focused mostly on quantifying a person's level of risk for evaluations that occurred only once (e.g., a sentencing evaluation) and in which there was little interest in prevention or management of potential violent behavior. He described the second approach as a risk management approach in contexts in which evaluations might occur repeatedly (e.g., for a person found not guilty by reason of insanity, or during probation) and in which the legal system was very concerned about reducing or preventing potential violence on the part of the person who was evaluated. Although Heilbrun's dichotomy is interesting, we believe the field has already moved forward into incorporating management and prevention principles into even the prediction context of evaluations.

Hart (2001) noted, "The ultimate goal of violence risk assessment is violence prevention" (p. 15); he stated that risk evaluations should also focus on consistency (which is arguably enhanced through the use of actuarial and guided clinical assessments), should be prescriptive in identifying and prioritizing interventions to reduce risk, and should be transparent and open to scrutiny. As Litwack (2002) noted, "A clinical assessment of dangerousness is not equivalent to a prediction of violence.... Rather, it is a determination that the individual poses sufficient risk of sufficiently serious violence in the near future which justifies his/her confinement under the law" (p. 172). Hart, Kropp, and Laws (2003) furthered this approach when they said,

> The primary decision to be made is preventive, that is, a determination of what steps should be taken to minimize any risks posed by the individual. The decision is not a simple prediction of whether or not the person will re-offend; such a prediction is meaningless without a more full discussion of the risks posed by the person... and the conditions under which someone is likely to live. (p. 3)

In addition to the role of the expert witness in these cases, one must also consider the methods used. This is an area hotly debated in the field. One consistent finding is with regard to unaided clinical judgment. This is not an acceptable practice in the field of risk management and should be avoided. A recent study by Odeh, Zeiss, and Huss (2006) found that the top 13 risk factors selected by practitioners to predict violence were not related to recidivism. The authors summarized a number of common issues associated with unaided clinical judgment. First, the risk factors deemed important varied greatly among clinicians. Second, risk factors tend to fluctuate by client, and some factors may have indirect effects. Third, the types of risk factors deemed important may depend on the type of recidivism decision being made (e.g., violent, sexual, or yes/no vs. severity). Indeed Huss and Zeiss (2004) found that the classification accuracy of clinicians improved when considered as a group and when they judged recidivism in terms of severity rather than dichotomy.

That said, deciding on methods to bolster clinical judgment can be a daunting task. The data on the predictive accuracy of measures or practices often involved in this endeavor are modest at best (Wollert, 2006). To further complicate the issue of accuracy, the literature is rife with information on different approaches (i.e., structured professional judgment vs. actuarial methods vs. measures that predict specific forms of violence or that pertain to specific offender characteristics or types). The results of these studies are often mixed mainly because of varying sample sizes, populations, and evaluators (Mills, Jones, & Kroner, 2005). For example, Wollert (2006) found that when recidivism rates are low, as is often the case for older sexual offenders or incest offenders, the predictive accuracy of actuarial measures decreased significantly. Specifically, he reported that the predictive efficiency (i.e., percentage of time the expert is right) of the Static–99 when applied to the original sample was .52. When applied to offenders with lower recidivism rates, the efficiency score dropped to .31. In fact Wollert found that the efficiency score for several actuarial measures steadily decreased as the age of the offender increased.

On the basis of the information reported above, one could focus on the benefits of a structured professional judgment tool such as the HCR–20 or an actuarial measure such as the Static–99 when used correctly (e.g., with the Static–99, the base rate recidivism for offenders placed in the high-risk group is four times the recidivism rate of those placed in the low-risk group) or the problems with the measures as we learn more about offender behaviors over time. The message here is that because the role of the expert is to inform the courts and manage risk with the best science available, it is imperative that experts select measures that have been developed and/or tested on a population similar to the case at hand. In addition, when evaluating a measure for potential use, experts should examine the literature and pay special attention to the time frames and methods used for assessing recidivism in the studies. When reporting the results of an assessment, experts should provide information on the decision rules applied (i.e., what constitutes high vs. low risk), sensitivity (i.e., hit rate), specificity (i.e., false-alarm rate), and efficiency or predictive power of the measures used. By acknowledging the fallibility of the measures to predict recidivism, the expert can educate the courts on the realities of the field and turn the focus back to the management of risk. Although we agree that the data on actuarial measures are not always earth shattering, significant progress has been made. There are a number of well-designed instruments available to trained, competent experts. For example, the PCL–R is an excellent measure of a relevant characteristic in the assessment of risk. In the most recent PCL–R manual (Hare, 2003), significant portions of the normative sample are ethnic minorities, particularly African Americans, and the base includes persons from Europe and a substantial number of female offenders (over 1,000). Hare's (2003) review of the data concluded that "PCL–R scores and their interpretation are not unduly influenced by the ethnicity of the inmate or patient" (p. 51) at least with regard to Caucasians and African Americans. He cited other research including sophisticated item response theory analyses (e.g., Cooke, Kosson, & Michie, 2001) that despite minor differences between the groups, the instrument appears to be "metrically equivalent across groups" (p. 51). Hare acknowledged that more work on the interaction of ethnicity and the manifestation of psychopathic traits is needed and that examiners should be cautious in interpreting the PCL–R scores of ethnic minorities for whom the PCL–R has not been well validated. For further information on psychopathy and the risk of recidivism, see Patrick (2006).

A thorough discussion of the many possible instruments available is beyond the scope of this article; we have mentioned the HCR–20, COVR, VRAG, and Static–99, but there are others, such as the Level of Service Inventory (Andrews & Bonta, 1995), Sex Offender Risk Appraisal Guide (Quinsey et al., 1998), Rapid Risk Assessment for Sex Offender Recidivism

(Hanson, 1997), and Sex Offender Need Assessment Rating (Hanson & Harris, 2001). The choice of measure depends on the individual case. To aid the reader, we recommend the following: Weiner and Hess (2006) for a summary of the research on violence risk instruments; Quinsey, Harris, Rice, and Cormier (2006) to provide support for the use of actuarial measures; Webster and Hucker (2003) for broad, easily understandable information on risk assessment measures; and Douglas, Yeomans, and Boer (2005) for a comparison of several popular instruments.

Finally, some have worried (Campbell, 2000, 2003; Cunningham & Reidy, 2002) that courts will be unduly influenced by experts testifying about risk, particularly using actuarial data; the concern is that this increases the potential damage caused by purportedly "unscientific" risk evaluations and fosters the implication that such practice is unethical. However, in practice, the courts are not passive recipients of expert testimony. The courts are built on an aggressive adversarial system and assume that the fact finder is capable of sorting out bad science from good science through means available to them (e.g., discovery, cross-examination). For example, a Canadian judge stated: "Today, jurors are much better informed and more sophisticated. The days are over when an expert was an expert and that was the end of the matter" (Saunders, 2001, p. 112). Indeed, the Supreme Court's mandate regarding gatekeeping by the judiciary in Daubert, by its very nature, imposes more stringent reviews of the scientific soundness of expert-proffered testimony and increases opportunities for challenges and objections to be raised. These safeguards, strengthened by the Daubert decision, reduce the potential for harm from risk evaluations. Obviously, this does not reduce the ethical burden of the psychologist to present his or her conclusions as objectively and clearly as possible in accordance with ethical principles and highlights the need for experts to not only inform but also educate the court and court officers on matters relevant to risk (e.g., psychopathy).

Yet, some have raised concerns that judges may not be very proficient at deciding what "good science" is and is not (Kovera & McAuliff, 2000; Kovera, Russano, & McAuliff, 2002). Although we acknowledge this can be a problem, we offer two comments. First, the data on judges' decision making are equivocal. A review of federal district court cases (Dixon & Gill, 2002) found that following Daubert, judges more carefully reviewed the reliability of proffered evidence, applied stricter standards to admissibility decisions, and began to focus more often on the theories and methods used by experts in reaching their conclusions. Similarly, in an analysis of post-Daubert decision making by state and federal appellate courts, Groscup, Penrod, Studebaker, Huss, and O'Neil (2002) found that while rates of admissibility of expert testimony in criminal cases did not change, judges began to evaluate evidence differently, particularly with regard to the use of the Federal Rules of Evidence. Second, there are data indicating that when judges do not make use of sound expert input, their decisions can be flawed. Krauss (2004) found that when judges departed from federal sentencing guidelines, their predictions regarding recidivism were worse than chance and slightly less impressive than the formulistic methods. He suggested that this was due to bias or improper application of knowledge. Englich, Mussweiler, and Strack (2006) reported that judges appeared to be vulnerable to irrelevant anchors in sentencing. Other research indicated that judges exhibited significant variability in pretrial (bail hearing) decision making (Dhami, 2005).

In a past review on this issue, Saks and Kidd (1986) noted that factors that affect human decision making (e.g., heuristics and biases) actually reduce the likelihood that a jury or judge will understand or consider statistical data presented as evidence and that potentially more harm could accrue should "probabilistic tools" not be used to inform judicial decision makers. They noted that statistical information such as base rates were likely to be weighed less than "case-specific" or narrative information by judges and juries, making judicial decisions more likely to be biased or flawed. They stated, "The more realistic problem is presenting statistical evidence so that people will incorporate it into their decisions at all" (Saks & Kidd, 1986, p. 235). Krauss and Sales (2001) provided evidence for this concern. In their mock jury study, jurors preferred clinical opinion testimony to actuarial testimony. It is interesting that a later study by Krauss, Lieberman, and Olson (2004) indicated that jurors' perception of testimony was at least partially influenced by the juror's mode of processing information (i.e., experiential vs. rational). This pair of studies highlights the interactive nature of expert testimony.

Saks and Kidd (1986) also cogently argued that to omit the use of statistical or actuarial data in legal proceedings is to choose "a comforting ritual over accurate decisions" (p. 233). This point is especially valid when considering judicial decisions that may involve persons who are accused or convicted of very serious crimes or potential crimes (such as violence against their children in a custody case). For example, any professional who has worked with sexual offenders realizes that the public greatly misperceives the estimated base rates of sexual recidivism. Many perceive all sex offenders as dangerous and violent and have little understanding of specific risk factors that may play a role in elevating the risk potential of a given individual. Campbell (2004) acknowledged this point in the first chapter of his book when he stated, "The fear and prejudice elicited by sex offenders encourages public policy premised on emotional appeal" (p. 4). We argue that comprehensive, careful, competent forensic risk evaluations (as compared with general clinical evaluations) can provide legal decision makers with information that may help them adjust their expectations and reduce their biases. In the absence of such information, decisions will likely be made on the basis of bias, salient and irrelevant specific features of the case (e.g., a yuck factor), social stereotypes and myths, and other unknown factors. Risk evaluations are not a perfect tool, need further research, and have a potential for being misused (e.g., Hare, 1998), but they represent, in our opinion, a step forward in improving judicial decision making to both protect the public and guard individual rights. Saks and Kidd (1986) said it very well:

> The comparison is not between humans and mathematics, but between humans deciding alone and humans deciding with the help of a tool....Moreover, as a matter of developing and introducing new tools from what might be called decision-making technology, the identification of flaws does not imply that the tools ought not to be used. The proper question is whether the tool, however imperfect, still aids the decision maker more than no tool at all. (p. 235)

One issue that deserves further comment is Campbell's (2004) claim that the use of the term psychopathy would be prejudicial in court and should not be used. This concern has also been raised by others (e.g., Cunningham & Reidy, 2001). Campbell (2004) cited Guy and Edens (2003), who found that describing a sex offender as psychopathic by using PCL–R testimony increased the rate of civil commitment by female mock jurors. For male mock jurors, the psychopathy term had the opposite effect. It is interesting to note that Edens, DesForges, Fernandez, and Palac (2004) found that describing a defendant as psychotic had the same impact on juror perceptions as describing a defendant as psychopathic. In another study, Edens, Colwell, DesForges, and Fernandez (2005) found that in a mock jury trial, describing the defendant as psychopathic in a capital murder case resulted in increased support for a death sentence. Given these mixed findings, the impact of describing a defendant as psychopathic is not yet clear. Although it appears that Edens et al. (2005) made some significant improvements in their methodology over time, several points are worth noting. All studies involved mock jurors reviewing a brief case summary who were asked to decide on death or life in prison, with minimal facts and no deliberation. It is wise to use language carefully and to define one's terms in a forensic report, regardless of the term being used. In fact one could avoid the specific term psychopathy (as described by the aforementioned studies) and simply note the personality characteristics that put the defendant at risk for future recidivism. This may be the most prudent course of action for practitioners.

Conducting Ethical Risk Evaluations

In summary, the goal of ethical practice is not to categorically predict with a high rate of accuracy the likelihood that a given offender will commit a future violent crime. The goal of ethical practice is to provide the court with information on risk factors, describe whether or not those factors apply in the current context, describe and elaborate the person's history of previous violent behaviors and relate those previous contexts to the person's current and reasonably estimated future situations, and suggest strategies to reduce risk. Ethical and effective risk evaluations are highly responsive to the legal context in which the evaluation is performed (e.g., sentencing evaluations vs. release evaluations in a forensic hospital), consistent with the review by Heilbrun (1997). Ethical practice in this area is based on competent and relevant forensic assessment using modern instruments and methods; education of legal decision makers, if necessary, regarding the elements of the report; careful delineation of the limits of our technology and knowledge; and effective use of scientific reasoning. The role of the risk evaluator as a neutral party and educator for the court on risk issues is consistent with the role of an expert witness and appears to be one of the defining characteristics of forensic evaluators versus clinicians (Tolman & Mullendore, 2003). As an example, there is evidence that judges often may confuse distinct terms such as psychopath with psychosis and may need assistance in interpreting the risk factors that are present (Tolman & Buehmann, 2004).

It seems obvious to recommend that a mental health professional be competent in the field of risk assessment before stepping into a courtroom, but unfortunately there is evidence that professionals become involved in these cases without adequate preparation (Haag, 2006; Tolman, 2001; Tolman & Mullendore, 2003). Given that the field of risk assessment is rapidly developing and changing, any professional practicing in this field must stay abreast of the evolving guidelines and methods of evaluation. For professionals conducting forensic evaluations, ethical standards have existed for some time, as reflected in the Specialty Guidelines (Committee on Ethical Guidelines for Forensic Psychologists, 1991). These guidelines are currently under revision, but they originally built on and supported the American Psychological Association's Ethical Standards at the time. They emphasize competence, understanding of legal standards and contexts, protection of the legal rights of evaluees, maintenance of objectivity in practice, clarification regarding the boundaries of testimony or reports, and preservation of scientific knowledge regarding one's specialized area of practice. Other professional standards of practice for risk assessments exist such as for evaluating sexual offenders (Association for the Treatment of Sexual Abusers, 2005); these standards have been debated in professional circles and are published and available. Heilbrun (2001) described a set of general principles that apply to most forensic evaluations, depending on the evaluation context. Heilbrun, Marczyk, and DeMatteo (2002) also gave examples of how specific principles apply to risk assessment, including use of relevance and reliability as guides for seeking information and data sources, use of scientific reasoning in assessing the causal connection between clinical condition and functional abilities, identification of relevant forensic issues, clarification of one's role with an attorney, and use of nomothetic evidence in reaching conclusions. Ethical forensic evaluations emphasize the role of the psychologist as an objective evaluator, not an advocate, regardless of which side retained the expert. Practicing psychologists should be aware of and adhere to these ethical principles in conducting evaluations (see also American Educational Research Association, 1999; American Psychological Association, 2002).

Apart from ethical standards, practitioners should be aware that even a cursory review of the scientific risk assessment literature indicates some broad areas of agreement on practice standards for ethical risk evaluations. First, there is almost universal agreement that unstructured clinical techniques are insufficient (e.g., Monahan, 1981). Second, given the strength and stability of the relationship between psychopathy and recidivism, this is a factor that should probably be assessed when evaluating a person's risk for future violence, using an instrument designed for that purpose (e.g., Hare, 2003) and after having received training in its use (see also Gacono, 2000; Hart, 1998; Monahan et al., 2001). Antisocial traits such as poor self-regulation (Hanson & Morton-Bourgon, 2005) have also been linked to violent recidivism. Specific to sexual violence, there is evidence that sexual deviance is strongly related to recidivism (Hanson & Morton-Bourgon, 2005). Miller, Amenta, and Conroy (2005) noted that assessment devices for sexual deviance are limited; however, Hanson and Morton-Bourgon (2005) found that many experts use clinical interviews and self-report measures to diagnose pedophilia or paraphilias. Although some clinicians may shy away from self-report measures with offenders, a recent meta-analysis by Walters (2006) indicated that self-report measures and standardized risk appraisal measures performed equally in predicting institutional adjustment and recidivism. According to Walters, the self-report measures that tap into issues directly related to recidivism (e.g., criminal attitudes) perform better than more general instruments such as personality inventories. In addition, most actuarial measures designed for evaluating sexual offenders include items for assessing sexual deviance. Walters also found that self-report measures and risk appraisal measures account for unique variance in outcomes. This provides some support for combining these methods.

Third, risk evaluations should review other known risk factors related to the context of the evaluation (e.g., Hanson & Bussiere, 1998; Harris et al., 2003; Quinsey et al., 1998), a task that is enhanced through the use of actuarial (e.g., Quinsey et al., 1998) and guided clinical instruments (e.g., Webster et al., 1997) and not rely solely on traditional clinical instruments and techniques. Earlier we provided several comprehensive resources for more information on these instruments.

Fourth, an expert should consider dynamic risk factors as well as potential protective factors and base rates (Douglas & Skeem, 2005; Rogers, 2000; Webster, Hucker, & Bloom, 2002) in evaluating risk; it should be noted that the guided clinical instruments such as the HCR–20 already enjoin consideration of dynamic factors as part of the instrument. The impact of treatment on dynamic factors and consequently recidivism is not yet clear (Miller et al., 2005). However, Douglas and Skeem (2005) provided an excellent review of the most promising dynamic factors with regard to violence risk assessment.

Fifth, forensic evaluators should make use of collateral data sources and assess multiple domains of functioning, as well as address issues of risk management and risk reduction (e.g., Hart, 2001). We acknowledge that integrating these sources and variables can be difficult. We have found Heilbrun (2001), Heilbrun et al. (2002), and Gacono (2000) particularly helpful with regard to synthesizing report information.

Conclusion

The debate about the nature and ethics of conducting risk evaluations has been going on for more than two decades and will continue. We note that the issue of admissibility of risk evaluations under Daubert v. Merrell Dow Pharmaceuticals, or even the older Fry v. United States (1923) standard, is not a psychological determination. The trial judges, as monitored by the appellate courts, determine what proffered evidence or testimony will be admitted under Frye or Daubert. Preliminary evidence (Tolman & Rhodes, 2005) suggests that 96% of cases involving the PCL–R (Hare, 2003) and 93% of cases involving the Static–99 (Harris et al., 2003) in at least 23 jurisdictions were found by U.S. federal and state courts to be admissible either explicitly or implicitly. In addition, the number of articles, books, and conference talks dedicated to issues of risk management would certainly suggest that the practice is generally accepted.

The real-world context of risk evaluations is that courts want and need information about individuals' potential risk of engaging in future violence to make crucial decisions on a regular basis. The reality of risk evaluations is that substantial and compelling progress (e.g., Hanson, 2005) has been made in our identification of risk factors known to be linked to violence and in the development of both actuarial and guided clinical instruments to assist practitioners in reducing bias, ensuring adequate review of key known risk factors, and improving consistency in their reports compared with the past. The practical reality for many involved with the justice system would be that without state-of-the-art risk assessment and management information, decisions would be made about their future and their liberty based on prejudice, bias, social myths, and irrelevant contextual factors. The real world of risk evaluations is that a decision on whether these evaluations are ethical or not hinges on the context in which the evaluations occur and in the degree of knowledge, competence, and proficiency of the examiner.

We suggest that it is time to move beyond simple black-and-white questions of whether risk evaluations are ethical or not. Psychologists involved in training and continuing education programs need to more clearly define the boundary lines between forensic and clinical practice (e.g., Greenberg & Shuman, 1997; Tolman & Mullendore, 2003) and should develop and implement explicit empirical and theoretical models for teaching psychologists about issues related to risk factors, dangerousness, and ethical assessment (e.g., Tolman, 2001). Practicing psychologists should become involved in educational innovation and interdisciplinary efforts between psychology and law to enhance the understanding of the legal system among psychologists and to enhance attorneys' and judges' abilities to recognize unethical and improper evaluations when they see them. Research psychologists should continue research into understanding how to improve the ability to predict and manage violence risk based on dynamic and protective factors (e.g., Douglas, Webster, Hart, Eaves, & Ogloff, 2001). The literature base needs to be expanded in contexts in which there is relatively little current information (e.g., risk evaluations in spousal abuse cases, stalking, custody). Further clarification and consensus building regarding a more specific standard of practice for risk evaluations would enhance psychologists' standing in the courts and in our profession.

References

Addison v. Texas, 441 U.S. 418 (1979).

American Educational Research Association (1999). *Standards for educational and psychological testing.* Washington, DC: Author.

American Psychological Association (2002). *Ethical principles of psychologists and code of conduct.* American Psychologist, 57, 1052–1059.

Andrews, D. A., & Bonta, J. (1995). *The Level of Service Inventory—Revised.* Toronto, Ontario, Canada: Multi-Health Systems.

Association for the Treatment of Sexual Abusers (2005). *Practice standards for the evaluation, treatment and management of adult sexual abusers.* Beaverton, OR: Author.

Banks, S., Robbins, P. C., Silver, E., Vasselinov, R., Steadman, H. J., Monahan, J., et al. (2004). A multiple-models approach to violent assessment among people with mental disorder. *Criminal Justice and Behavior*, 31, 324–340.

Barbaree, H. E., Seto, M. C., & Langton, C. M. (2001). Evaluating the predictive accuracy of six risk assessment instruments for adult sex offenders. *Criminal Justice and Behavior*, 28, 490–521.

Becker, J. V., Stinson, J., Tromp, S., & Messer, G. (2003). Characteristics of individuals petitioned for civil commitment. *International Journal of Offender Therapy and Comparative Criminology*, 47, 185–195.

Behnke, S. (2005). On being an ethical psychologist. *Monitor on Psychology*, 36 (7), 114–115.

Benda, B. B., Corwyn, R. F., & Toombs, N. J. (2005). Recidivism among adolescent serious offenders: Prediction of entry into the correctional system for adults. *Criminal Justice and Behavior*, 28, 588–613.

Berlin, F. S., Galbreath, N. W., Geary, B., & McGlone, G. (2003). The use of actuarials at civil commitment hearings to predict the likelihood of future sexual violence. *Sexual Abuse: A Journal of Research and Treatment*, 15, 377–382.

Breyer, S. (2000). Introduction. In Reference manual on scientific evidence (2nd ed.). Washington, DC: Federal Judicial Center. Retrieved October 16, 2005, from http://air.fjc.gov/public/f%20jcweb.nsf/pages/16

Campbell, T. W. (2000). Sexual predator evaluations and phrenology: Considering issues of evidentiary reliability. *Behavioral Sciences and the Law*, 18, 111–130.

Campbell, T. W. (2003). Sex offenders and actuarial risk assessments: Ethical considerations. *Behavioral Sciences and the Law*, 21, 269–279.

Campbell, T. W. (2004). *Assessing Sexual Offenders: Problems And Pitfalls.* Springfield, IL:

Charles C Thomas.

Committee on Ethical Guidelines for Forensic Psychologists (1991). Specialty guidelines for forensic psychologists. *Law and Human Behavior*, 15, 655–665.

Cooke, D. J., Kosson, D. S., & Michie, C. (2001). Psychopathy and ethnicity: Structural, item, and test generalizability of the Psychopathy Checklist Revised (PCL–R) in Caucasian and African-American participants. *Psychological Assessment*, 13, 531–542.

Cunningham, M. D., & Reidy, T. J. (2001). A matter of life or death: Special considerations and heightened practice standards in capital sentencing evaluations. *Behavioral Sciences and the Law*, 19, 473–490.

Daubert v. Merrell Dow Pharmaceuticals, Inc., 509 U.S. 579 (1993).

DeMatteo, D., & Edens, J. F. (2006). The role and relevance of the Psychopathy Checklist—Revised in court: A case law survey of U.S. courts (1991–2004). *Psychology, Public Policy, and Law*, 12, 214–241.

Dhami, M. K. (2005). From discretion to disagreement: Explaining disparities in judges' pretrial decisions. *Behavioral Sciences and the Law*, 23, 367–386.

Dixon, L., & Gill, B. (2002). Changes in the standards for admitting expert evidence in federal civil cases since the Daubert decision. *Psychology, Public Policy, and Law*, 8, 251–308.

Douglas, K. S., & Skeem, J. L. (2005). Violence risk assessment: Getting specific about being dynamic. Psychology, *Public Policy, and Law*, 11, 347–383.

Douglas, K. S., Webster, C. D., Hart, S. D., Eaves, D., & Ogloff, J. R. P. (Eds.). (2001). *HCR–20 Violence Risk Management Companion Guide.* Burnaby, British Columbia, Canada: Simon Fraser University, Mental Health, Law, and Policy Institute.

Douglas, K. S., Yeomans, M., & Boer, D. P. (2005). Comparative validity analysis of multiple measures of violence risk in criminal offenders. *Criminal Justice and Behavior*, 32, 479–510.

Edens, J. F. (2006). Unresolved controversies concerning psychopathy: Implications for clinical and forensic decision making. *Professional Psychology: Research and Practice*, 37, 59–65.

Edens, J. F., Colwell, L. H., DesForges, D. M., & Fernandez, K. (2005). The impact of mental health evidence for support of capital punishment: Are defendants labeled psychopathic considered more deserving of death? *Behavioral Sciences and the Law*, 23, 603–625.

Edens, J. F., DesForges, D. M., Fernandez, K., & Palac, C. A. (2004). Effects of psychopathy and violence risk testimony on mock juror perceptions of dangerousness in a capital murder trial. *Psychology, Crime and Law*, 10, 393–412.

Englich, B., Mussweiler, T., & Strack, F. (2006). Playing dice with criminal sentences: The influence of irrelevant anchors on experts' judicial decision making. *Personality and Social Psychology Bulletin*, 32, 188–200.

Frye v. United States, 293 F. 1013 (D.C. Cir. 1923).

Gacono, C. B. (Ed.). (2000). *The clinical and forensic assessment of psychopathy: A practitioner's guide.* Mahwah, NJ: Erlbaum.

Greenberg, S. A., & Shuman, D. W. (1997). Irreconcilable conflict between therapeutic and forensic roles. *Professional Psychology: Research and Practice*, 28, 50–57.

Grisso, T., & Appelbaum, P. S. (1992). Is it unethical to offer predictions of future violence? *Law and Human Behavior*, 16, 621–633.

Groscup, J. L., Penrod, S. D., Studebaker, C. A., Huss, M. T., & O'Neil, K. M. (2002). The effects of Daubert on the admissibility of expert testimony in state and federal criminal cases. *Psychology, Public Policy, and Law*, 8, 339–372.

Guy, L. S., & Edens, J. F. (2003). Juror decision-making in a mock sexually violent predator trial: Gender differences in the impact of divergent types of testimony. *Behavioral Sciences and the Law*, 21, 215–237.

Haag, A. M. (2006). Ethical dilemmas faced by correctional psychologists in Canada. *Criminal Justice and Behavior*, 33, 93–109.

Hanson, R. K. (1997). *The development of a brief actuarial scale for sexual offense recidivism*. Ottawa: Public Works and Government Services of Canada.

Hanson, R. K. (2005). Twenty years of progress in violence risk assessment. *Journal of Interpersonal Violence*, 20, 212–217.

Hanson, R. K., & Bussiere, M. T. (1998). Predicting relapse: A meta-analysis of sexual offender recidivism studies. *Journal of Consulting and Clinical Psychology*, 66, 348–362.

Hanson, R. K., & Harris, A. (2001). *The Sex Offender Need Assessment Rating (SONAR): A method for measuring change in risk levels*. Ottawa: Public Works and Government Services of Canada.

Hanson, R. K., & Morton-Bourgon, K. E. (2005). The characteristics of persistent sexual offenders: A meta-analysis of recidivism studies. *Journal of Consulting and Clinical Psychology*, 73, 1154–1163.

Hare, R. D. (1991). *Psychopathy Checklist—Revised*. Toronto, Ontario, Canada: Multi-Health Systems.

Hare, R. D. (1998). The Hare PCL–R: Some issues concerning its use and misuse. *Legal and Criminological Psychology*, 3 (1), 99–119.

Hare, R. D. (2003). *Psychopathy Checklist—Revised* (2nd ed.) technical manual. Toronto, Ontario, Canada: Multi-Health Systems.

Harris, A. J. R., Phenix, A., Hanson, R. K., & Thornton, D. (2003). *Static–99 coding rules revised*. Ottawa, Canada: Office of Public Safety and Emergency Preparedness. Retrieved November 8, 2005, from http://www.sgc.gc.ca/corrections/publications_e.asp#2003

Hart, S. D. (1998). Psychopathy and the risk for violence. In D. J.Cooke, A. E.Forth, & R. D.Hare (Eds.), *Psychopathy: Theory, research, and implications for society* (pp. 355–373). Dordrecht, the Netherlands: Kluwer Academic.

Hart, S. D. (2001). Assessing and managing violence risk. In K. S.Douglas, C. D.Webster, S. D.Hart, D.Eaves, & J. R. P.Ogloff (Eds.), *HCR–20 violence risk management companion guide* (pp. 13–26). Burnaby, British Columbia: Simon Fraser University, Mental Health, Law, and Policy Institute.

Hart, S. D., Kropp, P. R., & Laws, R. D. (2003). *The Risk for Sexual Violence Protocol (RSVP): Structured professional guidelines for assessing risk of sexual violence*. British Columbia, Canada: Simon Fraser University, Mental Health, Law, and Policy Institute.

Heilbrun, K. (1997). Prediction versus management models relevant to risk assessment: The importance of legal decision-making context. *Law and Human Behavior*, 21, 347–359.

Heilbrun, K. (2001). *Principles of forensic mental health assessment*. New York: Kluwer Academic/Plenum.

Heilbrun, K., Marczyk, G. R., & DeMatteo, D. (2002). *Forensic mental health assessment: A casebook*. Oxford, England: Oxford University Press.

Hemphill, J. F., Hare, R. D., & Wong, S. (1998). Psychopathy and recidivism: A review. *Legal and Criminological Psychology*, 3, 141–172.

Huss, M. T., & Zeiss, R. A. (2004). Clinical assessment of violence from inpatient records: A comparison of individual and aggregate decision making across risk strategies. *International Journal of Forensic Mental Health*, 3, 139–147.

Kovera, M. B., & McAuliff, B. D. (2000). The effects of peer review and evidence quality on judge evaluations of psychological science: Are judges effective gatekeepers? *Journal of Applied Psychology*, 85, 574–586.

Kovera, M. B., Russano, M. B., & McAuliff, B. D. (2002). Assessment of the commonsense psychology underlying Daubert: Legal decision makers' abilities to evaluate expert evidence in hostile work environment cases. *Psychology, Public Policy, and Law*, 8, 180–200.

Krauss, D. A. (2004). Adjusting risk of recidivism: Do judicial departures improve or worsen recidivism prediction under the federal sentencing guidelines? *Behavioral Sciences and the Law*, 22, 731–750.

Krauss, D. A., Lieberman, J. D., & Olson, J. (2004). The effects of rational and experiential information processing of expert testimony in death penalty cases. *Behavioral Sciences and the Law*, 22, 801–811.

Krauss, D. A., & Sales, B. D. (2001). The effects of clinical and scientific expert testimony on juror decision making in capital sentencing. *Psychology, Public Policy, and Law*, 7, 267–310.

Litwack, T. R. (2002). Some questions for the field of violence risk assessment and forensic mental health: Or, "back to basics" revisited. *International Journal of Forensic Mental Health*, 1, 171–179.

Miller, H. A., Amenta, A. E., & Conroy, M. A. (2005). Sexually violent predator evaluations: Empirical evidence, strategies for professionals, and research directions. *Law and Human Behavior*, 29, 29–54.

Mills, J. F., Jones, M. N., & Kroner, D. G. (2005). An examination of the generalizability of the LSI–R and VRAG probability bins. *Criminal Justice and Behavior*, 32, 565–585.

Mills, J. F., Kroner, D. G., & Hemmati, T. (2004). The Measures of Criminal Attitudes and Associates (MCAA): The prediction of general and violent recidivism. *Criminal Justice and Behavior*, 31, 717–733.

Monahan, J. (1981). *The clinical prediction of violent behavior. In Crime and delinquency issues: A monograph series* (Publication No. ADM 81–921). Washington, DC: U.S. Government Printing Office.

Monahan, J. (1984). The prediction of violent behavior: Toward a second generation of theory and policy. *American Journal of Psychiatry*, 141, 10–15.

Monahan, J., Steadman, H. J., Robbins, P. C., Appelbaum, P., Banks, S., Grisso, T., et al. (2005). An actuarial model of violence risk assessment for persons with mental disorders. *Psychiatric Services*, 56, 810–815.

Monahan, J., Steadman, H. J., Silver, E., Appelbaum, P. S., Robbins, P. C., Mulvey, E. P., et al. (2001). *Rethinking risk assessment: The MacArthur Study of Mental Disorder and Violence*. Oxford, England: Oxford University Press.

Odeh, M. S., Zeiss, R. A., & Huss, M. T. (2006). Cues they use: Clinicians' endorsement of risk cues in predictions of dangerousness. *Behavioral Science and the Law*, 24, 147–156.

Patrick, C. J. (Ed.). (2006). *Handbook of psychopathy*. New York: Guilford Press.

Quinsey, V. L., Harris, G. T., Rice, M. E., & Cormier, C. A. (1998). *Violent offenders: Appraising and managing risk*. Washington, DC: American Psychological Association.

Quinsey, V. L., Harris, G. T., Rice, M. E., & Cormier, C. A. (2006). *Violent offenders: Appraising and managing risk* (2nd ed.). Washington, DC: American Psychological Association.

Rice, M. E., & Harris, G. T. (1997). Cross-validation and extension of the Violence Risk Appraisal Guide for child molesters and rapists. *Law and Human Behavior*, 21, 231–241.

Rogers, R. (2000). The uncritical acceptance of acceptance of risk assessment in forensic practice. *Law and Human Behavior*, 24, 595–605.

Saks, M. J., & Kidd, R. F. (1986). *Human information processing and adjudication: Trial by heuristics*. In H. R.Arkes & K. R.Hammond (Eds.), *Judgment and decision making: An interdisciplinary reader* (pp. 213–242). New York: Cambridge University Press.

Saunders, J. W. S. (2001). Experts in court: A view from the bench. *Canadian Psychology*, 42, 109–118.

Seto, M. C., & Barbaree, H. E. (1999). Psychopathy, treatment behavior, and sex offender recidivism. *Journal of Interpersonal Violence*, 14, 1235–1248.

Skeem, J. L., Miller, J. D., Mulvey, E., Tiemann, J., & Monahan, J. (2005). Using a five-factor lens to explore the relation between personality traits and violence in psychiatric patients. *Journal of Consulting and Clinical Psychology*, 73, 454–465.

Skeem, J. L., Mulvey, E. P., Applebaum, P., Banks, S., Grisso, T., Silver, E., & Robbins, P. C. (2004). Identifying subtypes of civil psychiatric patients at high risk for violence. *Criminal Justice and Behavior*, 31, 392–437.

Tolman, A. O. (2001). Clinical training and the duty to protect. *Behavioral Sciences and the Law*, 19, 387–404.

Tolman, A. O., & Buehmann, E. (2004, June). Judicial perceptions of expert risk assessment. Paper presented at the Fourth Annual Conference of the International Association of Forensic Mental Health Services, Stockholm, Sweden.

Tolman, A. O., & Rhodes, J. (2005, March). The admissibility of actuarial risk instruments in federal and state courts: Current status. Paper presented at the annual conference of the American Psychology-Law Society, San Diego, CA.

Tolman, A. O., & Mullendore, K. B. (2003). Risk evaluations for the courts: Is service quality a function of specialization? *Professional Psychology: Research and Practice*, 34, 225–232.

Walters, G. D. (2006). Risk appraisal versus self-report in the prediction of criminal justice outcomes: A meta-analysis. *Criminal Justice and Behavior*, 33, 279–304.

Webster, C. D., & Douglas, K. S. (2001). *Purpose of the companion guide*. In K. S.Douglas, C. D.Webster, S. D.Hart, D.Eaves, & J. R. P.Ogloff (Eds.), *HCR–20 violence risk management companion guide* (pp. 1–12). Burnaby, British Columbia, Canada: Simon Fraser University, Mental Health, Law, and Policy Institute.

Webster, C. D., Douglas, K. S., Eaves, D., & Hart, S. D. (1997). *HCR–20: Assessing risk for violence(Version 2)*. Burnaby, British Columbia, Canada: Simon Fraser University, Mental Health, Law, and Policy Institute.

Webster, C. D., & Hucker, S. J. (2003). *Release decision making: Assessing violence risk in mental health, forensic, and correctional settings.* Hamilton, Ontario, Canada: St. Joseph's Healthcare.

Webster, C. D., Hucker, S. J., & Bloom, H. (2002). Transcending the actuarial versus clinical polemic in assessing risk for violence [Special issue: Risk assessment]. *Criminal Justice and Behavior, 29,* 659–665.

Weiner, I. B., & Hess, A. K. (Eds.). (2006). *The handbook of forensic psychology* (3rd ed.). Hoboken, NJ: Wiley.

Wollert, R. (2006). Low base rates limit expert certainty when current actuarials are used to identify sexually violent predators: An application of Bayes's theorem. *Psychology, Public Policy, and Law, 12,* 56–85.

Teaching, Writing
& The University

Dr. Rick McDonald

The Role of a Mentor: How One Teacher Got Started

by
Mary Ellen Greenwood

In Homer's Odyssey, Mentor is a trusted friend of Odysseus and advisor to his son, Telemachus. It comes as no surprise that Athena—great goddess of wisdom, justice, and skill— disguises herself as Mentor to assist Telemachus. ("Mentor." Encyclopedia Mythica.) I imagine the younger man, troubled with doubt and struggling to find the best path in the absence of his father, and Athena is there to offer welcome advice. Telemachus becomes a strong and capable man and there is no doubt that the guidance of a mentor made a difference ("Telemachus"). Professionally, we could all use Athena whispering guidance in our ears and encouraging us to make ethical and sound decisions regarding our curriculum, our students, and ourselves. But we can—and ought to—take that spirit and find and become mentors in the academic community. I remember my own personal Athena very well.

When I met Lynn Langer Meeks—the Director of the Writing Program at Utah State University—in 2001, I believed that teaching college composition was a temporary job, a way to get through grad school and pay the rent in my rundown cinderblock-walled apartment. Six years and a Masters degree later, and I'm still here—though "here" is now UVSC, nearly 120 miles to the south of Utah State—discovering new groups of freshmen and sophomores who are discovering new concepts and life experiences themselves. And, no matter what lesson plan I create or how many times I get up in front of a class, Lynn is there, whether I realize it or not.

You could say that she embodied my image of a modern Athena. She wore more jewelry than the display case at Macys and towered over even the tallest male students. The walls of her home were red, a reflection of her fearlessness. Imposing, confident, and devoted to the new English teachers she mentored every fall, Lynn was simultaneously a ferocious champion of the novice (pushing for smaller class caps was a favorite battle of hers) and a gentle nurturer who helped her charges find something within themselves that they could share with their English 1010 students. It didn't matter that we graduate students were inexperienced and often not much older than those students in our composition classes; she believed that we could teach, and so we did.

Who I am professionally and ethically has been influenced by her dedication to the three responsibilities of academia: service, research, and teaching. First, her take on service: "You have a responsibility to the academic community," Lynn said, and so, within days of my arrival on campus, I found myself placed on departmental committees with my fellow grad instructors. A sign-up sheet was passed around, we each selected the two committees we were most interested in, and we were off. Over the course of three years, I served on committees with names like the Textbook Committee, Library Committee, Scholarships and Awards Committee, Computer Facilities Committee, Travel Committee, Website Committee, and Office Space Committee. You name it, we probably had a committee for it. And if we didn't have our calendars with us to synchronize schedules and plan our meetings, we were met with Lynn's perplexed query, "And where is your planner?" A new concept initially, committees empowered us and gave us a voice while strengthening and developing our sense of community—however small and low on the totem pole we knew we really were as graduate students. I remember attending meetings with the Library Committee, composed of a variety of individuals who represented librarians, adjuncts, professors, and graduate instructors, where we discussed a common concern—the research needs of students—and we developed strategies to address that concern together.

It was that focus—working together to accomplish goals—that led Lynn to implement a generational approach to mentoring. Each year, she would select two second-year graduate students to assist her in instructing and supporting the incoming first-year teachers. While Lynn would discuss theory, her experienced assistants would offer the hands-on, in-the-trenches guidance that included sharing lesson plan ideas, modeling the creation of an effective syllabus, integrating helpful classroom management techniques, and providing invaluable peer moral support. During my second year, I had the opportunity to serve as one of Lynn's Assistant Directors of Writing. I wrote curriculum, listened to concerns from the first years, and began to understand just how tough (and rewarding) an administrative role can be. Lynn's trust in her assistants allowed them to experiment, practice, and learn—all while under her watchful eye. Teach a man to fish, goes the saying. Well, teach someone to lead and you create a new generation of leadership.

Along with service, Lynn emphasized research: "Publish or perish," Lynn would quote over and over. "I'm working on a book," she would mention and with each mention we knew she probably meant a different book. She was always working on a book and she was always excited about it. It was contagious. In addition to my thesis defense, I pushed myself and presented at five different conferences from Westminster College in Salt Lake City to Utah State to Albuquerque to Park City, Utah, and saw my own writing published in a few small journals. It was the trip to Park City—where the Writing Program Administration Conference was to be held—that I saw Lynn in true form. Because a number of us—including her—would be presenting, she had taken the mandatory driver training course in order to operate one of the university's large 15-passenger vans. This Amazon of a woman, with bracelets and bangles jingling and clacking as she maneuvered the steering wheel, delighted in her role as conference chauffeur and got us safely there and back, all the while discussing our presentations and offering pointers and encouragement. Now that I think about it, my panel wasn't very well attended, but it was my first conference and it was a success.

While service and research were important, the third emphasis, teaching, was Lynn's love. She started out as an English teacher in the Arizona public school system and spent her life exploring the way students learn and finding the most effective teaching methods. Some of the things she told us—several times—have remained with me and have become part of my own teaching philosophy.

Regarding the cap on composition classes: We need to offer quality instruction. Do not add students. Do not add students. Do not add students past the cap.

Regarding grading: Use a rubric, a scoring standard. It's what keeps us honest and fair. It's how students understand how we have assessed their writing. It's how they determine what is working in their writing and what isn't.

Regarding Pedagogy: Variety is the key to good teaching. Break them into groups and get them thinking and discussing. Don't lecture them to death: that only bores them and drains you of your precious energy. Teach the way they learn by placing learning in their hands; they learn it when they do it. Approximate, approximate, approximate in the classroom.

And, regarding the freshman students: You are probably their first experience with college. They are taking English 1010 this semester and we want them to go on and succeed in the world. Challenge them and care about them. Conference with them. Help them see what they can do. Every student can learn to write.

On September 11, a few weeks after we'd begun our first semester of teaching, the terrorist attacks left our campus, like all others, reeling. We would be heading to our 1010 classes the next day, facing students who had seen trauma unfold on television screens. Lynn offered advice I'll never forget: "Put your lesson plans aside tomorrow. Let your students talk. Talk with them. They will need a place to find room for their feelings. And sometimes the lesson plan isn't the most important thing."

There are some things, though, that even the most careful and prepared mentor cannot do. In October, Lynn's life ended quietly after an eighteen-month struggle with pancreatic cancer. Memory is a funny thing. We remember certain events and not others and certain variables, like attitude and emotion, can affect how we construct a memory.

Obviously, I've had time for reflection, though I realize it is easy to sentimentalize a person after her death, turning her into a wondrous model of perfection and professionalism. But I think it is human to canonize. It gives us peace of mind amid confusion and frustrating loss. And while I am keenly aware of my tendency to idealize, there are truths about the legacy of a good mentor: how that individual teaches, motivates, and guides the novice to a sense of independence and confidence. But no matter how independent the new teacher becomes, he or she is also a product of environment. Nurture and nature. The mentor and the mentored. In examining the Greek roots of the word mentor, we have the noun mentos, which means intent, purpose, spirit, and passion ("Mentor" Online Etymology Dictionary). All of these descriptive words can be highly affecting and highly contagious. Highly Lynn.

Coincidentally, a campus-wide memorial service was held at Utah State where Lynn was posthumously honored for her years of contributions to education on the day I gave this paper. The people there shared memories and placed her on the pedestal that she deserves. I'm could not be there; I was at UVSC giving this paper because Lynn said that true commitment to academia means that we do not stagnate: we write, we share our ideas, we go to conferences, and we build communities. And, if given the choice, she too would have attended a conference like this. A mentor, defined, is a wise and trusted counselor or teacher. A mentor, defined, is an influential supporter. I can only hope to be that for my students at UVSC.

Notes

An earlier version of this paper was presented at the Center for the Study of Ethics Annual Faculty Conference: "Ethics in the Professions," Utah Valley State College, Orem, Utah, January 25, 2007.

Works Cited

"Mentor." *Encyclopedia Mythica*. 21 December 2006 www.pantheon.org.

"Mentor." *Online Etymology Dictionary*. 21 December 2006 www.etymonline.com.

"Telemachus." *Encyclopedia Mythica*. 21 December 2006 www.pantheon.org.

Ethics and the Part-Timer

By
Mary Allen

I'm Nobody! Who are you?" - Emily Dickinson

No one knows what to call them. Part-timers? Ad hoc? Adjuncts? Adjunct: "something added to another thing but not essentially a part of it." They are the phantom corps on campus, the bottom feeders, not to be glanced at or acknowledged. Here come the cockroaches. A regular faculty member may incur whiplash turning away from the unseemly sight.

Losers? Masochists? Saints? All of this and more.

Part-timers aren't mentioned in the catalog. They don't have offices. Yet they teach half the classes in college these days, keeping them afloat.

Part time doesn't necessarily mean temporary. There is the Adjunct Professor, someone eminent, who offers an occasional course after a day job. And others pick up a class from time to time for extra change. But the career part-timer survives by the teaching life, taking on six, seven—a dozen courses a semester.

Qualifications

An advanced degree is required and a superior mind, as you must absorb the part-timer schedule—classes scattered across three states, six campuses. Which room? Time? What book? Where next?

Infallible health is a must. Should you miss class because you are dying, with your hours and locations, no secretary is there to go and explain.

You need the endurance of a trucker. Indeed, trucking is what you do—hurtling from one location to another, plowing through blizzards heading north, swirling waters going south, at the mercy of traffic backups.

No personal life. This qualification may seem extreme. But family things takes time. Avoid child abuse by not having a child. Stay single. More time to grade papers.

Intimacy with failure is a plus. Here you shine. You know insults. Let those suckers roll off because you are, well, nobody. Not a rising scholar, not even a recognizable instructor.

Liabilities

Yes, the liabilities of this life. There's the comical pay, not to be compared to a full-timer salary. And pay raises are bizarrely construed. When other faculty receive a three-percent raise, part-timers, where the amount would be minuscule, may get one percent. Why is this? Plus, timing of the adjunct paycheck is diabolical. They who need it most might not get paid until mid-semester. One institution held off all moneys until the end, after grades were turned in.

No health insurance. You can't get sick.

No office and likely no office space. Part-timers must meet students in the hall. Or for privacy, try the restroom.

No funding to attend conferences to improve your professional standing. But, then, you have no standing. Forget these silly events.

Never a promotion. As one seasoned adjunct was told when she asked about advancement, "But you don't have a job."

All this, and still the saddest thing about the part-timer life is—the insecurity. It's like the Woody Allen quip that the food at a resort was terrible, and the portions were so small. Getting a class the night before the semester makes you scramble, but you do it. The ugly, miserable, inhumane deed is the snatching of what is yours at the last instant, as crudely as the old-time hook that plucked an unwanted performer, in mid-motion, off a stage.

The Case of Dr. Dana Shaughnessy

It was the first day of the semester, January sleet, as Dana headed from George Mason University in Fairfax, Virginia, to the community college in Alexandria, wipers flapping. She galloped up to room 310.

The department secretary stepped in Dana's way.

"Excuse me, Dalinda, this is my class."

"Not really. They gave it to regular faculty. We tried to call." Dalinda did not make eye contact.

"I've made out the syllabus. They can't do this," Dana countered, her windpipe shrinking.

"Says so in your agreement."

"What agreement?"

"It's in the mail."

Ah. "So who got this class?"

Dalinda ran a fingernail down her roster. "Moon."

"Lester Moon? With no PhD? And where is he?"

Dalinda backed off, hugging her secretarial goods. Do not strike the messenger, Dana.

With no other instructor in sight, she went in the classroom and passed out the syllabus, with its color icons for holidays, a masterpiece. "Dr. Dana Shaughnessy." She swallowed. "I'm an adjunct."

"What's that?"

"We teach in various places. Any of you work part time?" Many nodded.

"No benefits," someone said.

About then Lester Moon wandered in. "Wrong room?" He scratched himself.

Yes. Yours is in motorcycle maintenance. Go there now.

He pulled out a wrinkled paper. "Says 310."

He stood there. Dana did. "Nice meeting you," she finally said to the class, and with a small bow strode out in the hall, where she bit the handle of her briefcase to staunch the scream of mortification that would have alerted security.

Dana watched as Lester went to the trash can, plucked out a Slurpee cup, and sloshed it on the table. "Write about that."

This then, my friends, can be the fate of a part-timer.

Not that our indomitable Dana was destroyed by this slight. She'd had worse. And she couldn't afford the puffy eyes you get from weeping. She had a class in Maryland that night.

Campuses and Facilities

Part-timers expand to many campuses, in a widening trajectory that can make you feel like Willy Loman. Or you could end up on a cruise ship. Yet again, in a prison. Know where you are or you may find yourself giving the wrong lecture. Having designated briefcases can help, but be sure to grab the right one. For your considerable travel, stock your car with an ice chest, a change of hats, books on tape. You'll be able to digest entire classics.

Have a car that runs.

If you are assigned a regular rectangular room, don't be fooled. This is an aberration. Yours may be wide and shallow, the class split to the sides, forcing you to swivel. Or the deep, narrow room, with everybody in the back. You could end up in a science lab with sinks, gas spigots, the aroma of fetal pig. Even worse is the closet, a triangular slot left over in a bad building plan. Tables nailed to the floor, instructor pinned to the blackboard.

The key to all this, to the part-timer life, is to realize you are a joke. Then enjoy.

A Trailer

Dana was assigned to a trailer, out behind an elementary school. The low toilets there suited her fine, as she was a small person. But a cheap trailer for people who paid full tuition? Packed in like passengers on a bus.

Yet a good thing happened. It was impossible to be serious in a trailer. This was a class that laughed. A Vietnamese couple smiled all the time. A fellow inseparable from his laptop came early to play games with his mates. Arnie.

Maybe it was the trailer, as if this were a trip instead of school. Or just a lucky group without one lunatic or whiner. They liked each other. They liked her. The end came too soon.

The night of the final was an ice storm. A teacher's dread is not making it. You'd never see these people again. They'd come prepared, wait. Not fair. How would you grade?

The taillights on the beltway wouldn't move. Please go. Dana vowed that if she got there, she would forever be a caring teacher.

When the blurry pink in front of her spurted forward, a prettier sight she had not seen. And she got to the trailer, fine. But it was dark. Vehicles in the lot blinked their headlights hello.

She got out, slipping, sliding, and inched over to try the freezing doorknob. Of course. Locked.

A light in the elementary school and she hustled over there, down halls of crayon drawings, gulping a cafeteria smell, looking for somebody with a key. That wouldn't be a teacher. But no custodian tonight.

Back to the dark parking lot, where somebody called, "Dr. Shaughnessy?"

Warming to that melodious sound, she saw that it was Hugh, who worked construction and usually came late. "Trailer locked?"

"Yup."

"I can get you in."

Dear Hugh. Sweet Hugh. Deserving-of-an-A Hugh.

Dana recalled that Hugh had served a prison term and hoped it was for breaking and entering. He got a bag out of his truck, whose contents Dana did not question as she watched the working saint. The trailer door shuddered, popped open, and she loved him.

People thronged out of their cars, giddy coming into the trailer. Most everyone was there.

But where was Arnie? He never missed. Wrecked on a slick road somewhere so he couldn't call? He would do that. A favorite here. But he needed this final to get an A. She so wanted him to get an A.

When the only sound was scratching pens, a pounding came at the door. An administrator on the prowl, seeing that they had broken in?

Dana opened. It was Arnie, bearing an armload of pizzas, delivering that delicious smell.

So it was that a few souls in a trailer on this wintry night did "gladly lerne" and their instructor "gladly teche."

Advocates for Adjuncts

Indeed, the adjunct system needs fixing, and many these days are trying. Not an easy job. Imagine the full-timer assigned to supervise adjuncts. Facing these malcontents, this under-privileged horde, best ignored. Fielding complaints that are impossible to resolve. Giving part-timers the schedules they request, as they hound with a hundred e-mails. Whoever succeeds at this deserves tenure.

Some who take charge of adjuncts are so miserable that you pity them. They're jumpy. Afraid to look at you. They may bring pastry to the meetings. Doesn't help. Gatherings are cut short. Or canceled.

Then one dear day you get a supervisor who is a genuine advocate for adjuncts. Kindly, he listens; amazed, he learns. He asks part-timers for teaching tips. A mediator collects adjunct concerns. She delivers them to the Dean and actually gets back to you with the response.

Advocates who take on part-timer pain, when they have their own tenure-track terrors, are the part-timers' heroes. And if they can't make improvements, they try.

Benefits

On to the benefits of the part-timer life. Benefits, you say?

Many, for those who embrace it. Backdoor benefits to be sure. But dear. Whether you're down-and-out driven or called to this life, it can be rich and comic.

The variety is a hoot. A job in one place, how paltry. You have many homes. The rolling college campus is yours. Military base, warehouse, trailer. You adapt incredibly, widening your world. This flexilife keeps you from a midlife crisis, the malaise of the settled, the safe. For those tethered to a desk or tucked into an ivory tower, sameness petrifies. You, my friend, are as fluid as water.

With your many work sites, you can also escape. Most people ticked off at work have no place to go. You do. Have a rotten class? You're outta there. You'll be great at the next campus. Quit a school if you want. No explanation needed. No red tape. You have other jobs and can get more. A call to a desperate department could do it.

Your inscrutable schedule gives an excuse to avoid any activity. Drive a relative to the airport? Darn, gotta class at that hour. Red Cross campaign? If only you had the time.

Like anyone given to a high calling—monk, scientist, terrorist—you have a reason for not having a life.

Part-timers let loose of scholarship, if ever they cared. They're glad not to face graduate students, who can be jaded by theory, above story. Literature courses, being the elite, are gleaned by full-timers. So what. Adjuncts, relegated to composition, prefer essays. Short ones. They don't read weighty novels any more. Unload your academic baggage. Notes from graduate school? Burn 'em. You don't have to know that stuff. No scholarship at all. It's best if you don't cite academic journals.

You don't have to publish. You're not encouraged to publish. Nobody wants you to publish. If you do, you won't be praised. Possibly shunned. A part-timer never has to write a word.

Does this bring a grin?

Or maybe you hanker to do something entertaining on the side. Now's your chance. Try a romance novel. That screenplay about homicide in the workplace you've been thinking about. Knock off a how-to manual. You might even find a reader.

No required meetings. Curriculum committees. Search committees. The hosting of visiting celebrity professors. You don't have to do these things. What a boon. All other faculty are forced to meetings. Part-timers, never. You may choose to attend adjunct gatherings, and it's nice to go. Meet your compatriots. But if you can't make it, that's OK. The many who aren't there are assumed to be in class.

Feel bad you don't have an office? Of course you do. But this way no office hours. Nobody likes them. With no status you won't be advising anyone and don't need an office for that. You're lucky. No need to learn pesky requirements. What the heck it takes to graduate.

If you find obscurity degrading, you may want to find another career. But a taste for anonymity can be acquired. The ambition that once spurred you may have become a thorn. It is a scientific fact that stress results from self-importance. Give it up. Discover the giddiness that comes from being a nobody.

You have no professional enemies. Nowhere in all your places of employment do others have the least worry that you will overtake them. You aren't in the race.

Not that obscurity is to be confused with nothingness. An adjunct may be obscure in the system but will still reign in class. You don't have to announce that you're a part-timer. By sharing your underdog status, though, you can bond with students.

"I'm Nobody! Who are you?"

Security for a part-timer? In a weird way, yes. Consider this: You aren't important enough to be fired. As the adjunct was told when she asked about a promotion—she didn't have a job. Well, then, no need to delete her. And when you have no rigidity about hours, locations, last-minute classes, your name moves up the list. While a course can be taken away, you will pick up others. Colleges are fickle. One has no need; another calls back begging.

It's those on the tenure track who are tormented with insecurity. Poised to receive life's plum—or be let go, into oblivion.

No one will suggest that you retire. (From what?) You may continue in your non-job forever. To survive, well yes. But if you love it, to be alive.

Your experience is stunning. Look at it. No single school can hone a teacher as the many do. In one place you're taught student portfolios. In another the art of the positive syllabus. Your expertise burgeons as you amass tips, wisdom, nifty handouts from your various places. Best of all, the crowds of diverse students in your wake train you.

Part-timers may thus become master teachers.

The secret joy of the adjunct life is the adult students. You get them because they come out at night to the offbeat places where you are sent. Don't tell.

They have the best stories. Jobs they've had, families, divorces, every kind of wreck. And some brave triumphs. They know plenty. Adult learners are also modest, afraid they can't keep up, yet glad to be in school. They've learned there are worse places. They're the nurturers in your groups. Ah, and they like the teacher.

It is said that children are the most thrilling pupils.

Adults, I say.

And you, a part-timer, are still a college teacher. You hurry to class, pulsing at the door, students waiting within. What today? Today? Again they lift you up. Again.

Writing Steel-Toed Poems, Indictment Poems, I-See-Your-Bet-and-Raise-You Poems: The Poet as Ethicist

by
Rob Carney

People don't tend to think of poems as ethical guideposts. Words about the beauty of nature, words that rhyme—that's a poem. Outpourings about love or loss or meeting hard times with perseverance—that's a poem. And sometimes some of these assumptions turn out to be right. But that's not the whole story. Poets engage the world through their craft but also with the whole of themselves: mind, heart, and guts. Their acts of imagination are sometimes, ideally, a bit like digging post holes, planting sign posts, and saying, "Hey, humanity, go this way not that way." Just because we aim at making art doesn't mean we never touch on the philosophical, on what's ethical. And because poems are art rather than essays or pamphlets or slogans or talking points, when we do touch on ethics, ideally our words should sink deep . . . should go to the heart and guts, and therefore also upward into the mind.

I'm thinking of William Butler Yeats, for example, of his poem "The Second Coming," for example. Yeats wrote it in 1939, undoubtedly influenced, at least somewhat, by global events. Events?—I should say horrors; and after 1939, there were more and worse horrors to come. So, yes, Yeats's poem was contemporary then, but that doesn't make it historical today. Ethics, if they really are ethics, don't become dated; the poem and its warning are still plenty relevant right now. In it he writes, "The best lack all conviction, while the worst / Are full of passionate intensity."[1] It's worth hearing again: "The best lack all conviction, while the worst / Are full of passionate intensity" (lines 7-8). Oh man, if that doesn't explain bad government and status quo voters, then I don't know.

He ends his poem with a question rather than a statement, and doing so is both artistically and ethically right; for poets, when they're good at their job, make strong declarative statements, yes, but their poems, their very best ones, don't so much provide a final answer as concern themselves with raising, and raising, and raising the necessary questions . . . then hoping the listener will join in the effort to seek. In the end of the poem, he asks, "And what rough beast, its hour come 'round at last, / Slouches toward Bethlehem to be born?" Amen.

I don't intend to answer that question. Rather, I'll be sharing four of my own poems, for whatever they're worth. To me, the subject of each—or one subject of each—is Ethics. Maybe

---

[1]   This poem is in many books, but I'm specifically using The Collected Poems of W.B. Yeats, revised 2nd edition, Richard J. Finneran, ed. (New York: Scribner Paperback Poetry, 1996), whose table of contents is arranged both by poem number (200) and page number (187).

I'm wrong; maybe it's moral outrage or a plea for wider empathy. In any case, my intent—besides Art—is Ethics, which these days would mean their stance is "political." And because they don't condemn homosexuals, or brand Mexicans "illegals," or cotton to the Newspeak term "family values" (as if that has any inherent meaning, or even makes accurate use of the word family or the word values), you could fairly conclude my poems lean center-left. I don't apologize for that. I shouldn't have to.

Now, often what a poet does is introduce each poem with some background context or some paraphrase of its intended subject, and I do indeed have a back story. After the poems, before I wrap up, I'll share it. But for now I think it's enough to say that I didn't have our Utah legislature in mind when I wrote these. One poem, the zebra fable, was triggered by Salt Lake City's Evergreen Institute, not by the Hill. Local TV news was trumpeting the success of Evergreen's so-called "Reparative Therapy," which apparently gets gays to straighten out. And the one about sphinxes (sphinxes, as in the mythical lioness woman who'd kill and eat you if you couldn't solve her riddle)—that poem is twelve years old so in no way occasioned by the recent huffing over border control. I only mention it to remind people that twelve years ago this wasn't an issue to campaign on. . . . I think that's enough jabber, so here are the poems:

Now Hiring Sphinxes For Border Patrol. Must Be Willing To Relocate

It begins with the riddle:
"A man lies dead in a field beside his pack.

Inside, had he opened it,
is something that would have saved his life.

Answer correctly or die."
And I know where we're headed now:

aerial view of the Rio Grande, a dizzying
zoom, a panicked latina pleading uselessly for clues . . .

Ellis Island where the corpses pile in heaps,
their throats bruised black, backs

snapped in two . . . Seattle, Washington,
and 13 Cantonese busboys

down the hatch.
Such desperate guessing:

"Is it water?" "A sandwich?"
"Geiger counter?" "Insulin?"

"Swiss Army knife?" "A lightning rod?" "A gun?"
Lo siento. Sayonara. Nyet.
The bleaching wishbones.
The deliberate picking of teeth.

Ah! sweet success. Now how about a squadron
in the Bronx, a kind of pilot program;

issue tear gas and bullet-proof vests,
and see how it goes; take a bite out of crime.

But suppose some sneak through anyway?
Suppose thousands cross over in airplanes,

stow aboard air balloons,
illegally parachute in,

which is the answer—a chute
still stuffed inside the dead man's nylon pack.

Then sic 'em with gryphons, too.
Whip us up another riddle. Start again.

The Professor's Attempting To Disprove An Axiom;
you can change a zebra's stripes.
He's got notebooks full of entries,
a hundred studies on microfiche,

and a grant to finance his field tests
from the Conundrum Think Tank in D.C.
They're banking on him big time. Reparative Zoology is in.

The professor starts with measurements—
calipers, an abacus—
then experiments with tasty solutions of bleach.

And the zebras cooperate:
they listen to his lectures,
watch slides of Realist paintings,

patiently sit through charts and graphs tracking predatory ratios,
and eat his enchanted apples, three bags full.

But nothing happens.
He whips out his Bible and quotes from Leviticus,
makes worried and threatening faces—no result.
These zebras are stubborn, he concludes, boneheaded as mules.

Don't they know my time is valuable?
Don't they know what's best for them?
Don't they know it makes our hearts ache to see them this way?

Some Things Have One Meaning, Some Things Don't:
"I do," for instance, is conditional;
the truth, it turns out, is political;
and equal means that most have equally less.

But words are like elastic, and unless
you're careful not to stretch too far, they won't
snap back. . . .

I know what it is to be in love,
and no one has the right to disapprove
of who I love. They might, but they'd be wrong.

What else? Our lives are loaned to us. Not long.
And not to pile up money. Not for power.
And how we pay that loan back does matter:

with interest, yes—with being interested;
by promising and keeping promises;
by caring more and minding much less instead.

Every four years we get an extra day for what?
If I were a saw, I'd cut wood with my teeth,
        but I'm not.

        If I were my yard, I'd grow grass instead of hair,
        have trees instead of arms

        and shake hands with birds,
        but I'm not.

        I'm a man with a mind, heart, and language,
        so I'll speak:

A hundred crows can crash their voices into anything,
    take fish away from an osprey,

    drive stellar jays off
    of every fence post, they're still just crows.

    I'd rather be corn and take my chances;
    corn has ears.

In Stout Grove, a temple of sequoias—
    these thousand-year coastal redwoods thirty feet around—

    I startled a mountain lion.
    It turned from the road and was gone

    in so much silent fern.
    Like animal lightning, like a green green sky.

    If anyone ever kills it,
    he'll have taken more wild beauty than he can ever make.

    He'll owe the universe a cougar,
    and I hope in my too tame guts he has to pay.

How can God, the size of all creation,
    be buried alive in one book?—

    we can't even forecast the weather,
    who's fooling who?

How can salmon that spawned by the millions
    and fed ten thousand bears

    disappear in the power grid,
    only swim a while longer up the channels of TV?

Or crows, the whole harangue of them,
    so mistake their own croaking?

I mean people, of course,
people with their black rag hearts. . . .

I'm just a man, not even an osprey,
    and I can't saw off what's rotten,

    but maybe there are still enough ears out there.
    Maybe there's still a language enough of us can speak.

Earlier, I told you I had a back story to go with them. This is it: Last year our part-time legislature was roosting on an unexpected budget surplus, some hundreds-of-millions bonanza. So during the 45-day session, non-profits and the poor attempted to lobby for a restoration of dental benefits for the neediest Utahns on Medicare. Rather than listen, or even just put up with this perceived nuisance, state troopers were dispatched to dispose of offending leaflets and clear these citizens away from their capitol. The leaflets showed photos of decaying teeth. I guess that was the "offensive" part: Eeeeeew ick. In the remaining days, no discussion of benefits being restored was allowed out of committee. In the remaining days, they budgeted a new parking lot for themselves instead. One that cost more, by the way, than restoring dental coverage. One allowing free year-round parking to lobbyists; that was a nice touch. Further, when the state was sued for denying free speech and public access, the plaintiffs won. This led the folks in charge of Capitol Preservation to draft new regulations establishing so-called "free speech zones"—as if this can be said with a straight face—and these zones virtually guarantee that no one in our House, Senate, or Governor's office ever has to cross paths with their constituents, at least not the ones whose concerns don't concern them. That's really cute.

(I'm not making this up. I'm not mischaracterizing. All of this has been reported in print journalism and on the radio, and you can read and listen, the same as me.)

The poet and scholar, T.S. Eliot, coined the term "the objective correlative," and this crummy little saga is mine. By objective correlative, Eliot meant a specific, concrete image that stands in for the emotion or idea. I suppose it's just a fancier way of saying "show, don't tell," which is pretty standard advice, actually. What our representatives did last winter was rotten, as rotten as the teeth in those displeasing photographs. And their worming out from under the court's ruling against them is just as bad. To me, this stands out as a concrete example of what the Republican party, both locally and nationally, has done wrong. Wrong, as in unethical.

Or, As you've done it unto the least of these, you've done it unto me.[2]

---

2   This is slightly paraphrased from my King James Version. The exact wording in Matthew 25:40 is " . . . Inasmuch as ye have done it unto the least of these my brethren, ye have done it unto me." But since I am actually objecting to legislators not doing unto—to their withholding from the naked, hungry, imprisoned, etc.—perhaps Matthew 25:45 is the better, more accurate verse: " . . . Inasmuch as ye did it not to one of the least of these, ye did it not to me."

That's the back story. That was my reason for choosing to share these particular poems today, to last fall ask Dr. Keller to include me in this conference. In mid- to late-September 2006, this business over free speech rules to shut up people like the Medicare-Dental protesters made the news. I knew right then that I wanted to address this come January, and even what I would say in conclusion. In wrapping up, I told myself, I will say this:

We just had elections for state and federal office. I don't know who you voted for, or if that person won. That was November, and it's January now. We're just beginning new Congressional sessions here and in D.C. It would seem important to watch what gets prioritized by these representatives. And to pay attention to how your representatives vote. Ethics better count for something.

That's the pulse inside Yeats's "The Second Coming," and it's beating in the ribs of my poems too. We're not nihilists; nihilists don't bother to write poetry. Writing is hopeful, celebratory, consoling, lusting, seeking, grieving, and more; and when it's angry, when it's condemning, it's aiming to be corrective rather than merely resigned to the way things are: "Oh well, that's life, best to put it all behind you and move on." I don't buy that crap, and neither should you.

It's better to want the best to have conviction.

It's better to go on believing there's a language that enough of us still speak.

Creativity and Community Come to College

By
Jans Wager
(from the panel discussion: On the Corporate University)

L et's begin with a question.
What does the corporate university look like?

1. The corporate university pays lip service to undergraduate education while leaving the bulk of the teaching to adjunct instructors, inexpensive labor unprotected by tenure.
2. Instead of shared governance between students, faculty, and administration, the corporate university follows a business model, with the president of the college appointing individuals with strong business backgrounds to key academic positions such as dean or vice president.
3. Academic freedom, the keystone of public higher education, also gets short shrift in the arrangements, since the paying customer, often the parents of the students, feels fully justified in determining curriculum. In other words, if you want fries with that, you can get 'em.
4. In the sciences, research which once enriched the public domain becomes privatized; instead of providing scientific stepping stones for others, the work of corporate university scientists and students fills the pharmaceutical company's coffers.[1]

Is Utah Valley State College (UVSC) a corporate university? Well, we see aspects of what I describe above here--and also, no, not at all. UVSC has always emphasized teaching over research and insisted that its tenured faculty spend time in the classroom, giving students access to thinkers, writers, and researchers who have achieved the highest academic levels. UVSC has managed to keep class sizes small; most of our undergraduate required classes are taught in classrooms, not lecture halls. Although an overabundance of our lower division teaching is done by part-time labor, a situation exacerbated by consistent legislative underfunding, I still think that the administration is devoted to reducing that adjunct ratio by increasing the number of tenure track faculty. My experience as Associate Dean of the School of Humanities, Arts, and Social Sciences suggests that we are not hiring star professors by promising them little or no teaching. Instead we hire the best of recent Ph.D.s from around the country and put them into the classroom. High quality undergraduate education is alive and well at UVSC.

But quality education must be nurtured and its value reiterated to the students, faculty, administration, and community. And more of the community needs to be invited to campus. Education writer James Fallows notes that the "fastest growth in America's college-age population...will be a group that has had the lowest college attendance rate."[2] Lee Caldwell, President of Dixie state, adds that "Utah Hispanics go to college at one-third the national rate."[3] Instead of marketing primarily to the local white population, UVSC must invite the Hispanic population to the campus. The college's future, as well as the state and the nation, depend on it.

The future also depends on the quality of education we offer. If we only educate the students according to the values and knowledge of the previous generation, we will produce mediocrity--workers without the ability to think. The world changes constantly, faster now than ever. A liberal arts education, including coursework in the humanities, social, and natural sciences designed to challenge students to think deductively, provides the context for creative work in any discipline including daily life.

Higher education has long had the dual and often dueling missions of training workers (Horace Mann) and educating thinkers (John Dewey). UVSC's varied programs ensure that we continue to graduate individuals ready to work in a variety of trade, technology, academic and business venues. But given the rate of information technology growth and change, by the time a student graduates much of the technical information she or he has learned to use is already out of date. What will help most is that our graduates know how to think critically, creatively, and flexibly, how to articulate complex ideas verbally and in writing, and how to continue to learn and grow outside the academic setting. In order to train workers we must educate thinkers; an educated labor force is our only real natural resource.

But Utah is failing to do that. According to a recent Deseret News article, "Utah ranks 45th in the nation in the number of its high school graduates moving directly on to college;... Utah ranks 33rd in the nation in the percentage of young people ages 25-34 who have college degrees and that the number continues to drop;...Utah is at or near the bottom in manufactured exports and venture capital activity and...in patent rates," reflecting a serious deficiency in educating creative and original thinkers—inventors and innovators.[4] These statistics point to the fact that higher education in Utah is failing to do what it should—and what I believe the administration, the trustees, the citizens of Utah Valley, and the state legislators must really want--educate thinkers. We have a strong, highly qualified faculty committed to teaching in the undergraduate classroom. We need to support that resource by rigorously protecting academic freedom and engaging in shared governance to fill key academic positions.

Every time I go into the classroom at UVSC I recognize the potential of the students sitting there. In order to truly educate them to become the creative forgers of a better future for Utah and the nation, UVSC might have corporate links, but we must realize that what counts is building not a corporate university culture but an rich and vibrant academic culture—one that attracts and retains both a diverse mix of students and the best intellectuals, scientists and researchers as faculty members and teachers. As a public institution of higher education with a focus on undergraduate teaching, UVSC is in a unique position to do so much more than train workers. Let other institutions of higher education in Utah fully exploit the corporate university model. UVSC should nurture an academic model, one that responds to the whole community and supports and rewards quality faculty dedicated to teaching. UVSC can and should engage the future and educate thinkers.

Notes

1   Jennifer Washburn's University Inc. provided a context for some of these definitions.

Jennifer Washburn, University Inc.: The Corporate Corruption of Higher Education (New York: Basic Books, 2005).

2   James Fallows, "College Admissions: A Substitute for Quality, Decline by Degrees: Higher Education at Risk (New York: Palgrave Macmillan, 2005) 45.

3   Lee Benson, "Utah rates critically low in its higher education," Desert Morning News 17 Dec. 2006. 1Jan. 2007 <http://deseretnews.com/dn/print/1,1442,650215746,00.html>

4   Benson.

Fast Food Education: Do You Want Fries with That?

By
Richard McDonald
(from the panel discussion: On the Corporate University)

I've spent almost all of the last 22 years of my life attending or teaching in colleges and universities of different sizes. That doesn't make me an expert in how colleges should be run—but it makes me invested in the future of what colleges will be—especially this one (where I've now been for more than 9 years). "Fast Food Education: Do You Want Fries with That," my funny or provocative title (depending on what you think about the current state of education) came long before the idea for this paper or this panel. As I mentioned I have worked in a number different educational settings and I guess there have been times, even in recent history, where I wondered whether I was working at an institution of higher education or a Burger King. I am reminded of Burger King's "special orders don't upset us" credo and the business motto that created it— "The Customer is Always Right" far too often in the world of academia. And even though I like my Whopper with extra pickles and ketchup, I struggle with the idea that the customer is always right in a higher-education setting. What I'm getting at is that there is an attitude becoming more prevalent at colleges that the student as customer should determine what she or he learns. And while I recognize that as much as I detest the idea that the student (or the tax payer) is my (gulp) customer, I think we need to look closely at what colleges are doing—because if they are a business, they're not selling Whoppers—or widgets for that matter. Students come to my classroom expecting me to teach them something. In order for them to consume my product, I actually can't allow them to hold the pickle–the pickle may be an integral part of the lesson. So, if we are going to adopt a business model for higher education—there are definitely some prominent business concepts that just can't work. Nevertheless, as stodgy as universities like to pretend they are, the history of colleges in America is one of making and remaking themselves to serve the needs of their constituencies.

When I created the ambiguous title "Corporate Education" for this session, my intention was to try to take a closer look at some of the business models and business procedures that are more and more becoming a part of higher education. The fact is that as money from states and the federal government has tightened and the number of students has increased (an increase that has lead to educating a larger and overall less prepared portion of the population), colleges have been forced to consider new attitudes about financial planning. As much as it bothers me to say it, colleges are businesses. There is no doubt about it—even from their 12th century beginnings--universities were places where students paid money to receive an education. Additionally, colleges have adapted over the years to offer more practical knowledge to larger numbers of people—especially in the last 30 or so years. Fifty years ago—something like 5%

of the population received college educations—30 years ago—16%. Now something like 75% of high school graduates enroll in Bachelors programs (Schneider 62). Most Americans firmly believe that one needs a college education to succeed in life.

As college becomes the destination for the majority of the population, attitudes about what one learns in college have changed. The American public wants a college that helps this growing number of young people attain the skills necessary for the working world. Although most employers surveyed desire that their new employees possess skills in analytical thinking, problem solving, oral and written communication, ethical reasoning, and to have scientific and technological competence, and an understanding of the world in which they live (the typical expectations of General Education)(Schneider 65), there is often pressure from the public to reduce the time spent on general college courses and either increase the number of specialized major-specific courses or shorten the overall length of college (Kirp 128). The idea being that learning that applies specifically to the students intended work field is the overwhelmingly important element of college education.

In doing the research for this presentation I looked at quite a bit of literature about higher education and the public's satisfaction with it, past and present. It appears that the most successful time period for education were the years between World War II and the end of the Vietnam war (Sperber 133). During that time education expanded to fill the needs of the middle class and there was an emphasis on strong general education with specialization occurring during the last two years of college. Education commentators, and to a certain extent the general public, assert that starting in the 1970s the trend (at large universities, especially) toward large-roomed lecture classes eroded the quality of education and broke the link between professor and student established in smaller classes (Sperber 134). This change, too, was in response to pressure to economize on college's spending.

So what does all of this mean for UVSC or higher education in general in the 21st Century. As the university has done in the past, we must make some difficult choices about what students should get out of a university education. Do we want our colleges merely to train students for their future careers? Colleges have always prepared students for jobs in fields related to their course of study, but from the inception of the university the idea that a college should broadly educate students has also been present. College has been a place where students get exposed to a wide variety of subjects and ideas that they may never have the opportunity to study again. This information about fields different from the one they intend to pursue helps them to understand the world around them. Additionally, learning how to learn leaves students with the ability to pursue topics that interest them throughout their lives. With the fluidity of the job market today and the near inevitability of changing not only jobs but careers, broad training in college is even more essential. But regardless of the possible application of knowledge to one's work, colleges have always taught people to love learning for their personal satisfaction. The science student taking a humanities elective might develop a life-long love of art that has negligible value in her 9-5 job, but provides her with a life-long interest. The same is true of the humanities student who is introduced to a life-long, fulfilling hobby during his introductory astronomy course.

Let me finish up my bit by going back to my initial conundrum. If universities are a business, but a business where we don't let the customers decide exactly what they get–what the heck kind of business are they? Well, it turns out I have a friend who actually runs such a business. Jans Wager's partner, Bill, runs a back-country skiing business that takes people to remote areas for ski tours. He has numerous stories—some pretty funny—of customers who wanted to do things that he or one of his guides would not let them do. If the customer wants to do something that could be hazardous for them or others in the party, they are forbidden to do it. Maybe back-country ski touring should be the new university business model. O.K. so maybe no students will die if they receive a less well-rounded education, but diminishing the breadth of education could very well cripple their personal and professional happiness and diminish the amount of pleasure they experience over their lifetimes.

Influential Sources

Gregorian, Vartan. "Six Challenges to the American University," *Declining by Degrees*. 77-96.

Hersh, Richard H. and John Merrow. Eds. Delining By Degrees:*Higher Education at Risk*. New York: Palgrave, 2005.

Kirp, David L. "This Little Student Went to Market," *Declining by Degrees*. 133-29.

Maeroff, Gene I. "The Media: Degrees of Coverage," *Declining by Degrees*. 11-22

Schneider, Carol. "Liberal Education: Slip Sliding Away," *Declining by Degrees*. 61-76

Sperber, Murray. "How Undergraduate Education Became College Lite," *Declining by Degrees*. 131-43.

Wadsworth, Deborah. "Ready or Not? Where the Public Stands on Higher Education Reform," *Declining by Degrees*. 23-38.

Washburn, Jennifer. University Inc.: *The Corporate Corruption of Higher Education*. Cambridge, MA: Perseus, 2005.

The Culture of UVSC and How it is Communicated

By
F. Dennis Farnsworth, Jr.
(from the panel discussion: On the Corporate University)

I wasn't recruited by UVSC. I was a walk-on, but soon had contract in hand. I wasn't hired because I was brilliant. I was hired because I was a low-cost producer, and the administration was able to spot a "good buy!" When I first started here, life was all work and no money; fortunately, things have improved greatly since then!

When I arrived at the college I noticed that the floors were tilted and the mirrors crazed. The natives spoke gibberish and engaged in strange rituals. Today the floors are straight, the mirrors are normal, I speak the language of the natives and engage in their rituals. Apparently, I have come to be fully socialized! This was a slow process and not carried out in a formal way (I was not assigned a mentor, for example, but learned on my own). This socialization occurred fairly rapidly, for I enjoyed being here and was eager to learn, fit in, and make my contribution.

The primary attitudinal change was increased self-confidence, especially where relating to my faculty peers was concerned.

Rituals are significant at Utah Valley State College. When employees are about to retire, a reception is held for them, tributes are paid, and everybody shakes hands and applauds. These ceremonies have emotional as well as symbolic content: they result in additional bonding among faculty.

Indeed, retirement is a significant rite of passage. But other rites of passage exist as well. These include tenure, promotion, and the acquisition of degrees. Degrees confer credibility and get us in the door; tenure confers job security; and promotion communicates worthiness. The priests who mediate do so with solemnity befitting the occasion. They render the incantations appropriate to the rite. Graduation of students each year, for example, while obviously a rite of passage for them, is for faculty as well. They carve another notch in the stock of their rifles, don their feudal robes and participate in a rite rooted in the medieval culture that is the common heritage of Western higher education. This being the case, then, it may well be that my socialization has been more completely to the generality of higher education than to the specificity of UVSC.

Rituals continue at the heart of the tribal relations which constitute UVSC's interactions with peer institutions. Presidents meet, shake hands, smoke the peace pipe, and plot their attack on the regents and the legislature. It is all highly symbolic and political. On the first of July I saw the president in the hallway and wished him "happy new year!" He didn't hesitate in returning the greeting. Is there any reckoning other than the fiscal year? Oh yes, the academic year!!

Cultures are identified in part by their norms and values. What are ours?

One of the most dominant norms is that students come first. In most situations students probably do come first. Instructors treat students as customers and go to pains not to take advantage of them.

A puritan ethic prevails here. First of all, UVSC is a "dry" campus. Secondly, while student and faculty are not prohibited from fraternizing with each other, everyone seems to understand where the line is that is not to be breached: consensual relationships are a non-issue.

Everyone agrees they are a bad idea. Mating calls are restricted to the single and available. (while I have not done a formal study to validate these perceptions – they are largely anecdotal – nevertheless, I am certain my colleagues would agree).

The prevalent ideology here is liberalism: enlightened self interest is pursued within the overall framework of concern for the public interest. Rights (especially academic freedom) are enthroned with reverence and jealously guarded. While there may be potential conflicts between liberalism and the Puritan Ethic, I am unaware as to what they might be.

Business, Ethics & Law

Dr. Hugh Rode, Dr. Stott Harston, Dr. Carolyn Howard-Morris

Teaching Ethics and Honesty in Business Classrooms: A Study of Changes in Student Perceptions

By
Susan R. Madsen, Ovilla Turnbull,
Troy R. Nielson & Larry D. Hartman

Abstract

With recent highly publicized breaches of ethics among members of the business community (e.g., Enron, WorldCom, Adelphia, Global Crossing, and Tyco), there is a need to re-examine specific strategies employed in colleges and universities to influence business students toward increased ethics and honesty. The purpose of this study was to examine whether perceptions and attitudes toward ethics and honesty could be influenced during a semester-long college business course. A survey was administered to students in six human resource management classes taught by four different faculty members. The Likert scale questionnaire utilized the 20-item Ethics Position Questionnaire (Forsyth, 1980) as well as eight original honesty items created by Madsen (2006). In addition, it included two short cases written by Denisi and Griffin (2001) which asked for qualitative student responses. The questionnaire examined four aspects of ethics in two categories: 1) honesty (i.e., plagiarism and cheating) and 2) ethics (e.g. idealism and relativism.) To measure student changes in perceptions and attitudes, the survey was administered both at the beginning and end of the semester. During the semester instructors placed particular emphasis on integrating the study of ethics into the teaching of human resource management.

According to Baird (1980) and McCabe and Trevino (1995), business students are more likely to engage in academic dishonesty than non-business majors. In addition, business students have more tolerant attitudes toward cheating (Roig & Ballew, 1994) and tend to believe that they need to have unethical beliefs and behaviors in order to successfully complete their college degrees (Crown & Spiller, 1998; Lane & Schaupp, 1989). Since this literature was published, there have been highly publicized breaches of ethics among members of the business community (e.g., Enron, WorldCom, Adelphia, Global Crossing, and Tyco). With these concerns in mind, it is clear that there is a need to re-examine specific strategies employed in colleges and universities to influence business students toward increased ethics and honesty. We argue that it is not only essential, but outright imperative that business faculty foster and encourage honesty in whatever reasonable and effective capacity possible. This means that faculty must act as exemplar models of morality (Cabral-Cardosa, 2004).

The recent ethical breaches among top corporate leaders has fueled interest and the desire for educators and scholars to study college and university curriculum in order to discover the types of lessons, assignments, activities, and methods that are most effective in positively changing students' ethical perceptions and behaviors. This study was designed specifically to look at a portion of these concerns, as its purpose was to examine whether perceptions and attitudes toward ethics and honesty could be influenced during semester-long college business classes, more particularly six sections of a human resource management survey course.

Literature

Ethics researchers are now arguing that there has never been a more critical time for faculty to teach ethics than now (e.g., South, 2004). However, some researchers have purported that teaching ethics cannot do much for those who, at a fundamental level, don't care about doing the right things (South, 2004). Dowd (1992) studied ethics among students in general and found that many students perceive the action of cheating as harmless. Yet, research (Dowd, 1992; Hilbert, 1987) has reported connections between unethical classroom behaviors and unethical workplace behaviors. Therefore, hedging the cheating behavior and especially changing the lax attitudes of students may have positive societal impact. According to Robinson and Moulton (1985), institutions of higher learning "must decide whether [they are] going to try to direct values, influence them in any way, or ignore them for good or ill" (p. 28).

Dowd's (1992) research focused specifically on plagiarism by students. He posited that there may be a wide variety of reasons that students cheat and/or plagiarize the work of others. These reasons include the following: alienation of students, a desire for good grades, immaturity, personality, poor college policy on academic honesty, public figures serving as poor role models, and self-centeredness. More than ten years and numerous public scandals later, many of the reasons enumerated by Dowd still appear to be relevant.

Although there is a plethora of research on the topic of testing and reporting the statistical prevalence of cheating and plagiarism in the classroom, there is also some discussion of whether honor codes, written and enforced, can help minimize the incidences of college cheating and plagiarism. Cabral-Cardosa (1994) and McCabe and Trevino (1993) suggested that implementing strongly-worded and strictly followed codes of ethical conduct within business schools decreases incidence of cheating. Crown and Spiller (1998) found a significant reduction in cheating for students with honor codes. Brown and Howell (2001) noted that a worded statement about plagiarism appears to be an effective way to change student's perceptions of the issue and is likely to have positive effects on their future behavior. Busby, Sorenson, and Anderson (2004) reviewed many related studies between 1972 and 2003 and concluded that the serious problem of student cheating in higher education can be addressed in part by educators emphasizing "honor codes-pledges established by the university, employing classroom procedures to inhibit cheating, assigning projects dealing with ethical questions (including cases studies), and helping identify worthy role models" (p. 22). Others (e.g., Brown & Howell, 2001; Cabral-Cardoso, 2004; Dowd, 1992; Crown & Spiller, 1998) argued that having a poor or no college policy on plagiarism and academic integrity might send the wrong message to students and faculty regarding the importance of these issues. Indeed, having an unambiguous policy regarding academic expectations with defined consequences for failure to comply is critical. Cabral-Cardoso (2004) reported that this type of policy is needed to thwart future incidences. This researcher also found that faculty members involved in academic dishonesty are typically not effective in teaching ethics and honesty to their students.

There seems to be a lack of helpful instruments to measure changes in ethical perceptions that can be used in business school classrooms. The Ethics Position Questionnaire (EPQ)

(Forsyth, 1980) is one of the few that seemed applicable to use for the purpose of this study. It was developed by Forsyth (1980) and then replicated in a variety of arenas (e.g., Davis, Anderson & Curtis, 2001; Redfern & Crawford, 2004; Treise & Weingold, 1994) in the decades since its inception. The EPQ is a means of classifying respondents into four quadrants "as a general measure of ideology applicable to almost any context of ethical judgment" (Treise & Weingold, 1994, p. 63.) These quadrants can be represented visually by a bisecting scale ranging from universalism, on one hand, and relativism on the other; and with pragmatism as opposed to idealism on the bisecting axis. Hence, it purports to be a measure of ethics by rating individuals on the basis of universalism as compared to relativism and pragmatism as compared to idealism. The traits measured as defined as follows:

1.   **PRAGMATIST:** "A person who focuses on consequences produced by an action" (Treise & Weingold, 1994, p. 61). In other words if an action is likely to produce good consequences it is viewed as ethically superior to one that is likely to produce a negative outcome.

2.   **IDEALIST:** "A person who focuses on the inherent rightness or wrongness of an action regardless of the consequences" [(Treise & Weingold, 1994, p. 61). This could also be said that an action is either right or wrong and is separate from the outcome. If something that is wrong produces desirable results, it is still wrong. Employees lower in idealism were more likely to engage in both organizational and interpersonal deviance (Henle, Giacalone, & Jurkiewicz, 2005].

3.   **RELATIVISM:** "The degree to which individuals believe moral questions should be decided by universal moral rules" (Treise et. al, 2005, p. 224). Henle et al., (2005) found that employees who were higher in relativism appeared to disregard socially accepted codes of conduct. They argued that this would then predispose them toward workplace deviance.

4.   **UNIVERSALISM:** "Moral systems can be ordered in accord with their inherent 'rightness' or in accordance with natural law" (Treise & Weingold, 1994, p. 63). This is to say that an action is right or wrong in itself and the rightness or wrongness does not depend on the situation or locale.

A number of researchers have used the EPQ to measure ethics. In one pertinent example, O'Higgins and Kelleher (2005) used the EPQ to compare the ethical sensitivity of managers in the human resources, marketing, and finance functional areas of business. They proposed that the differences may come from education and training for the different role types, external legal and social pressures for performance, or emphasis on showing positive results (e.g., financial growth). For example, Singhapakdi, Vitell, and Craft (1996) argued that due to the nature of human resources and the moral intensity that practitioners are likely to experience, human resource managers would be more ethically sensitive than both the marketing and the finance managers. They discovered that, in fact, there was a significant difference between the ethical sensitivity of human resource managers as compared to marketing managers. Yet, there was not a measurable difference between human resource managers and finance managers. It appears that the higher than expected level of ethical sensitivity by finance managers was a result of the external legal pressure they experience which, over time, may have ingrained in them internal values (O'Higgins & Kelleher, 2005).

Muijen (2004) addressed appending the teaching of ethics onto the regular business curricula. She added an ethical reflection component to the various ethics curriculum and integrated it by providing subject relevant ethical questions to which the students respond by describing their individual behavior. No pre-post tests were done to determine whether this approach effectively increases ethical sensitivity. Muijen (2004), who performed her research at a religious based institution, concludes that "the implementation of a reflective approach to value learning is a 'more' encompassing educational aim than the 'mere' inclusion of applied ethics in the curriculum and why it cannot be bound to conveying specific Christian values to the students" (p. 239). The aim of the approach, which Muijen counts successful, was to turn "Un-reflective value judgments [about what one might do in situations represented in the case-studies used] to philosophical reflection on the relevant values" (p. 239). Muijen and others believe that successful ethics education include reflective components designed within the curriculum.

Purpose and Research Methods

This study examined whether business faculty can teach ethical sensitivity and improve present and future ethics-oriented behavior through a specific focus on its importance and by integrating it into lessons and coursework throughout a given semester. Two major categories were addressed with two sub-categories under each: 1) honesty (plagiarism and cheating) and 2) ethics (idealism and relativism). Two research questions were posed in the design of this study:

1.   By appending onto classroom lecture and activities a strong emphasis on the soundness of ethical and moral behavior, can faculty induce an increased attitude of honesty in students as manifested by an increase in perceptions of the importance of and perceived future behavior of not being involved in cheating and/or plagiarizing?

2.   Can added emphasis on the propriety of honest, ethical behavior in a given course improve students' ethics scores on relativism and idealism scales (as defined by Forsyth, 1980) from the beginning to the end of a semester?

Basically, the educators posed the question of whether ethics can be learned by students in the business classroom.

This study was conducted on a large college campus during the Spring semester of 2006.

Students (n=110) in six sections of an introductory human resource management course taught by any one of the four faculty members were surveyed. Identical survey instruments were distributed to the students at the start and end of semester instruction (pre- and post-test design). A research assistant (non-instructor) compiled all of the data and analyzed the qualitative responses. Of the respondents, 84 provided enough information for gender data to be gathered, with 19 female, 65 male, and 36 unknown respondents. Also, of the 110 participants, 53 completed only one administration of the survey or did not provide enough information to match the pre-survey with the post-survey. This meant that the final statistical tests could only use the 57 completed pre- and post-test surveys.

The instrument was divided into three sections. Parts A and B contained general statements to be rated by respondents and measured on a seven-point Likert scale with a response of one being "Strongly Disagree" and a response of seven being "Strongly Agree." The first section (Part A) tested students' honesty by asking about attitudes toward cheating and plagiarism. Items included the following eight items:

1.   A student should understand and be aware of all aspects of plagiarism.

2. Plagiarizing is a serious offense.
3. Top (successful) students are ones who adhere to plagiarism rules and guidelines.
4. Decisions in college related to plagiarism have no impact on the way a person will make decisions in future employment.
5. A person would be considered honest even if he/she occasionally misleads others.
6. It is dishonest for a person to act or say he/she is prepared for class when he/she is not.
7. Sometimes it is okay to cheat if a person believes he/she has good reasons.
8. Being honest in college directly relates to being honest in a person's future career.

The second section (Part B) utilized the EPQ (as previously described) that measured the students' ethical attitudes on idealism and relativism scales. Sample items included
1. People should make certain their answers never intentionally harm another even to a small degree (idealism scale).
2. Whether a lie is judged to be moral or immoral depends upon the circumstances surrounding the action (relativism scale).

The third section (Part C) measured qualitative data by asking students to type their responses to questions regarding two vignettes found in Denisi and Griffin's (2001) human resource management textbook.

It is important to note a few limitations to this research study. First, as already mentioned, the small sample size particularly in end of semester responses is a major weakness of this research. The post sample size is too small to show statistically significant changes. Secondly, the intensity of delivery between instructors was not standardized. Each instructor was just instructed to make ethics a priority during the semester in his or her classes. There was no uniformity of curriculum in implementing this in each section. Finally, the questions may or may not measure the change in ethical reasoning and sensitivity among business students. As already mentioned, the relativism scale did not appear to measure the ethical construct that was intended to be measured in this study. More research, including the use of a control group, is needed to determine the whether the questionnaire correctly measures the change.

Results and Discussion

Table 1 shows a comparison of the standard deviations and the mean scores for students who took both the pre-and-post as well as the scores for those who took only the pre-test. The data show that the pre-test mean scores for those students (n= 57) who completed the semester and completed both the pre-and-post portions of the test was higher (M= 6.13) than the pre-test mean scores for all students (n=110) including those who completed a pre-test only (M=5.91). Part of this difference may be that some students who had less-ethical leanings dropped the course early on in the semester, possibly as a result of learning about the ethics component of the course curriculum.

Unfortunately, because one instructor did not require the return of the post-test survey the final sample size of 57 was insufficient to show significant results in statistical tests that compared the means of the pre- and post-survey samples. Intercorrelations run using a Pearson's statistical test (see Table 2) was done to compare the data based on fourteen items: instructor, gender of the participant, and then time-one (T1) versus time-two (T2) for each of the six items represented in the quantitative portion of the study (honesty, cheating, plagiarism, ethics, idealism, and relativism). Although this study was severely limited with the final sample size, some interesting correlations provide insight for further discussion.

Table 1. Means and Standard Deviations

Variables	Pre-test: All Students (n-110)		Pre-test: Students who completed both (n=57)		Post-test: Students who completed both (n=57)	
	M	SD	M	SD	M	SD
1. Honesty	5.91	.76	6.13	.61	6.37	1.35
a) Plagiarism	6.08	.88	6.36	.76	6.44	.67
b) Cheating	5.73	.96	5.88	.87	6.29	2.63
2. Ethics	4.60	.78	4.69	.8	4.57	.73
a) Relativism	3.91	1.29	3.9	1.46	3.67	1.61
b) Idealism	5.30	1.02	5.51	1.01	5.49	1.06

Although there was no correlation between the students' responses at the beginning of the semester and the instructor, there was a clear correlation between the students' responses in two sections with one particular instructor. Students who had this instructor had statistically higher responses related to the importance of not plagiarizing (plagiarism awareness) than students in other sections of the course. These students also responded more strongly to the question "Decisions in college related to plagiarism have no impact on the way a person will make decisions in future employment." These students had a clearer understanding that their choices in college influenced their honesty in future employment. It appears this instructor provided more dialogue and discussion in class related to these issues than did the other three instructors.

There were a number of other correlation results that should be highlighted. The sample had a low number of female students which may have explained no findings related to gender. As with the t-test, there were no statistically significant results between T1 and T2 on any of the constructions. This means that there wasn't a clear increase of student perceptions related to honesty or ethics awareness and understanding. Hence, these results do not show that the students increased their perceptions of these constructs throughout the course. One explanation is that the sample size was so small. Another is that their initial perceptions (T1) were fairly high to begin with. Another element to consider is that business students did not respond well to the relativism scale. In fact, after the study the researchers concluded that the relativism scale was not the best measurement to use for this type of research, particularly with business school students. Another ethics scale may have shown changes in attitudes and beliefs more than this scale. Basically, there was a high correlation between T1 and T2 in many constructs (e.g., plagiarism, r = .50; ethics, r = .47), meaning that the answers were very similar (no statistical change in perceptions occurred). A few other correlations that may provide ongoing dialogue include the following:

• Students who had high responses for honesty at the beginning of the semester also had higher perceptions of the importance of not plagiarizing at the end of the semester (r =. 45).

- Students who strongly agreed that honesty was important at the beginning of the semester also had high agreement with the idealism items at the beginning of the semester ($r = .39$).
- At the beginning of the semester, students responses between cheating and plagiarism items were similar ($p = .36$).
- Student at the beginning of the semester who had agreed strongly with the idealism items also agreed strongly with the four cheating items at the beginning ($r = .34$) and at the end of the semester ($r = .27$).

Table 2. Intercorrelations

Variables	1	2	3	3a	3b	4	4a	4b	5	5a	5b	6	6a
1. Instructor	--												
2. Gender	.47	--											
3. Honesty T1	.03	.07	--										
a Plagiarism T1	.00	-.01	.81**	--									
b. Cheating T1	.05	.12	.84**	.36**	--								
4. Honesty T2	.06	.28	.19	-.06	.32*	--							
a. Plagiarism T2	-.29*	.22	.45**	.50**	.20	.21	--						
b. Cheating T2	.14	.23	.08	-.19	.28	.97**	-.04	--					
5. Ethics T1	.07	.09	.19*	.17	.15	.08	.16	.04	--				
a. Idealism T1	.08	.13	.39**	.31**	.34**	.21	.21	.17	.57**	--			
b. Relativism T1	.02	-.03	-.09	-.03	-.11	-.05	.04	-.06	.76**	-.10	--		
6. Ethics T2	.13	.12	.10	.07	.10	.20	-.06	.22	.47**	.36**	.23	--	
a. Idealism T2	.11	-27	.34*	.26	.27*	.25	.26	.19	.26	.63**	-.17	.59**	--
b. Relativism T2	.05	-.11	-.17	-.14	-.11	.02	-.30*	.10	.34*	-.11	1.0	.67**	-.20
T1=Time 1 (Beginning of Semester); T2=Time 2 (End of Semester)													

On the qualitative section of the instrument students were asked to analyze vignettes relating to ethical decisions they may have to make as a human resource practitioner. The first described a situation in which the student is to imagine that he or she is a project manager in a human resource department charged with paring down the two human resource departments into one, which means laying off several individuals. The written instructions direct the project manager to be fair and keep the best people between the two companies, however the supervisor tells the project manager to "take care of as many of our own as possible." Students are then asked questions about whether they would follow the written instructions or the ones the supervisor gave. They are also asked how they would go about making the decision between who stays and who is let go.

In response to the first vignette the responses from student to student at the beginning of the semester compared to the end of the semester varied little. Most of the respondents agreed that the issue was who they should layoff. The respondents were also homogeneous in their solutions, saying that they would evaluate items such as "employees' past performance" and "time on the job." The conclusions were, almost wholly, that they would choose the "best candidates for the jobs" and not show favoritism to "insiders." One student, for example, stated that "I would base my decision strictly on merit. If a person has the skills, they should remain. If they don't, they get the axe." Interestingly, at the end of the semester the students gave similar answers but provided additional detail about how they would go about the selection process (e.g., evaluate "likelihood of future good performance," "past efficiency" and "reliability"). Although the answers did not vary much from the beginning to the end of the semester, the students were much more educated about the legal and ethical issues around their decisions.

The second vignette described a dilemma in which the student (as a hiring manager) must decide between two internal candidates for a job. Both have fairly equal qualifications. One is a black female with performance appraisal scores which are slightly lower than the white male that is also being considered. However, the hiring manager feels that the black female's supervisor consistently scores all individuals slightly lower than what they should be. Students are asked to answer questions about the ethical implications and about what they would do in this situation. This item proffered the most interesting results because of the varied responses to one of the questions which asked, "What do you think most managers would do? What would you do?"

Responses differed both from student to student and somewhat from beginning to the end of semester. Many students reasoned that they would choose to hire either the black female or white male, but felt that "Most Managers" would make the other selection or make the same selection for a different reason. For example, one student argued: "Most managers would choose the higher scoring white male; he is easier to defend as the right choice. However, I would choose who fits the job better. I would listen to my gut instincts and not worrying about my defense." Like this student, there were many who simply refused to make a selection about what they or the majority of managers would do. They did, however argue the merit of each choice. In fact, one respondent stated that "As far as the situations that were presented, I had no idea how they should be answered at the beginning of the semester. I didn't answer them because I didn't know how. After taking the class I can better understand what the ethical dilemmas of situations were, and now I understand the legal implications behind them."

A primary reason the students ascribed to the decision most managers would make about whether to hire the black female or the white male was related to legal issues. The students felt their own selections or reasoning differed from those made by "most managers". For example, one stated "I'd say to hire the girl, for she is just as good but the company will avoid possible litigation." Another stated that most managers would "Probably pick the black female because she is a protected class and this will eliminate litigation. I personally would pick whoever would add value to the position." This trend may indicate a lack of faith in "most managers" and/or the legal system. Even those that did not specifically mention the legal system had other reasons that they didn't seem to trust management reasoning. But these students asserted that they would be different. Respondents commonly made statements like "Most managers would select the black female because of status quo. I would pick her because of her performance." Others were harsher; one asserted that "Most managers would probably pick the worst candidate for the position because their decisions are based on subjective data/information so whoever can manipulate this data the best will get the job. I would get to know each person by actually spending time with them, not just asking them lame questions."

Conclusion

Given the results of the study, further questions are posed for future research. Do less-ethically minded individuals self-select out of courses in which great attention is given to ethical sensitivity? Do particular types of teaching methodologies (e.g., lecture, examples, guest speakers, cases, service-learning experiences) lead to increased ethical and honesty sensitivity? Does the EPQ measure the change in ethical sensitivity? If the questions related to ethics (EPQ) were more business relevant would a greater change in perceptions and attitudes be evident?

By finding better and more effective ways of directing students toward academic and professional honesty, the hope is that the overall standards and expectations these students have for themselves and their peers will increase. Accomplishing this aim may take a single approach (e.g., implementing and enforcing strongly-worded codes of conduct), but more likely, the optimal approach will include a meld of methods each of which must be studied for effectiveness. Here we examined the effectiveness of making the study of business and academic ethics an integral part of business coursework.

There is a lot more research that can be done on the subject of whether ethics can be learned in a business classroom setting appended onto the curriculum of some other subject. The literature (e.g., Dowd, 1992; Muijen, 2004; South, 2004,) suggests students—especially in business majors (McCabe & Trevino, 1995)—increasingly lax in their attitudes toward cheating and plagiarism, are wending their way through college. This is cause for alarm because of the recent highly publicized breaches of ethics among business practitioners. The question then becomes what can be done with current students to hedge this trend, especially in light of studies which indicate a connection between cheating and lax behavior while in school and after graduation. It is clear that more research needs to be conducted in this area. It is imperative that students learn ethics and honesty during childhood, adolescence, and college years. Future research on the most effective means to do this in college classrooms around the country continues to be needed and welcomed.

References

Baird, J. S. (1980). Current trends in college cheating. *Psychology in the Schools,* 17, 124-125.

Brown, V. J., & Howell, M.E. (2001). The efficacy of policy statements on plagiarism: Do they change students' views? *Research in Higher Education,* 42(1), 103–118.

Busby, C. H., Sorenson, P. S., & Anderson, D. S. (2004). Home, gender, and the social scene: Factors influencing and pedagogies discouraging cheating among college students. *Journal of Business Inquiry: Research, Education, and Application,* 3, 7-24.

Cabral-Cardoso, C. (2004). Ethical misconduct in the business school: A case of plagiarism that turned bitter. *Journal of Business Ethics,* 49(1), 75-89.

Crown, D. F., & Spiller, M. S. (1998). Learning from the literature on collegiate cheating: A review of empirical research. *Journal of Business Ethics,* 17(6), 683–700.

Davis, M. A., Anderson, M. G., & Curtis, M. B. (2001). Measuring ethical ideology in business ethics: A critical analysis of the Ethics Position Questionnaire. *Journal of Business Ethics,* 32(1), 35-54.

Denisi, A. S., & Griffin, R. W. (2001) *Human Resource Management.* New York: Houghton Mifflin.

Dowd, S. B. (1992). Academic integrity—A review and case study. Information Analyses; Reports-Research; Tests/Questionnaires. (*ERIC Document Reproduction Service No. ED349060*)

Forsyth, D. R. (1980). A taxonomy of ethical ideologies. *Journal of Personality and Social Psychology,* 39, 175-184.

Henle, C. A., Giacalone, R. A., & Jurkiewicz, C. L. (2005). The role of ethical ideology in workplace deviance. *Journal of Business Ethics,* 56(3), 219-230.

Hilbert, G. A. (1987). Academic fraud: Prevalence, practices, and reasons. *Journal of Professional Nursing,* 39,(3), 39-45.

Lane, M. S., & Schaupp, D. (1989). Ethics in education: A comparative study. *Journal of Business Ethics,* 8(12), 943-949.

McCabe, D. L, & Trevino L. K. (1995). Cheating among Business Students: A challenge for business leaders and educators. *Journal of Management Education,* 19, 205-218.

Muijen, H. S. C. A. (2004). Corporate social responsibility starts at university. *Journal of Business Ethics,* 53(1/2), 235-246.

O'Higgins, E., & Kelleher, B. (2005). Comparative perspectives on the ethical orientations of human resources, marketing, and finance functional managers. *Journal of Business Ethics,* 56(3), 275-288.

Redfern, K., & Crawford, J. (2004). An empirical investigation of the Ethics Position Questionnaire in the People's Republic of China. *Journal of Business Ethics,* 50, 199-210.

Robinson, G. M., & Moulton, J. (1985). *Ethical problems in higher education.* Englewood Cliffs, NJ: Prentice Hall.

Roig, M., & Ballew C. (1994). Attitudes toward cheating of self and others by college students and professors. *The Psychological Record,* 44, 3-12.

Singhapakdi, A., Vitell, S. J., & Kraft, K. L. (1996) Moral intensity and ethical decision-making of marketing professionals, *Journal of Business Research,* 36(3), 245–255.

South, J. (2004). Ethics in the classroom. *Quill,* 92(6), 10-13.

Treise, D., & Weingold, M. F. (1994). Ethics in advertising: Ideological correlates of consumer perceptions. *Journal of Advertising*, 23(3), 59-70.

Ethical Implications of Servant-Leadership within the Context of Business

By
Jeffrey McClellan & J.P Spagnolo

"Your Fired," Each week this cold, forceful declaration echoes throughout living rooms across the country as "employees" on *The Apprentice* are given their final notice of participation on the show. With unsympathetic, strictly business candor, the infamous business tycoon, Donald Trump, appears to end people's careers with little or no thought for anything beyond the needs of the business and the desire to entertain. The same coldness enshrouds the faces of executives under indictment for fraudulent financial practices and seems to permeate the entire world of business. Although at the very root of such actions lies the issue of ethical decision-making, it seems that amidst all of the bottom-line, self-serving behavior, business and leadership ethics may merely be an oxymoron.

Over the past few years, the study of ethics has proliferated in business programs throughout the country. Nonetheless, things do not appear to have changed much. As a result, some have wondered, "is there something about the entrepreneurial type or the organization man— or both—that leads to ruthlessness at worst, insensitivity to ethical nuances at best?" (Tell, Fall 2001, p. 201). The answer to this dilemma probably lies as much in an understanding of the theory of leadership that guides the traditional business leader as it does with the actual leader. If this is true then perhaps the solution lies not in simply trying to teach ethics to traditional leaders, but in exploring alternate paradigms of leadership. One such paradigm, which fundamentally reconstructs the notion of leadership from the inside out, is Greenleaf's philosophy of servant-leadership.

In order to understand the potential implications of servant-leadership in regards to ethical decision-making in business, this paper will first explore the traditional paradigm of leadership and its implications regarding ethical decision-making. Servant leadership will then be described as an alternate conceptualization of leadership. Finally, the relevance of this new way of viewing leadership within the world of business will be explored by describing the ethical implications of some of the fundamental tenets of the philosophy of servant-leadership.

Traditional Leadership

Traditional notions of leadership within organizations have focused on what leaders do to accomplish results (McGee-Cooper & Looper, 2001). From this perspective, "a successful leader is one whose group or organization gets things done" (McCaulley, 2004). Consequently, the focus of leadership development within this paradigm is on assisting leaders to acquire the skills necessary to encourage followers to perform in such a way that the organization's goals and objectives are achieved. To the extent that one achieves these objectives, he or she is viewed as an effective leader and receives the traditional rewards of leadership, position, status, power, and wealth. Consequently, this paradigm encourages leaders to focus their efforts on achieving results to obtain these tangible, personal rewards.

Because of the emphasis this traditional leadership model places on skills, its related development programs tend to focus solely on training leaders to attain and implement the skills necessary to get things done. As Northouse (2004) explained, "The skills approach [to leadership development] provides a structure that is very consistent with the curricula of most leadership education programs . . . . [that] have traditionally taught classes in problem solving, conflict resolution, listening, and team work" as well as other leadership skill sets (Northouse, 2004, p. 51).

While there is nothing necessarily wrong with developing the skills necessary to achieve results within an organizational context, the implications of this model of leadership and its associated development programs on ethical decision-making lies at the heart of the questionable validity of the idea of business ethics. These implications are particularly evident in an article written by Tell (2001). In this article, Tell seeks to answer the question "are ethics overrated" (p. 10). The conclusion appears to be no. However, the reason for answering no is that the appropriate ethical decision typically represents what is good for business within the traditional paradigm of achieving organizational results; however, the emphasis may be on longer-term results and "keeping faith with all constituencies" (p. 12). Herein lies the flaw. As long as the bottom-line measure of leadership success is tied to achieving results, and leaders receive self-serving rewards for doing so, the ability to justify one's behavior as ethical because it achieves results is facilitated. Thus "MBA students themselves rate business executives pretty low in ethical evolvement (though they think their own ethics are OK)" (p. 13).

Greenleaf and Servant-Leadership

In contrast to this traditional results-oriented philosophy of leadership, Greenleaf proposed a model of leadership that focuses on the motivation of the leader and alters the nature of the outcomes of leadership. In addition, servant-leadership shifts the paradigm of leadership development from a focus on skills to a focus on identity.

The term servant-leadership was coined by Robert Greanleaf in his essay, *The Servant-Leader*. As a result of his religious, philosophical, and experiential background and through the inspiration that came to him after reading Hesse's *Journey to the East*, Greanleaf (1977) proposed that leadership had less to do with oversight, position, and direction and more to do with service. He wrote, "The great leader is seen as servant first, and that simple fact is the key to his greatness" (p. 21). This servanthood is grounded not merely in the behaviors of the leader as servant, but rather in "a natural feeling that one wants to serve, to serve first." (p. 27). As a result of this deep, internal desire to contribute to the growth of others, "conscious choice brings [one] to aspire to lead" (p. 27). Once this choice is made,

> Servant-leaders do lead. They go on out ahead and lead the way. But there is a special quality to this—the quality of service. They take others with them because of their manner. . . . It is in serving that they gain the respect of others who know that the servant carries their interests in mind. (Young, 2002, p. 250-251)

At the core of this model of leadership, and what distinguishes it from all others, is the motivation and initiative of the individual. In a later revision of this original essay, Greenleaf (1977) explained this important point in the following terms:
The servant-leader is servant first . . . [it] begins with the natural feeling that one wants to serve, to serve first. Then conscious choice brings one to aspire to lead. (p. 27).
Thus, this natural feeling which begins "with caring for individual persons," propels the individual to choose to lead, "in ways that require dedication and skill and that help them to grow and become healthier, stronger and more autonomous" (Greenleaf, 2003a, p. 37).
In contrast to other models of leadership that focus on the achievement of organizational goals and individual skill development, Greenleaf (1977) proscribed a way of leading that focuses on serving the highest needs of individuals (p. 27). As a result, he argued that the "best test" of the servant leader is:

> Do those served grow as persons? Do they, while being served become healthier, wiser, freer, more autonomous, more likely themselves to become servants? And, what is the effect on the least privileged of society? Will they benefit or at least not be further deprived?" (p. 27).

Greenleaf (1977, 2003a) recognized that this standard created a challenge for leaders in that assessing the outcome of ones leadership is nearly impossible. Such leaders may not always achieve organizational goals and they may not be popular. In addition, they will likely be burdened with the conflicting needs of the multitudes of people whom they are called to serve. This, Greenleaf (1977) argued, "is part of the human dilemma; one cannot know for sure if he or she is having the desired impact" (p. 27-28). Consequently, within the paradigm of servant-leadership, effective leadership requires that leaders be grounded in their identity rather than in their skills and accomplishments.

From this core identity, and as the servant-leader develops and utilizes the knowledge and skills required to lead others, behaviors are engaged in and skills acquired as an extension of one's servanthood and as a means of pursuing the desire to serve. The expertise derived from this hard work and one's experiences are essential to leadership, but not sufficient. Greenleaf (2003b) wrote, "leadership overarches expertise" (p. 41). Furthermore, personality and style are also insufficient descriptors of and means for engaging in leadership (p. 41). What is essential is the integration of all of these actionable elements with the servanthood core of the person. This integration of intent and action is evident in the characteristics of servant-leaders (Greenleaf, 2003a). These included initiative, goal development, listening and understanding, language and imagination, the ability to withdraw effectively so as to engage creativity, acceptance and empathy, intuition and foresight, profound awareness and keen perception, persuasion over coercion, a strong awareness of self, patience, a willingness to define one's own roles, and healing and serving. When he revised this original essay, he added community building to this list of characteristics (Greenleaf, 1977).

While at first glance, these "characteristics" appear to describe behaviors; the reality is that fundamentally they do not. Consider, for example, listening. There is an astounding difference between a leader who listens and a listening leader. This difference is evidenced in the following statements, "listening is basically an attitude—really wanting to understand. It is also a technique. But the technique without the attitude is phony" (Greenleaf, 2003a, p. 46). This is because,

Given a little time, we can always tell when we're being coped with, manipulated, or outsmarted. We can always detect the hypocrisy . . . . It won't matter if the person tries sitting on the edge of the chair to practice active listening . . . or any other skill learned in order to be effective. What we'll know and respond to is how that person is regarding us when doing those things. (Arbinger Institute., 2000, p. 27)

Another example of how technique and attitude combine to identify the characteristics of servant-leadership is explained by Lad and Luechauer (1998),

Servant-leaders typically have a passionate zeal for creating a preferred future. Then again, Hitler, Mussolini and Jim Jones all had visions. What differentiates servant-leaders from maniacal dictators is their deep desire to pursue this vision from the basis of humility, empathy, compassion, and commitment to ethical behavior. In short, they articulate a vision and then enable, ennoble and empower those around them to work for the attainment of that vision. In essence, servant-leadership represents a pull rather than a push model of vision attainment. (p. 64).

Thus it is in the integration of the attitude and the action that behaviors become characteristics and the skilled leader becomes a servant leader. This same significant distinction can be applied to each of the characteristics delineated by Greenleaf.

Greenleaf's model of leadership identifies servant-leaders as individuals who, motivated by love and a desire to serve others, choose to serve. As a result, they integrate their expertise and actions with their motivational core in order to achieve the ends of the "best test."

Ethical Implications of Servant-Leadership

As a philosophy of leadership grounded in the servant-oriented identity of the leader, Servant-Leadership has many implications for ethical decision-making. These include specific implications of the "best-test," the essential need to recognize and embrace paradox, the call for intuitive, collaborative, in-the-moment decision-making.

The Ethical Implications of the Best Test

The literature on servant leadership refers to the following, previously cited, statement as the best test:

Do those served grow as persons? Do they, while being served become health- ier, wiser, freer, more autonomous, more likely themselves to become servants? And, what is the effect on the least privileged of society? Will they benefit or at least not be further deprived?" (Greenleaf, 1977, p. 27).

The implications with regards to business ethics are obvious. Within this paradigm, the results-oriented needs of the organization are not considered the primary focus of the leader. In- stead, Greenleaf wrote, "An institution starts on a course toward people-building with leadership that has a firmly established context of people first" (p. 54). Initially, this transition may mean placing the needs of people on par with those of achieving results (p. 155). However, "as the economy becomes even more productive and people get more sensible and settle for fewer 'things' in the new ethic, service to those who produce may rise in priority above service to those who use" (p. 155). When this occurs, organizations no longer see achieving results as a top priority, but rather as a means to the end of serving people to "become healthier, wiser, freer, more autonomous, more likely themselves to become servants?" (p. 27). If this tenant is accepted, the ultimate goal of business is no longer to achieve results, but to serve in the growth of human beings with an emphasis on doing no harm, results would ultimately give way to the ideal of service as the primary motivation of the leader. This ideal is what is meant by the ethical heart of the servant.

The Ethical Heart of the Servant

It is clear from Greenleaf's writings that the heart, or intentional nature, of the leader is the most fundamentally important element of servant-leadership. This is strikingly apparent in his (1977) claim that Servant-Leadership "begins with the natural feeling that one wants to serve, to serve *first*" (p. 27). In a similar vein, Patterson (2003) argued that "Servant leadership encompasses seven virtuous constructs, which work in a processional pattern" (p. 2). These virtues include *agapao* love, humility, altruism, vision, trust, empowerment, and service. Patterson proposed that these virtues build upon one another beginning in the heart of the leader with *agapao* love which nurtures and facilitates the virtues of humility and altruism. Foundational to this construct is the motivational core of love and a strong sense of servant-oriented purpose. As Lad and Luechauer (1998) wrote,

> Servant-leaders typically have a passionate zeal for creating a preferred future. . . . [However] what differentiates servant-leaders from maniacal dictators is their deep desire to pursue this vision from the basis of humility, empathy, compassion, and commitment to ethical behavior. (p. 64)

It is this heart of service that tempers the drive for power, status, position, and wealth and refocuses the leader, once again, on the growth of others instead of simply on accomplishing results. Consequently, the nature of ethical decision-making is fundamentally altered from the perspective of the servant-leadership paradigm; because instead of developing and using skills to serve the organization and the leader, such skills are used to legitimately serve the needs of the people through the accomplishment of results.

Admittedly, the implications outlined thus far, leave traditional leaders to query whether or not servant-leadership is even a realistic paradigm for dealing with the challenging and often paradoxical nature of the real world of business. However, embracing paradox is one of the fundamental themes of Greenleaf's writings and, consequently, one of the themes with the most significant implications in relation to ethical decision-making.

Recognizing and Embracing Paradox

The world we live in is deeply paradoxical. It is rare to find oneself, especially if one is a leader, in a situation that is not deeply challenging as a result of the paradoxes inherent within the situation. Regarding this reality, Greanleaf (1977) wrote,

> Just as there may be a real contradiction in the servant as leader, so my perceptual world is full of contradictions. Some examples: I believe in order, and I want creation out of chaos. My good society will have strong individualism amid community. It will have elitism along with populism. I listen to the old and to the young and find myself baffled and heartened by both. Reason and intuition, each in its own way, both comfort and dismay me. (p. 26-7).

These internal paradoxes are manifested in Greenleaf's conceptualization of the servant leader. Indeed, they are embodied in the very name he selected to describe his ideas. Both the term "leader" and the word "servant" bare powerful connotative, denotative and emotional meaning. Each has left a deep path across the history of time littered with meaning and emotion.

The word "leader" throughout time, and even today, has conjured up images of great men or women who, through the force of their own personality, characteristics, or skills, acted as the driving force of nations, armies, organizations, and groups of people (Carlyle, 1973; Northouse, 2004; Wren, 1995). At the same time, philosophers and scholars have challenged and continue to challenge this notion of great men or women as the driving force in society. These individuals have argued that the emergence of leaders is more a result of the interaction between individual leaders and society (Kelley, 1998; Michelet, 1973; Wren, 1995). Furthermore, leadership theorists have argued that leadership is a function of traits possessed by leaders, a reflection of the behaviors and skills exhibited by leaders, derived from the individual style of the leader, or a complex amalgamation of various situational or contingency factors such as leader-member relations, task structure, and a leaders positional power (Antonakis, Cianciolo, & Sternberg, 2004; Northouse, 2004; Smart, 2005). All of these competing and even paradoxical ways of defining leadership have thrust it into a realm of conceptual ambiguity (Antonakis et al., 2004; Dhar & Mishra, 2001; Thompson, 2000).

Although he recognizes that the terms "serve and lead are overused and words with negative connotations," Greenleaf (2003a) does not shy away from their use because the very paradoxes they contain make them essential to his theory (p. 31). Thus servant-leadership argues that leadership is both about the identity of the leader as servant, one who is humble and sincerely desires to improve the lot of all whom he contacts, and the choice of the servant to lead, to engage in the challenging act of trying to serve within the conflict laden context of leadership.

Consequently, leadership, according to Greenleaf, involves many of the elements that are found in any theory of leadership. Leaders must be self-driven, confident, provide ideas, take risks, provide vision, articulate and achieve goals, and lead the way (Greenleaf, 1977, 2003a). Paradoxically, however, they must also be concerned with the personal and emotional growth of others, humble, open and receptive, recognize great-ideas, act with responsibility and unlimited liability, identify and follow a vision, listen to and learn from others, and accept failure (Greenleaf, 1977, 1996b, 2003b). Additional paradoxes referred to by Greenleaf (1996a) include: the recognition that "evil is an aspect of good" (p. 44), absolute values become approximate in the minds of people (p. 45), any virtue or idea that, when carried to the extreme becomes absurd (p. 45), too much freedom is bondage (p. 45-46), perceived understanding reveals lack of comprehension (p. 46) sometimes the best way to serve others is to not give them what they want (p. 48), the ability to make creativity out of conformity (p. 50). The ability to balance such apparent contradiction is rooted in the leader's capacity to recognize and embrace such paradoxical perspectives.

The implications for ethical decision-making are apparent. Many leaders approach ethical decision-making by striving to find the right answer so as to achieve results. Once they think they have found it, they then simply commit themselves to following through to see it done. Furthermore, within a construct that places primary emphasis on achieving results, the question of what to do when one has the answer seems clear—get it done no matter what. Unfortunately, this myopic perspective fails to recognize the paradoxical reality that whatever is "right" is also "wrong." In other words, what may appear right from one perspective may not remain "right" when looked at from another vantage point. Furthermore, the paradoxical nature of servant-leadership requires that leaders both achieve results (the role of the leader) and nurture the development of others (the role of the servant) with neither outcome taking priority. Recognition of these implications requires that leaders approach ethical decisions with humility and willingness to seriously consider multiple viewpoints and strive to balance their leadership of the organization with their stewardship to serve people.

Intuitive In-the-Moment Decision-Making

Because of the need for respect for the paradoxical reality of ethical situations, leaders should enter challenging environments with a desire to embrace the servant leadership paradox. According to DeGraaf, Tilley, and Neal (2004):

> For leaders in a wide range of positions, dealing with change has created a sense of uneasiness in terms of how we serve and lead others in order to produce value for our organizations, our customers, our staff, and ourselves. In response to this balancing act, we often seek to take the easier route of selecting either serving or leading, but not both. The concept of servant-leadership challenges this approach and encourages us to disregard the *either/or* option and instead live in the paradox of *both/and* (p. 133).

Embracing this servant leadership paradox in changing environments and ethically challenging situations obliges leaders to be willing to make intuitive in-the-moment decisions in collaboration with others. In-the-moment decision making stands in sharp contrast to the decision-making paradigm of traditional leadership. The traditional leadership paradigm argues that decisions should be made by the leader based on objective, rational analysis and in accordance with predetermined policies and procedures. Thus leaders enter a situation much as Trump fires his fictional employees, with a pre-developed inalterable plan of attack.

In contrast, Greenleaf's concept of in-the-moment decision making asserts that effective decision making is grounded in the ability of leaders to, as a result of a heightened sense of awareness, intuition, and conceptualization combined with a servant's heart and the acceptance of paradox, engage in ethically challenging decision making. This they do without resorting to appeals to predetermined, often situationally inappropriate, responses that fail to address the unique and often troubling realities of immediate ethical quandaries that demonstrate deep respect for all persons involved. Such an approach is more realistic in true-to-life situations wherein ethical dilemmas arise, such as Trump's involvement in deciding what to do in response to the antics of Miss America. In that situation, the predetermined cold ideal of letting the person go came in conflict with the complex issues of "the moment."

As mentioned, this notion of in-the-moment decision-making is grounded in the leaders heightened sense of awareness and willingness to openly collaborate with followers. Such an approach requires a deep capacity and desire to open oneself to the perspectives of others and the input available through listening. Thus in-the-moment decision-making involves participation. However, according to Spears (1998) listening involves not only "listening intently to others," but also "getting in touch with one's inner voice" (p. 4). This willingness and ability to listen nurtures a keen sense of awareness within the leader. As a result, the leader is able to enter challenging situations with a deeper understanding of "issues involving ethics and values" and "to view most situations from a more integrated position" (p. 5). This deep understanding of the situation combines with the conceptual ability to "think beyond the day-to-day realities" of the immediate moment and to view it from a big-picture perspective. This heightened awareness in-the-moment and big-picture conceptual ability combines to foster foresight and nurture intuition. Thus, leaders develop the capacity to envision the future and to see how the immediate context contributes to its emergences. Consequently, as Stacey, Griffin, and Shaw (2000) declared, "what an organization becomes emerges from the relationships of its members [in the in-the-moment decisions of individuals] rather than being determined by the [structured and pre-planned] choices of individuals" (p. 123). Within this conceptualization of leadership, the role of leaders is not to "step outside [the system] to operate on it or use it," when facing difficult ethical dilemmas but rather to engage in a process of localized "interaction, or relating" as they struggle with the complexities of the issues, thereby opening themselves to deeper understanding and intuition from which emerges a capacity for more holistic, collaborative, ethical decision-making (Griffin, 2002, p. 187). As leaders engage in such deep interpersonal interaction and change, thereby co-constructing the future, they embrace and intuitively respond to complexity and generate novelty through intuitively engaging paradox. As a result, they increase their capacity to make appropriate ethical decisions, in-the-moment, that respect the complexity of such challenges even when the context of the decision is deeply challenging.

Conclusion

Although the current status of business ethics suffers from a lack of an effective foundation, in that it is upheld by the traditional paradigm of what it means to lead. This situation is not without alternatives. One such alternative involves uprooting the problem of ethical decision-making and overlaying it upon the foundation of servant-leadership. Such a shift alters the focus and process of ethical decision-making. Instead of focusing on achieving organizational goals, servant-leadership refocuses on serving human beings as the primary objective, with achieving organizational goals as a means to accomplishing that objective. In addition, it shifts the leadership development paradigm from a skills based approach to an identity-based approach. Finally, as a result of this shift servant-leaders engage ethical challenges with the heart of the servant, the objectives of the "best test," openness to paradox, and the awareness, foresight, conceptualization, and intuition resultant from deeply present, collaborative, in-the-moment decision-making.

References
Antonakis, J., Cianciolo, A. T., & Sternberg, R. J. (2004). Leadership: Past, present, and future. In J. Antonakis, A. T. Cianciolo & R. J. Sternberg (Eds.), *The nature of leadership* (pp. 3-15). Thousand Oaks, CA: Sage.

Arbinger Institute. (2000). *Leadership and self-deception: Getting out of the box.* San Francisco: Berrett-Koehler.

Carlyle, T. (1973). History as Biography: Thomas Carlyle on history. In F. Stern (Ed.), *The varieties of history: From Voltaire to the present* (pp. p. 90-107). New York: Vintage Books.

Degraaf, D., Neally, C. & Neal, L. (2004). Servant leadership characteristics in organizational life. In L. Spears & M. Lawrence (Eds.), *Practicing servant- leadership: Succeeding through trust, bravery, and forgiveness* (p. 133-166). San Francisco: Jossey-Bass.

Dhar, U., & Mishra, P. (2001). Leadership effectiveness: A study of constituent factors. *Journal of Management Research, 1*(4), 254-256.

Greenleaf, R. K. (1977). *Servant leadership: A journey into the nature of legitimate power and greatness* (25th Anniversary Edition ed.). New York/Mahwah, NJ: Paulist Press.

Greenleaf, R. K. (1996a). *On becoming a servant-leader.* San Francisco: Jossey-Bass.

Greenleaf, R. K. (1996b). *Seeker and servant: Reflections on religious leadership.* San Francisco: Jossey-Bass.

Greenleaf, R. K. (2003a). The servant as leader (Original 1970 edition). In H. Beazley, J. Beggs & L. C. Spears (Eds.), *The servant-leader within: A transformative path* (pp. 29-74). New York: Paulist Press.

Greenleaf, R. K. (2003b). Teacher as servant. In H. Beazley, J. Beggs & L. C. Spears (Eds.), *The servant-leader within: A transformative path* (pp. 75-239). New York: Paulist Press.

Griffin, D. (2002). *The Emergence of Leadership: Linking self-organization and ethics.* London: Routledge.

Kelley, R. E. (1998). Followership in a leadership world. In L. C. Spears (Ed.), *Insights on Leadership: Service, stewardship, and servant leadership* (pp. 170-185). New York: John Wiley & Sons, Inc.

Lad, L. J., & Luechauer, D. (1998). On the Path to Servant-Leadership. In L. Spears (Ed.), *Insights on Leadership: Service, Spirit, and Servant Leadership* (pp. 54-67). New York: John Wiley.

McCaulley, C., D. (2004). Successful and unsuccessful leadership. In J. Antonakis, A. T. Cianciolo & R. J. Sternberg (Eds.), *The Nature of Leadership* (pp. 199-221). Thousand Oaks, CA: Sage.

McGee-Cooper, A., & Looper, G. (2001). *The essentials of servant-leadership: Principles in practice.* Waltham, MA: Pegasus Communications.

Michelet, J. (1973). History as a national epic: Michelet. In F. Stern (Ed.), *The varieties of history: From Voltaire to the present* (pp. 108-119). New York: Vintage Books.

Northouse, P. G. (2004). *Leadership: Theory and practice.* London: Sage.

Patterson, K. (2003). *Servant leadership: A theoretical model.* Paper presented at the Servant Leadership Research Roundtable, Regent University.

Smart, M. (2005). *The role of informal leaders in organizations: The hidden organizational asset.* Unpublished Dissertation, University of Idaho.

Spears, L. (1998). Tracing the growing impact of servant-leadership. In L. Spears (Ed.), *Insights on leadership: Service, spirit, and servant-leadership* (pp. 1-14). New York: John Wiley and Sons.

Stacey, R. D., Griffin, D., & Shaw, P. (2000). *Complexity and management: Fad or radical challenge to systems thinking?* London: Routledge.

Tell, D. (Fall 2001). Are ethics overrated? *Future: The magazine of the University of Phoenix*, 10-13.

Thompson, C., Michael. (2000). *The congruent life: Following the inward path to fulfilling works and inspired leadership.* San Francisco: Jossey-Bass.

Wren, J. T. (Ed.). (1995). *The leader's companion: Insights on leadership through the ages.* New York: The Free Press.

Young, D. S. (2002). Foresight: The lead that the leader has. In L. Spears & M. Lawrence (Eds.), *Focus on leadership: Servant-leadership for the twenty-first century* (pp. 245-255). New York: John Wiley & Sons.

Ethics in Federal Income Tax Legislation: Expectations vs. Reality for Low-Income Taxpayers

By
Sheldon R. Smith, Katherine D. Black, & Lynn R. Smith

Abstract

Federal income tax laws often provide potential tax benefits for various groups of taxpayers based on specific social or economic policies. Some of these benefits are targeted specifically at low-income taxpayers while other benefits are targeted more generally but can still apply to low-income taxpayers. In certain cases the benefits actually available to low-income taxpayers may be less than expected when the legislation was passed. This paper discusses some tax benefits that presume to benefit low-income taxpayers. Discussion of these specific tax benefits will lead to discussion of ethical issues that may arise for those who legislate these tax provisions. Legislators might be deceptively creating discrepancies in a complicated tax code to appear to provide benefits for low-income taxpayers when, in fact, they know these benefits are limited or nonexistent. In the alternative, the ethics of competence in understanding the tax laws legislated is relevant; legislators may be voting on legislation they do not really understand.

Introduction

Federal income tax laws often provide potential tax benefits for various groups of taxpayers based on specific social or economic policies. Some of these benefits are targeted specifically at low-income taxpayers. An example of this benefit is the earned income credit which provides a tax benefit for working taxpayers with low incomes. Other tax benefits are targeted more generally but can still apply to low-income taxpayers. An example of this benefit is the child tax credit.

In some cases the benefits actually available to low-income taxpayers may be less than what taxpayers are led to expect when the legislation was passed. Discrepancies can arise because of (1) specific qualifications and limitations within certain tax provisions, (2) evolution of tax laws over time which change the available benefits, (3) complications in coordinating multiple potential tax benefits, and (4) mistakes or errors in the law because of the legislative process. Some of the results can be quite counterintuitive.

This paper will first introduce and discuss selected tax benefits that are potentially available for low-income taxpayers. The benefits discussed will include the dependent care credit and exclusion, the child tax credit, the adoption tax credit and exclusion, and the retirement savings contribution credit. These examples will lead to a discussion of the ethical issues that may arise for those who legislate these tax provisions. Legislators might deceptively create discrepancies in a complicated tax code to appear to provide benefits for low-income taxpayers when, in fact, they know these benefits are limited or nonexistent. In the alternative, the ethics of competence in legislating tax laws may be applicable. For example, 1) in some cases, inadequate calculations have been performed to determine the actual effects of tax laws on taxpayers with various income levels; or 2) legislators may be voting on legislation they do not really understand. This type of issue focuses on individual competence. However, another type of competence is also relevant-systemic competence. This is the competence of the entire legislative process related to tax legislation. The ethics of systemic competence will also be discussed.

Although social, economic, and political viewpoints are important to policy decisions, the paper will not include a discussion of these different viewpoints as to whether tax benefits targeted for the poor are appropriate. Instead, the focus will be on the ethical issues related to legislation of tax laws which may seem to benefit low-income taxpayers when they do not necessarily provide the claimed benefits.

Tax benefits

Federal income tax benefits potentially available for individuals include exclusions, deductions, exemptions, and credits. Generally, all income is taxable, but an exclusion is an income item which is specifically excluded from taxation by law. Deductions are expenses, either business or personal, that the law allows a taxpayer to subtract in calculating taxable income. An exemption is an amount set by law that the taxpayer is allowed to subtract in calculating taxable income even though the exemption is not directly related to an expense incurred by the taxpayer. Generally, taxpayers are allowed a personal exemption (and one for the spouse as appropriate) plus another exemption for each person who qualifies as a dependent. These three tax benefits reduce taxable income, either by being excluded or by being subtracted. Taxable income is then used, applying the tax rates, to determine the amount of tax owed. A tax credit is a reduction of the taxes otherwise owed rather than an amount used in calculating taxable income. Most personal tax credits are nonrefundable, meaning they can reduce an individual's tax liability, but not below zero. A few personal tax credits are refundable, meaning they can reduce the tax liability down to zero with any excess being paid to the taxpayer by the government.

Dependent Care Credit and Exclusion

The Internal Revenue Code provides two related tax benefits for people who need to pay for dependent care to allow them to work. One is a nonrefundable child care credit of up to 35 percent of the first $6,000 ($3,000 if only one child) a taxpayer pays for dependent care[1]. The second is an exclusion from income of up to $5,000 of dependent care costs paid by the employer (or by the employee using a salary reduction agreement through an employer's plan[2]). The same expenses cannot qualify for both the exclusion and the credit. One potential problem for very low-income taxpayers such as those on a low hourly wage is that they are more likely to work for employers who offer no dependent care assistance plans. Therefore, these individuals will not be able to take the exclusion and will have to rely on whatever benefit they can obtain from the credit.

---

1   Internal Revenue Code (IRC) section 21.

2   IRC section 129

Exhibit 1[3]
Maximum Effective Dependent Care Credit—2007
Two Qualifying Individuals

Adjusted Gross Income	Applicable Percentage	Maximum Potential Credit	Head of HouseholdB Maximum Effective Credit		Married Filing JointlyB Maximum Effective Credit	
			Amount	Percent	Amount	Percent
$11,250 or less	35%	$2,100	$0	0%	$0	0%
$11,251 - 15,000	35%	$2,100	$375	6.3%	$0	0%
$15,001 - 17,000	34%	$2,040	$575	9.6%	$0	0%
$17,001 - 19,000	33%	$1,980	$775	12.9%	$0	0%
$19,001 - 21,000	32%	$1,920	$975	16.3%	$0	0%
$21,001 - 23,000	31%	$1,860	$1,203	20.0%	$0	0%
$23,001 - 25,000	30%	$1,800	$1,503	25.0%	$70	1.2%
$25,001 - 27,000	29%	$1,740	$1,740	29%	$270	4.5%
$27,001 - 29,000	28%	$1,680	$1,680	28%	$470	7.8%
$29,001 - 31,000	27%	$1,620	$1,620	27%	$670	11.2%
$31,001 - 33,000	26%	$1,560	$1,560	26%	$870	14.5%
$33,001 - 35,000	25%	$1,500	$1,500	25%	$1,070	17.8%
$35,001 - 37,000	24%	$1,440	$1,440	24%	$1,270	21.2%
$37,001 - 39,000	23%	$1,380	$1,380	23%	$1,380	23%
$39,001 - 41,000	22%	$1,320	$1,320	22%	$1,320	22%
$41,001 - 43,000	21%	$1,260	$1,260	21%	$1,260	21%
$43,001 and over	20%	$1,200	$1,200	20%	$1,200	20%

Calculations in which the maximum effective credit is less than the maximum potential credit were made assuming the top level of income within each bracket. The maximum effective credit is the smaller of the tax liability or the maximum potential credit, and the maximum effective credit percent assumes $6,000 of qualifying dependent care expenses. For head of household, a standard deduction of $7,850 (2007) and one personal exemption of $3,400 (2007) was used for a total of $11,250. For married filing jointly, a standard deduction of $10,700 (2007) with four exemptions at $3,400 were used for a total of $24,300. 2007 tax rates were used. For the head of household example, the maximum effective credit equals the maximum potential credit starting at an AGI level of $26,583. For the married filing jointly example, the maximum effective credit equals the maximum potential credit starting at an AGI level of $38,100.

The amount of the credit is equal to the percentage applicable to the taxpayer's adjusted gross income (AGI) multiplied by the dependent care expenses paid by the taxpayer during the year

---

3   Updated from Katherine D. Black and Sheldon R. Smith, Dependent Care Tax Benefits: A Sham and a Scam,@ Tax Notes, Vol. 113, Number 2, October 9, 2006, pp. 175-180.

(reduced by any amounts received through an employer's plan that are excluded from income). The percentage for the credit ranges from 35 percent of expenses for those with AGI under $15,000 to 20 percent of expenses for those with AGI over $43,000. The percentage is reduced by one percentage point for each $2,000 of AGI, or fraction thereof, in excess of $15,000.

Exhibit 1 shows the applicable percentages for the credit for different AGI levels and the maximum potential credit for each of these AGI ranges, assuming taxpayers have two qualifying children for the dependent care credit and will spend at least $6,000 on child care during 2007. Because the credit is nonrefundable and some taxpayers will not have a tax liability large enough to absorb their potential dependent care credit, the maximum effective credit for taxpayers in the lowest AGI ranges is less than the maximum potential credit.

Two different scenarios are illustrated in Exhibit 1. The first assumes a taxpayer filing as head of household with two children but who cannot claim the dependency exemption for his/her children because the exemptions will be taken by an ex-spouse. This scenario is illustrated because it represents the situation where the taxpayer is most likely (at smaller income levels) to have a tax liability against which to use the credit. Notice that under this scenario, the maximum effective credit is smaller than the maximum potential credit until the taxpayer's AGI is in the $25,001 - $27,000 bracket. The actual amount where the maximum effective credit and the maximum potential credit are first equal is $26,583. The effective credit percentage (out of $6,000 of expenses) is less than the applicable percentage credit until this level of AGI is reached and the effective credit percentage is only 29 percent.

The second scenario assumes a married couple filing jointly with four exemptions (taxpayer, spouse, and two children). While this might be a common situation, no effective credit is available until the taxpayers' AGI reaches $24,300. Even then, the maximum effective credit does not match the maximum potential credit until the taxpayers have $38,100 of AGI. Thus, the effective percentage (out of $6,000) does not equal the applicable percentage in the tax code until the percentage drops to 23 percent. Thus, no taxpayer can ever get a dependent care credit even approaching the 35 percent credit "promised" by the tax code and perhaps expected by those who do not know otherwise. The maximum percent credit is 29 percent in an extreme case and 23 percent in a reasonably likely case.

Even for taxpayers who do have an employer dependent care assistance plan that allows them to pay through a salary reduction option on a pre-tax basis, the choice between the exclusion and credit is not obvious. Black and Smith[4] illustrate how, depending on the AGI level, different taxpayers may be better off with one option versus the other, but taxpayers have no advance knowledge as to which might be better for them. In addition, an employer's plan can only qualify for the exclusion if it meets certain nondiscrimination tests such that the contributions or benefits provided under the plan do not discriminate in favor of employees who are highly compensated. Thus, low-income taxpayers who may unknowingly be better off with the credit may be encouraged to participate in the employer plan because of the nondiscrimination rules that must be met in order for highly paid employees to qualify for the exclusion.

---

4   Katherine D. Black and Sheldon R. Smith, "Dependent Care Tax Benefits: A Sham and a Scam," Tax Notes, Volume 113, Number 2, October 9, 2006, pp. 175-80.

Child Tax Credit

The Internal Revenue Code also provides a taxpayer with a credit for 2007 of up to $1,000 for each qualifying child (under age 17)[5]. This credit is generally nonrefundable, but part or all of it can actually become refundable as an "additional child tax credit" under certain conditions. Under the original legislation which provided for this credit, any or all of it could be refundable only for taxpayers who had three or more qualifying children, and the amount refundable was limited to a taxpayer's social security taxes in excess of his/her earned income credit.

Exhibit 2 2007 Income Needed to Fully Claim Child Tax Credit (CTC) (based on 2007 standard deduction and exemption amount and the 2007 tax rate schedule for a married couple filing a joint return)						
Number of Children	1	2	3	4	5	6
Potential Credits	$1,000	$2,000	$3,000	$4,000	$5,000	$6,000
Income Needed to Fully Claim CTC as Non-refundable	$30,900	$42,850	$52,917	$62,983	$73,050	$83,117
Income Needed to Fully Claim CTC as Refundable	$18,417	$25,083	$31,750	$38,417	$45,083	$51,750
Income Needed to Fully Claim CTC as a Combination of Nonrefundable and Refundable Credits	$18,417	$24,770	$30,130	$34,590	$40,850	$46,210
Assumes all income is earned income, taxpayers have no other exemptions besides the parents and the children who qualify for the credit, taxpayers have no other nonrefundable tax credits, and the taxpayers do not itemize deductions.						

However, the refundability was later liberalized so that for 2007, taxpayers with fewer than three children might qualify to the extent of 15 percent of earned income in excess of $11,750. Taxpayers with three or more qualifying children can claim a refundable credit based on the greater of these two limitations[6].

---

5   IRC section 24.

6   Congressional committee reports make it clear that taxpayers are still supposed to be able to use the greater

Exhibit 2 shows the amount of income needed to fully claim the child tax credit for married taxpayers filing a joint tax return who have one to six qualifying children. The bottom row of the exhibit indicates the minimum level of income needed to fully claim the credit as a combination of both the nonrefundable and refundable portions. Taxpayers who, for other reasons, do not have any tax liability at these income levels and need to take the entire credit as a refundable credit would need more income in five of the six cases as shown. It is certainly feasible that low-income taxpayers may earn less than these amounts and thus lose some of the child tax credit that they may have been expecting. Furthermore, the assumptions used for the exhibit were conservative. If the parents have additional dependents who are not qualifying children for the child tax credit or they itemize deductions, the income numbers needed to fully claim the credit would increase.

Adoption Tax Credit and Exclusion

The Internal Revenue Code also has provisions to help taxpayers who adopt a child. An adoption tax credit is available of up to $11,390 per adoption[7]. A related exclusion of up to $11,390 per adoption also exists for employer adoption assistance payments[8]. However, the situation for the exclusion for the lowest-income taxpayers may be the same as it is for dependent care benefits. Those with very low paying jobs are less likely to have employer adoption assistance plans available.

For those taxpayers who have adoption assistance available from an employer, the choice between the exclusion and the credit is far from straightforward. In some cases the optimal coordination of these benefits is extremely complicated or even impossible, even for a tax expert, partially because of the uncertainty of the timing of adoption payments and adoption finalization[9].

The adoption tax credit is nonrefundable but can be carried forward for up to five years beyond the year of the original claim, perhaps because of the potentially large dollar amount of this particular credit. The option to carry the credit forward to future years provides a greater probability that taxpayers will be able to claim more of the credit. However, even with this provision, some low-income taxpayers will lose some or all of the credit because it will expire before it is used. Even if a taxpayer can fully use the credit, it may take up to six years (a significant amount of time) to claim a credit that taxpayers may have thought they would be able to claim almost immediately.

Exhibit 3 shows how much income taxpayers would need to be able to fully use the adoption tax credit over a six-year period for one, two, or three adoptions. For one adoption, the income needed is $38,772. Obviously, the amount goes up for adoptions of two or three children

---

of these two limitations. The 2006 tax forms prepared by the IRS also reflect this committee intent. However, as noted later in the paper, because of a "technical correction" which was made contrary to the committee intent, the actual wording of the tax code now limits the refundability for taxpayers with three or more children to the social security taxes minus earned income credit test.

7   IRC section 23.
8   IRC section 137.
9   Sheldon R. Smith and Glade K. Tew, "The Adoption Exclusion: Complications for Employees," Tax Notes, Vol. 90, Number 5, January 29, 2001, pp. 659-664 and Sheldon R. Smith, "Adoption Tax Benefits: Emphasizing the Exclusion Before the Credit," Journal of Accounting, Ethics & Public Policy, Vol. 4, No. 4, Fall 2004, pp. 299-321.

which may occur if a sibling group is adopted. For two children the amount of income needed is $54,828, and for three children the amount of income needed is $70,833.

Exhibit 3[10]

2007 Adjusted Gross Income Levels Needed to Take Advantage of a Full $11,390, $22,780, or $34,170 Adoption Tax Credit Over Six Years* (based on 2007 standard deduction and exemption amounts and the 2007 tax rate schedule for a married couple filing a joint return)						
	One child adopted/ no other children		Two children adopted/ no other children		Three children adopted/ no other children	
Total Potential Adoption Tax Credit (ATC)	$11,390		$22,780		$34,170	
Tax Liability Needed to Take 1/6 of the ATC	$1,898		$3,797		$5,695	
Split between tax brackets	$1,565	$333	$1,565	$2,232	$1,565	$4,130
Divided by Tax Rates	0.10	0.15	0.10	0.15	0.10	0.15
Taxable Income Needed (Sum)	$17,872		$30,528		$43,183	
Add: Standard Deduction	$10,700		$10,700		$10,700	
Add: $3,400 per Exemption	$10,200		$13,600		$17,000	
Adjusted Gross Income Needed	$38,772		$54,828		$70,883	

* Table works backwards from the tax liability needed to take full advantage of one-sixth of the ATC to arrive at the AGI necessary to reach this tax liability.

Similar calculations show what income level is needed to fully use the adoption tax credit in just one year for adoptions of either one or two children. For one adoption, the income level

---

10   Adapted and updated from Sheldon R. Smith and Glade K. Tew, "Ironies of the Adoption Tax Credit," Tax Notes, October 4, 1999, 83-89 at 85 and Sheldon R. Smith, "The Adoption Tax Credit: Problematic Implications for Low-Income Taxpayers," forthcoming in the Journal of Accounting, Ethics & Public Policy. The child tax credit is not included in this exhibit because of more generous rules about the refundability of the child tax credit which now exist. However, the child tax credit could still be an issue in some cases.

needed would be $95,070. For two adoptions, the income level needed would be $144,030. Obviously, these amounts would not be considered low incomes. However, even the amounts required in Exhibit 3 to take the full credit over six years may be more than what low-income taxpayers might make.

Retirement Savings Contribution Credit

The Internal Revenue Code also has a provision to encourage some low- and medium- income taxpayers to contribute to a retirement savings plan. The retirement savings contributions credit is a nonrefundable credit of up to 50 percent of the first $2,000 contributed to a qualifying retirement savings plan ($4,000 for a married couple filing jointly).[11] For taxpayers filing jointly, the credit is 50 percent for those with income between $0 and $31,000. It drops to 20 percent for those with income between $31,001 and $34,000 and drops again to 10 percent for those with income between $34,001 and $52,000. The credit is not available for taxpayers filing jointly if their income is above $52,000.

Exhibit 4 2007 Adjusted Gross Income Needed to Take Advantage of Maximum Retirement Savings Contribution Credits At Various Levels* (based on 2007 standard deduction and exemption amounts and the 2007 tax rate schedule for a married couple filing a joint return)				
Income Range	$0C31,000		$31,001C34,000	$34,001C52,000
Total Potential Contribution	$4,000		$4,000	$4,000
Applicable Rate for Credit	50%		20%	10%
Maximum Credit (Tax Liability Needed)	$2,000		$800	$400
Split between tax brackets	$1,565	$435	$800	$400
Divided by Tax Rates	.10	.15	.10	.10
Taxable Income Needed (Sum)	$18,550		$8,000	$4,000
Add: Standard Deduction	$10,700		$10,700	$10,700
Add: $3,400 per Exemption	$6,800		$6,800	$6,800
Adjusted Gross Income Needed	$36,050		$25,500	$21,500
Upper Income Limit Allowed for Applicable Credit	$31,000		$34,000	$52,000
*Table works backwards from the tax liability to take full advantage, if possible, of the credit to arrive at the AGI necessary to reach this tax liability. No credit is available if AGI exceeds $52,000. This assumes that there are no additional personal exemptions other than the filers.				

Exhibit 4 shows the income needed to claim the full potential credit in each of the income brackets. Interestingly, those whose income is less than $31,000 and who are therefore in the income bracket to claim a 50 percent credit, would need $36,050 of AGI to have a tax liability large enough to get the $2,000 credit. Thus, it is mathematically impossible for anyone to get

---

11   IRC section 25B.

the full 50 percent credit. The maximum credit that could be used for taxpayers with income equal to $31,000 is $1,350 ($650 less than the statutory credit). A similar situation exists for those filing singly or as head or household. Taxpayers with incomes in the $31,001 to $52,000 brackets can possibly use the entire credit, but the credit is much less to start with because the percentage is only 20 percent or 10 percent rather than 50 percent.

If taxpayers have additional exemptions above the two assumed in the table calculations or if they itemize deductions rather than claiming the standard deduction, the availability of this credit would be reduced or eliminated. Also, it is unlikely that taxpayers in the lowest income range shown above will be financially able to make $4,000 of contribution to retirement savings plans.

Multiple Tax Credits and Progressivity of Tax Structure

The tax benefits discussed above have been examined in isolation. Some taxpayers may qualify for more than one of the nonrefundable credits discussed above. In addition, several other nonrefundable personal tax credits exist that have not been specifically discussed. If taxpayers are eligible to claim multiple nonrefundable tax credits, the income level necessary to claim all of the credits is even higher than what has been illustrated with each credit in isolation.

Also, the progressive nature of the federal income tax rate structure makes it more difficult for low-income taxpayers to benefit from nonrefundable tax credits. Information from the Congressional Budget Office indicates that income tax rates for low-income taxpayers are negative.[12] For 2003, the lowest quintile has a -5.9 percent tax rate and the second quintile has a -1.1 percent tax rate. Because many low-income taxpayers already have a negative tax due to refundable credits, it is even more difficult to legislate nonrefundable credits that can help this type of taxpayer. However, this is not an excuse to legislate credits that claim to help these individuals when they do not.

While it is true that an argument can be made that taxpayers "do not deserve" tax credits that will reduce their tax liability below zero, the point is that taxpayers may not get all of the tax benefits they are led to believe they may receive. Thus, ethical issues exist for those who are involved in the process of legislating these tax laws. Some of these issues will be discussed in the next section.

Ethical Issues In Tax Legislation

Ethics reform seems to be the watchword on Capitol Hill these days. Fingers are pointed whenever there is a breach of ethical or moral conduct. Perhaps it is time to scrutinize not only the obvious moral and ethical breaches, but also the accepted, standard moral and ethical breaches that have become pervasive. Is it possible that legislators pass tax legislation, either knowingly or unknowingly, that seems to provide tax benefits for low-income taxpayers when, in fact, it does not? If this is done knowingly, then the ethics of deception is relevant. If it is done unknowingly, then the ethics of competence is relevant.

---

12   Historical Effective Federal Tax Rates: 1979-2003, December 2005, Congressional Budget Office, accessed at http://www.cbo.gov/ftpdoc.cfm?index=7000&type=1 on February 6, 2007.

Ethics of Deception

If legislators pass tax laws that they know will not accomplish what they seem to do, have they breached an ethical duty? Might they gain politically by passing legislation that seems to benefit certain parties such as low-income taxpayers when the real effect of the legislation is different than it seems?

Ethics of Competence

Competence in tax legislation can refer to individual competence. Do legislators read and understand the tax legislation they are voting on? Most of our Senators and Representatives have no specific training in accounting and taxation. Many likely do not prepare their own tax returns. Most likely have not read much, if any, of the tax code. The tax code is extremely complex. Even the "tax experts" have commented on the complexity.

> The distressingly complex and confusing nature of the provisions of subchapter K present a formidable obstacle to the comprehension of these provisions without the expenditure of a disproportionate amount of time and effort even by one who is sophisticated in tax matters with many years of experience in the tax field. . . . Surely, a statute has not achieved "simplicity" when its complex provisions may confidently be dealt with by at most only a comparatively small number of specialists who have been initiated into its mysteries.[13]

Even though this quotation comes from a 1964 tax court case, it seems relevant to the current tax code. Despite calls for simplification, the code seems to only become more complex over time. Since the tax code is complex and tax legislation which adds to or changes it is also complex, do the legislators really know what the ramifications are of proposed tax legislation? Do we really believe that all the legislators carefully work their way through every tax act? Competence in tax legislation can also refer to systemic competence. Does the legislative process work such that tax legislation is drafted and passed appropriately to achieve stated and/or intended results? Are errors made in the legislative process which result in tax legislation that is not consistent with intent?

Examples of Deception or Incompetence

It may be difficult to distinguish problems with tax legislation that are a result of deception from those that are a result of incompetence. However, regardless of the reason, problems exist. These problems can relate specifically to misunderstanding by low-income taxpayers or others.

As illustrated earlier in the paper for the dependent care tax benefits and the adoption tax benefits, the difficulties for taxpayers in knowing whether to take the credit or the exclusion is not straightforward. What seems to be an obvious choice for one benefit over the other may counterintuitively become suboptimal. In addition, taxpayers, as a group, are not very sophisticated in their knowledge of the tax code. Low-income taxpayers cannot be expected to be any more sophisticated than other taxpayers, let alone more sophisticated than their legislators. Thus, any expectation that low-income taxpayers would even know there is a non-obvious

---

13   Foxman V. Commissioner 42 T.C. 535, 551 n. 9 (1964).

choice to be made may be inappropriate.

It is one thing when qualifications and limitations on certain tax benefits make it unlikely for low-income taxpayers to get full advantage of them, especially when multiple tax benefits are involved. It is quite another thing when, as illustrated earlier in the paper, for the dependent care credit and the retirement savings contribution credit, it is mathematically impossible for any taxpayer to get the full statutory benefit of a tax credit. The calculations to determine the ability of a specific credit to provide the statutory benefit are not difficult but are either sometimes not performed or are ignored if performed.

Because of the evolution of tax law, tax code limitations which may have made sense may no longer make sense. As discussed previously, the child tax credit can be partially or fully refundable in some circumstances, but the limitations on refundability have changed over time. The limit on refundability originally existed only for taxpayers with three or more qualifying children. These taxpayers could qualify for a refundable tax credit to the extent their social security taxes exceeded their earned income credit. To provide greater refundability, the limit was changed so that all taxpayers could claim a refundable credit to the extent of 10 percent of their earned income in excess of $10,000 (taxpayers with three or more children were allowed to use the greater of this test or the original social security taxes in excess of earned income credit test). Over time, the refundability was liberalized even more by changing the 10 percent test to a 15 percent test. In addition, the $10,000 amount has been indexed. For 2007, this amount is $11,750.

By changing the 10 percent test to a 15 percent test, Congress has made the original social security test obsolete. Chart 1 illustrates what happens in 2007 for a married couple filing jointly. The social security taxes do not equal the earned income credit until earned income reaches $29,183. However, by this time, 15 percent of earned income in excess of $11,750 is already greater than the social security taxes. For any higher levels of earned income, the 15 percent test exceeds the social security taxes test, so the social security taxes test is moot.

Another problem with the refundable portion of the child tax credit exists because of a slight wording change in the tax law which makes the tax code inconsistent with the Congressional committee intent.[14] It is unclear whether the wording change was an intentional attempt to change the tax law or simply an ill-advised attempt to clarify the wording. However, the result of the change in wording is that the 15 percent test on refundability was removed for taxpayers with three or more qualifying children, thus meaning these taxpayers have a smaller portion of refundable child tax credit than do other taxpayers. The same legislation that changed this wording also inadvertently left out a tax code section number that was intended to be referenced in the sentence but which was left out as a typographical error which was not caught in the proofing process.

The wording problems just discussed are the result of legislation of the Gulf Opportunity Zone Act of 2005.[15] These changes were billed as "technical corrections." Technical corrections

---

14   See Katherine D. Black and Sheldon R. Smith, "The Refundable Child Tax Credit: Now You See It, Now You Don't" Tax Notes, Vol. 113, Number 11, December 11, 2006, pp. 1015-1020 for an explanation and discussion of the change.

15   P.L. 109-135.

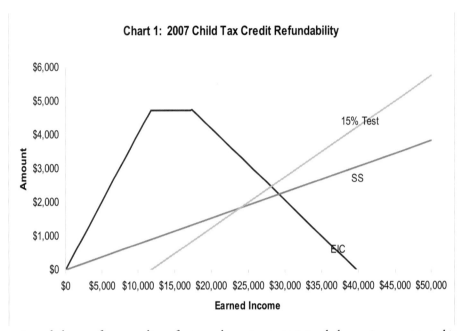

Chart 1: 2007 Child Tax Credit Refundability

are intended to conform wording of a tax code section to its intended meaning as expressed in legislative committee reports or to coordinate among the myriad, complex tax code sections. However, tax technical corrections are often passed as part of other large bills and are often added at the last minute. It is also likely that some of the technical corrections included in the Gulf Opportunity Zone Act affected the 2005 tax reporting year, so these "corrections" may have been hurriedly added to a bill so they could be passed before the Congressional holiday break at the end of 2005. This bill was passed and signed late in December.

Because technical corrections are supposed to correct prior errors and are not intended to change tax policy, this type of tax bill probably receives even less scrutiny by Senators and Representatives and their aids than other tax bills. However, it seems that, because of the way these technical corrections are made law, it is again an opportunity for either deception or incompetence to creep into the legislative process without much oversight.

Conclusion

Discrepancies between expected and actual tax benefits for low-income taxpayers can arise for a number of reasons: (1) specific qualifications and limitations of certain tax provisions; (2) evolution of tax laws over time which change the available benefits; (3) complications in coordinating multiple potential tax benefits; and (4) mistakes or errors in the law because of problems with the legislative process-individual or systemic, intentional or unintentional. The problems with misunderstanding the tax law and having false expectations of what it will provide are not unique to low-income taxpayers; other taxpayers can encounter problems as well. There is a difference between incompetently passing legislation that does not work and deliberately passing legislation that does not work. However, either scenario still harms the public and deteriorates the integrity and efficacy of Congress. The ethics of deception and competence with respect to the legislative process for tax laws should be reviewed and improved.

The Case of the Overambitious Ambulance Chaser: Rules of Professional Conduct for Lawyers in Advertising and Solicitation

By
Jill O. Jasperson

The overambitious ambulance chaser case is a United States Supreme Court case that was decided in 1978. It is the premiere case for lawyer solicitation, and is taught in every law school. The author also teaches this case in her legal ethics class here at UVSC. The citation for this case is Ohralik v. Ohio State Bar Assn.,436 U.S. 447 (1978)

Here are the details of our famous ambulance chaser, in the court's own words:

Mr. Ohralik, a member of the Ohio Bar, lived in Montville, Ohio. He practiced law in Montville and Cleveland. On February 13, 1974, while picking up his mail at the Montville Post Office, Mr. Ohralik learned from the postmaster's brother about an automobile accident that had taken place on February 2 in which Carol McClintock, a young woman with whom Mr. Ohralik was casually acquainted, had been injured. Mr. Ohralik made a telephone call to Ms. McClintock's parents, who informed him that their daughter was in the hospital. Mr. Ohralik suggested that he might visit Carol in the hospital. Mrs. McClintock assented to the idea, but requested that Mr. Ohralik first stop by at her home.

During Mr. Ohralik's visit with the McClintocks, they explained that their daughter had been driving the family automobile on a local road when she was hit by an uninsured motorist. Both Carol and her passenger, Wanda Lou Holbert, were injured and hospitalized. In response to the McClintocks' expression of apprehension that they might be sued by Wanda Lou, Mr. Ohralik explained that Ohio's guest statute would preclude such a suit. When Mr. Ohralik suggested to the McClintocks that they hire a lawyer, Mrs. McClintock retorted that such a decision would be up to Carol, who was 18 years old and would be the beneficiary of a successful claim.

Mr. Ohralik proceeded to the hospital, where he found Carol lying in traction in her room. After a brief conversation about her condition, Mr. Ohralik told Carol he would represent her and asked her to sign an agreement. Carol said she would have to discuss the matter with her parents. She did not sign the agreement, but asked Mr. Ohralik to have her parents come to see her. Mr. Ohralik also attempted to see Wanda Lou Holbert, but learned that she had just been released from the hospital. He then departed for another visit with the McClintocks.

On his way Mr. Ohralik detoured to the scene of the accident, where he took a set of photographs. He also picked up a tape recorder, which he concealed under his raincoat before arriving at the McClintocks' residence. Once there, he re-examined their automobile insurance policy, discussed with them the law applicable to passengers, and explained the consequences of the fact that the driver who struck Carol's car was an uninsured motorist. Mr. Ohralik discovered that the McClintocks' insurance policy would provide benefits of up to $12,500 each for Carol and Wanda Lou under an uninsured-motorist clause. Mrs. McClintock acknowledged that both Carol and Wanda Lou could sue for their injuries, but recounted to Mr. Ohralik that "Wanda swore up and down she would not do it." The McClintocks also told Mr. Ohralik that Carol had phoned to say that Mr. Ohralik could "go ahead" with her representation. Two days later Mr. Ohralik returned to Carol's hospital room to have her sign a contract, which provided that he would receive one-third of her recovery.

In the meantime, Mr. Ohralik obtained Wanda Lou's name and address from the McClintocks after telling them he wanted to ask her some questions about the accident. He then visited Wanda Lou at her home, without having been invited. He again concealed his tape recorder and recorded most of the conversation with Wanda Lou. After a brief, unproductive inquiry about the facts of the accident, Mr. Ohralik told Wanda Lou that he was representing Carol and that he had a "little tip" for Wanda Lou: the McClintocks' insurance policy contained an uninsured-motorist clause which might provide her with a recovery of up to $12,500. The young woman, who was 18 years of age and not a high school graduate at the time, replied to Mr. Ohralik's query about whether she was going to file a claim by stating that she really did not understand what was going on. Mr. Ohralik offered to represent her, also, for a contingent fee of one-third of any recovery, and Wanda Lou stated, "O. K."

Wanda's mother attempted to repudiate her daughter's oral assent the following day, when Mr. Ohralik called on the telephone to speak to Wanda. Mrs. Holbert informed Mr. Ohralik that she and her daughter did not want to sue anyone or to have Mr. Ohralik represent them, and that if they decided to sue they would consult their own lawyer. Mr. Ohralik insisted that Wanda had entered into a binding agreement. A month later Wanda confirmed in writing that she wanted neither to sue nor to be represented by Mr. Ohralik. She requested that Mr. Ohralik notify the insurance company that he was not her lawyer, as the company would not release a check to her until he did so. Carol also eventually discharged Mr. Ohralik. Although another lawyer represented her in concluding a settlement with the insurance company, she paid Mr. Ohralik one-third of her recovery in settlement of his lawsuit against her for breach of contract.

Both Carol McClintock and Wanda Lou Holbert filed complaints against Mr. Ohralik with the Grievance Committee of the Geauga County Bar Association. The County Bar Association referred the grievance to the state bar association, which filed a formal complaint with the Board of Commissioners on Grievances and Discipline of the Supreme Court of Ohio. After a hearing, the Board found that Mr. Ohralik had violated Disciplinary Rules (DR) 2-103 (A) and 2-104 (A) of the Ohio Code of Professional Responsibility. The Board rejected Mr. Ohralik's defense that his conduct was protected under the First and Fourteenth Amendments. The Supreme Court of Ohio adopted the findings of the Board, reiterated that Mr. Ohralik's conduct was not constitutionally protected, and increased the sanction of a public reprimand recommended by the Board to indefinite suspension.

The case went from the Supreme Court of Ohio to the Supreme Court of the United States. After analysis, the US Supreme Court affirmed the decision of the Ohio Supreme Court. Mr. Ohralik was indefinitely suspended from the practice of law in the state of Ohio.

What is the ethical responsibility of a lawyer regarding solicitation and advertising in most states? Each state passes their own set of professional responsibility rules, but rules are very similar. Nowadays, lawyer solicitation is still frowned upon in most instances, and the Utah Code of Professional Responsibility Rule 7.3 makes that clear:

Rule 7.3. Direct Contact with Prospective Clients.

(a) A lawyer may not solicit, in-person, professional employment from a prospective client with whom the lawyer has no family or prior professional relationship, when a significant motive for the lawyer's doing so is the lawyer's pecuniary gain. The term "in-person" includes in-person and telephonic communication directed to a specific recipient, but does not include letters addressed or advertising circulars distributed generally to persons not known to need legal services of the kind provided by the lawyer in a particular matter, but who are so situated that they might in general find such services useful.

(b) A lawyer may not solicit, by mail or other written communication directed to a specific recipient concerning a specific cause of action, professional employment from a prospective client with whom the lawyer has no family or prior professional relationship under the following circumstances:

(1) The lawyer knows or reasonably should know that the physical, emotional or mental state of the person is such that the person could not exercise reasonable judgment in employing a lawyer;

(2) The person has made known to the lawyer a desire not to receive communications from the lawyer; or

(3) The communication involves coercion, duress, or harassment

Lawyer advertising is discussed in Rule 7.2. This rule was confirmed by a case the year before the Ohralik case. It was Bates v. State Bar of Arizona, 430 U.S. 350 (1977) that set the stage for Ohralik. The details of the case were:

The law firm of Bates included licensed attorneys and members of the Arizona State Bar, who were charged in a complaint filed by the State Bar's president with violating the State Supreme Court's disciplinary rule, which prohibits attorneys from advertising in newspapers or other media. The complaint was based upon a newspaper advertisement placed by appellants for their "legal clinic," stating that they were offering "legal services at very reasonable fees," and listing their fees for certain services, namely, uncontested divorces, uncontested adoptions, simple personal bankruptcies, and changes of name. The Arizona Supreme Court upheld the conclusion of a bar committee that Bates had violated the rule.

The United States Supreme court, however, did not find that they violated any professional rules. The court held lawyer advertising was protected and states could prohibit advertisements in only limited ways. Bates changed the way lawyer advertising was treated. The Utah Code of Professional Responsibility Rule 7.2 discusses lawyer advertising in a much more forward thinking way. Here is the text for that rule:

Rule 7.2. Advertising.

(a) Subject to the requirements of Rules 7.1 and 7.3, a lawyer may advertise services through public media, such as a telephone directory, legal directory, newspaper or other periodical, outdoor advertising, radio or television, or through written or recorded communication.

(b) A copy or recording of an advertisement or written communication shall be kept for two years after its last dissemination along with a record of when and where it was used.

(c) A lawyer shall not give anything of value to a person for recommending the lawyer's services, except that a lawyer may pay the reasonable cost of advertising or written communication permitted by this Rule and may pay the usual charges of a not-for-profit lawyer referral service or other legal service organization.

(d) Any communication made pursuant to this Rule shall include the name of at least one lawyer responsible for its content.

Twenty years later, in 1997, the Ethics Committee of the Utah State Bar answered questions about web advertising. In short, Utah attorneys may operate and maintain a web site and post advertisements to newsgroups, provided they comply with Rule 7. Advertising through e-mail messages, which are directed to specific recipients, is generally permissible unless it violates Rule 7.3 (b). Attorneys' participation in "chat groups" is considered to be an "in person" communication and subject to the restrictions of rule 7.3 (a).

In December 2006, the author attended a continuing legal education course on e-lawyering. It concerned attracting and servicing clients specifically through the internet. As lawyers approach more and more technological advances, the author believes lawyers will also breach the divide into the greater advertising world.

Victim/Offender Mediation & Restorative Justice

By
Carolyn Howard-Morris

In today's society, people are prosecuted for wrongdoings and generally either fined, incarcerated or suffer other consequences for committing such offenses. In the adult system, there is little emphasis on emotional or mental restitution. I do not believe that this lack of emphasis is because of a failure in the court system itself, rather given the lack of time and heavy case load the courts are carrying, it becomes difficult, if not impossible, to manage the emotional and mental suffering of every individual involved in a crime. Generally, an offender will have a monetary restitution amount imposed, but the court's involvement after such restitution is paid is somewhat limited with regards to emotional restitution for the victim.

One of the wonderful aspects of mediation, especially victim-offender mediation, is that the offender has an opportunity to sit face to face with the victim involved in the crime and speak to them. The offender may not initially consider this a desireable opportunity, but usually by the end of the mediation the offender has accepted mediation as a valid recourse. Although mediation occurs very rarely in the adult criminal system, it is becoming more widely accepted and practiced in the juvenile system. I have conducted dozens of victim offender mediations since the time that I graduated from law school. For example, years ago I mediated a case involving a young offender who had stolen his teacher's credit card. The time for mediation arrived and the young boy sat at one end of the table with his parents, and the teacher sat on the other side. The mediation began and the teacher asked the boy why he had taken the credit card. It was evident that this young boy was embarrassed and contrite about his past actions. The fact that he had to sit face to face with his teacher likely will leave a lasting impression on him. The next time that he considers committing wrong, his thoughts may race back to the moment of truth when he was forced to confront his victim. Hopefully, his actions in the future will reflect the good he learned from the somewhat "traumatic" experience of facing his teacher.

Many children commit crimes and do not truly appreciate the consequences until they see how their actions have affected the victims involved. A second case that I mediated involved another young child under the age of 10. He had committed some very serious property crimes with the damages estimated at over $75,000 dollars. Obviously, there was no way that this child could pay back the full amount. In many juvenile courts, there is a cap that juveniles should not be required to pay more than $1,000.00 in restitution. If I applied this general rule to my case, the young child would be leaving the victims in a deficit of tens of thousands of dollars. As the mediation began, the victims asked the child how the child felt after he committed the devastating crimes. The child explained, "Every night I sit in my bed crying and wondering why I chose to do wrong." The child's precious tears rolled down his cheeks. I had expected the victims to be quite angry, as they probably had every right to be. However, as I looked to the other side of the room, the victims were crying as well. They told the young child that they forgave and that all was well.

These experiences teach an important lesson. Mediation allows people, both men and women, girls and boys, who have committed wrongdoings to face the consequences of their actions. Although mediation might be embarrassing for an offender, they are so much more likely to refrain from committing future criminal acts when they know that they will be facing their victim one on one and having to explain their actions. Although it is embarrassing in the moment, it is highly preventative in helping the offender to choose a new path.

What is pertinent about restorative justice is that the offenders in a crime might also be viewed as victims, in a personal sense. To illustrate this example, there was a mediation that I conducted several months ago where a young teenage boy had broken into the business of an older man. He had taken cash from the register and destroyed much of the building property. As we sat in mediation with the teenage boy on one side of the table with his mother and the older man on the other side, I was not sure what to expect from the "offender." The young boy, rather the offender, explained to the older man that he had broken into his business because of a conversation he had prior to the crime with his mother. The young boy told of the pleas his mother had given just hours before, asking that the family pool all of their resources to try and pay the family bills. Although the mother obviously meant no harm, the young boy took the plea as his own personal obligation. He did not have a job; in fact, he was too young to work. And so, in a desperate moment, he ran into the streets searching for the answer to his mother's serious distress. Naturally, his crime was not the appropriate answer to the problem at hand, but as he explained the situation, there was a peace about the room. The peace didn't excuse the act; the peace didn't grant restitution to the victim in the matter; and the peace did not wisk away the harm. However, there was an understanding between the offender and the victim that took place that day. No longer did the victim feel that the offender had been personally out to injure him or his business. But rather the victim could see the obstacle this young boy had faced. It did not justify the young boy, but rather placed a real human being in front of the victim. The victim saw the good intentions of this boy and his intent to rectify his actions.

Imagine if the law had not required mediation in this instance. Would it have been better to place the boy in jail and throw away the key? Would it have been better for the victim to go on feeling injured, full of hate and anger? Some would say yes. Some would say that the only retribution is punishment. Some would argue that people need to be punished. Obviously, this is true, but punishment can take many different forms. For this young boy to sit across from the victim of his crime, to face him and to answer for his crime, I believe, was far greater punishment than facing a lonely cinderblock cell. The boy saw the impact his actions had on another person. He saw the pain someone else suffered because of his choices. Restitution occurred that day. In all of the mediations that I performed, rarely do I have individuals who leave the mediation without a true desire to rectify their actions. Restorative justice gives the offender the motivation to change their behavior. It provides a personal restitution to all victims. It provides justice.

Mediation is an incredible key to restoring justice, both monetarily and emotionally, to the victim of a crime. It also helps to promote a resolve in the offender not to pursue further criminal actions and to rise above wrongdoing. Society as a whole is benefited by this restorative process.

The Right to Choose Life or Death: A Nurse's Perspective

By
Dianne McAdams-Jones

The dictionary defines ethics as "principles of right or good conduct". It further defines a right as "something to which one has a just or lawful claim." Most people today have heard of the "right to die with dignity" or with the abortion issue, "the right to life." When does a person not have a right to live? When does a person have a right to die? Who makes the decision? These questions force us to think about our views on life, what constitutes a meaningful existence, and our attitudes about death. Few nurses I know have a fixed opinion on the discussions above. Nevertheless, we believe in life, the sustaining of life, healing patients and their families, and caring for and nurturing the sick and infirm. It is hard to ask nurses to separate themselves from their belief in promoting life, and it is difficult for nurses to choose death for a patient.

In a clinical setting, process and outcomes are a huge part of caring for the patient. The discipline of nursing respects a patient's choices, even when they do not conform to modern medical practices or when those very choices impose upon the nurse's rights. Typically, regardless of whether they agree, nurses will advocate the patients' rights and aspire to develop a trusting professional relationship with their patients. Nurses value respect for the patient's choice while providing the best patient care.

While nurses aspire to clinical competence, they also want to ensure a just system of health care (Taylor, 1998). Nurses often will admit that they have a "calling" to their profession. The profession targets a goal of providing the best of care to the whole patient. Because of this goal, nurses rarely see their role as a neutral one on issues of choosing life or death. Nurses choose to advocate for their patients.

Right-to-die advocate Jack Kevorkian has created controversy with his desire to assert the legality of physician-assisted suicide. However, the laws in some states have opened the door for the pursuit of murder charges against any physicians who assists with suicide. The courts have generally looked askance at efforts to gain legal recognition of a right to assisted suicide or, alternatively, to overturn state laws forbidding the practice (Rogatz, 2003). Reasonable people want to see the sick get well. This being true, how then does one determine who has the right to live or die? Is our difficulty with end-of-life decisions because we have been given the right to exercise choices in so many other aspects of our lives? A patient who chooses death poses a challenge for nurses who have been trained to care, to administer healing salves and pills, to nurse the patient back to health and to sincerely seek the best for all of their patients. How then do these same nurses choose death for the non-responsive patients placed in their care?

The right-to-die advocate would say that there are instances where patients experience terrible suffering that can not be relieved by any of the therapeutic or palliative techniques medicine and nursing have to offer and that some of those patients beg for deliverance (Rogatz, 2003). Can nurses be convinced of any truth in this statement? As a nurse, I would say "no." Nurses instead make every attempt to make patients comfortable until the end.

The Hippocratic injunction is to do no harm. Pain is often not the cause for a patient or the patient's family to choose peaceful transition into the next life. Families and patients are often more concerned about the loss of self, the wasting body, the urinary and bowel incontinence, the immobility and the total dependence on others for care. This loss of dignity, or the fear of this loss, often encourages a cognizant patient to decide that they want no heroic measures to restore their life if they should die. For the nurse who considers the patient's personhood, dignity, and wishes to be values the profession should honor, a request for hospice (a peaceful and comfortable death with dignity) is not a tragedy, but a celebration of the end of life. The ultimate tragedy would be a depersonalization/loss of self. Robert Veatch set out to affirm that deciding in individual cases that the struggle against death need not continue is not incompatible with a more general social commitment to a public policy that sees at least some deaths as evil (Potter, 2002). In other words, it is equally as sad to decide that death is evil as it is to struggle to save a life that has no quality.

Nurses demonstrate caring for the total being of patients by interacting with the family and patient. The social history gathered during admission gives valuable insight into family/patient dynamics. When the patient is no longer able to speak, is immobile, cannot respond to the environment, cannot acknowledge their surroundings, and cannot control any bodily functions, the public cannot communicate with the patient. Over time, a family, in many cases, may cease to make visits. Then, the health care providers become the only ones who communicate with the patient, through the care they administer, but family members still retain legal rights with regard to continuing or discontinuing treatment.

When the patient can speak, can communicate with their family and friends and faithfully goes to the mailbox to fetch the newspaper, but their kidneys no longer produce urine and there is no venous access left, does the patient and family have the right to request a donor kidney? Many might argue that this patient's life has significant value, and still possesses quality regardless of any long-term prognosis. Family and friends value the love and fellowship of this patient regardless of whether the general public may see this patient's life as contributing to society.

Contrary to the above scenario, if this same patient were bedridden and could not speak, society might say there is no quality in this life and she or he should not be given the opportunity for a donor kidney. Although nurses are trained to accept the sanctity of life, often decisions must be made concerning limited resources and the ethical use of those resources. How the nurse contributes to end-of-life decisions must sometimes be directed by the laws governing these issues and the options these laws provide to patients.

Experienced nurses are acutely aware of a person's experience with illness, and hence continue to integrate patient history with their treatment. In addition to the facts indicated on a patient's chart, nurses must integrate patient history and patient and family desires into the treatment plan. Being knowledgeable of local laws is imperative, along with fulfilling the

Hippocratic Oath while integrating safe treatment strategies. The patient's decisions are first and foremost. In the case where the patient is unable to make decisions, then his appointed power of attorney will make the decisions and direct the plan of care. In the unfortunate cases where the patient is unable to make decisions and there is no power of attorney, the case becomes one of the State.

The American Nurses Association defines nursing as "the diagnosis and treatment of human responses to actual or potential health problems" (Taylor, 1998). Each person has a core right to make decisions which determine the course of their life, even if the health care provider disagrees with that decision, that provider is responsible for granting the patient's wishes wherever possible and legal. Despite the theatrics of the Terry Schiavo case, the system currently in place has worked well and continues to work well for most of society. That system is the one that lets the patient make the choice in end-of-life decisions. It continues to ensure the rights of those to have medical treatment consistent with their personal values and choices (Smith, W. J., 2005).

Those who know a person best can say what that person would have wanted either on a basis of conversations or discussions. Congress has no role in the decision-making process (Smith, W.J., 2005). The nurse is there to give support to the patient and to ensure the patient exercises his/her right to make a choice and that these rights and choices are honored. The nurse is bound to provide care in the most safe, caring, diligent, and supportive manner possible considering the patient's circumstances.

The nurse applies this knowledge by becoming proactive in insisting that the legal system is attentive and carefully investigates all possible methods of achieving the patient's wishes. Nurses sometimes must become proactive in following cases with letters to lawyers and media alike. Further, nurses apply the knowledge gained through a complete social history upon admission and extrapolate data that helps steer the plan of care. If there is a living will, a copy should be placed in the patient's files. If there is not a living will, then the nurse should contact Social Services to help supply the patient and family with the necessary tools needed to formulate a living will. What matters in any and all of the cases is that the individual patient does the thinking; not congress or any other right-to-life or right-to-death activists. The patient has a right to make the choice.

The nurse is the patient's advocate. Nurses find motivation for their caring through their involvement in the wellbeing of their patient. The nurse has a responsibility for the promotion of the patient as a whole person. The human being has to be appreciated as a moral subject. It becomes a sad commentary on a human life when someone with no vested interest in the patient is afforded the opportunity to withdraw life support.

As an organization, nurses have a responsibility to educate the public. Nurses must work to educate one another about end-of-life issues. All nurses need to help ensure the entire patient treatment process, from admission assessment to treatment planning to end of life preparation, is thorough and patient- (and family) friendly. Teaching the patient and their family about the treatment plan and their legal options is imperative. Communicating this information throughout the care plan, and ensuring the patient has met with Social Services can forestall any unforeseen legal issues which may arise. Typically the nurse begins formulating a plan of care following the initial patient assessment. With a thorough knowledge of the patient's prognosis, treatment plan, and wishes, it becomes the nurse's duty to advocate for the patient. Educators in the health care profession have an inherent responsibility to explain the legal issues concerning a patient's case, especially the workings of the living will. Someone must be an effective legal advocate for the patient's rights in order to ensure that their end-of-life desires are honored.

Ensuring the patient's final wishes are followed is not always an easy or straightforward task. The Schiavo case clearly revealed what happens when a patient has no written wishes. Nurses need to educate patients and family to limit any possible misunderstanding when the time to make end-of-life decisions comes. The living will is the most effective way to ensure the process goes as planned. Living wills by and large have worked successfully in communicating the desires of the patient and avoiding misunderstandings between family and healthcare workers when end-of-life issues arise. Being sufficiently prepared for end-of-life decisions reduces the complex set of emotional, legal, and operational issues. Recognizing possible problems in the patients profile during the admission process allows the nurse to address these issues by developing an integrated treatment plan with the patient and family. The nurse must utilize the information gained from the assessment and use it to educate the patient. Healthcare is of special moral importance, because it helps to maintain our status as fully contributing citizens. In the absence of our health and ability to exercise our rights, we must have a plan in place to preserve our dignity. A living will is the tool each health care recipient and health care provider must seriously consider making an integral part of their healthcare plan.

References

Glassick, C. E., Huber, M. T., and Maeroff, G. I.. (1997). *Scholarship Assessed: Evaluation of the Professoriate*. San Francisco: Jossey-Bass. (Original work published 1997)

Gastmans, Chris., Dierckx de Casterle, Bernadette., & Schotsmans, Paul. (1998). Nursing considered as Moral Practice: A Philosophical-Ethical Interpretation of Nursing. *Kennedy Institute of Ethics Journal*, 8.1, 43-69.

Smith, W.J., (2005, April 19). Should Congress Make It Harder to Withdraw Food and Fluid from Incapacitated Patients? (*From testimony before the House Subcommittee on Criminal justice, Drug Policy and Human Resources*). Philadelphia: Caplan, Arthur L.

Boyer, Ernest L. (1990). *Scholarship Reconsidered: Priorities of the Professoriate*. Lawrenceville, New Jersey: Princeton University Press.

Potter, Van Rensselaer. (Series Ed.), & Yount, Lisa. (Vol. Ed.). (2002). *On Dying with Personhood. Contemporary Issues Companion Series*. San Diego: Greenhaven Press, 2002.

Rogatz, Peter. (2003). The Arguments of Those Opposed to Assisted Suicide Are Flawed. In Roman Espejo (Ed.), *Suicide*, San Diego, California: Greenhaven Press. (Original work published 2003)

Taylor, Carol R. (1998). Reflection on "Nursing Considered as Moral Practice". *Kennedy Institute of Ethics Journal*, 8.1, 71-82.

War, Politics & History

Lieutenant Colonel Ronald E. Fischer

Detainee Abuse and the Ethics of Psychology

By
Kathryn French

Beginning in 2004 (earlier at Guantanamo Bay) the United States and other nations reeled from revelations of torture and mistreatment of detainees at Abu Ghraib, the Black Room at Baghdad's Camp Nama (Schmitt and Marshall, 2006), Forward Operating Base Mercury outside Fallujah (White, 2005), Guantanamo Bay, even detainee abuse on American soil in South Carolina (Leoning, 2006). The abuse was so extreme that some prisoners were killed. Types of abuse included beating, sexual taunting, intimidation by dogs, shackling in stress positions for hours, subjection to temperature extremes, a form of water torture in which prisoners are threatened with drowning, food and water deprivation, and threat of harm to family members. Shocked Americans were asking, "How could we have done this?"

The Defense Department and the State Department had earlier protested the Administration's determination that the Geneva Convention and other safeguards need not apply to detainees, whether or not they were proven enemy combatants. Jarred by internal and world-wide criticism, at last the American government officially and begrudgingly disallowed physical and mental human-rights violations except under direct presidential order.

Debates about torture, coercive interrogations, and maltreatment were initiated in the many organizations whose members have professional interactions with detainees, including the American Psychological Association (APA). In August, 2005, at APA's annual convention, an active duty military psychologist stood up in a session and asked what he and other psychologists can do when their job by nature is in conflict with the ethics of the profession. The question was acknowledged but not answered by the panel, all military mental health professionals. The panel was then asked about their freedom to speak honestly and openly. They responded that when people work for the military, criticism is not allowed, though behind closed doors private opinions may exist.

Two dilemmas of military psychologists were thus articulated. First, a psychologist in war time may often find that orders conflict with personal or professional ethics. War itself violates the first ethics rule, "Do No Harm." Second, obedient silence is enforced in the military, except for "Yes, Sir! No, Sir!" Military psychologists' extensive knowledge about human behavior is often omitted from decision and feedback processes applied to the same human behavior. For example, research psychologists know that coercion does not yield good intelligence, yet it became a proscribed tool for obtaining intelligence in "The War on Terror."

This paper addresses both issues. First described are the ethics for psychologists regarding detainees and interrogations. Second is a brief overview of selected psychological explanations of how ordinary people become abusive in detention and interrogation facilities.

Psychological Ethics and Interrogations

Psychologists revisited their comprehensive ethics code in the wake of detainee abuse. Actions taken at Guantanamo Bay were especially disturbing, as psychologists had some involvement with torture at that location (American Psychological Association, 2006; Okie, 2005). Detainee fears and psychological vulnerabilities were used against them in such techniques as sexual humiliation, stress positions, threats with dogs and physical contact, and religious defamation. (APA, 2006; Okie, 2005; Savage, 2005).

According to Stephen Behnke (2006), director of APA's Ethics Office, psychologists have two principle responsibilities during interrogations. The first is "Do No Harm" to the person being interrogated. The second responsibility is to society. The responsibility to the individual requires the psychologist to "Never engage in, facilitate or countenance torture or other cruel, inhuman, or degrading treatment...(including)... coercion (Behnke, p. 66). APA (2005) defines coercion as ranging from physical torture to psychologically damaging techniques such as threats of severe harm, sexual humiliation, defilement of religious objects, manipulation of a prisoner's fears, and techniques to "shock the conscience."

Psychologists are prohibited from conducting interrogations (Behnke, 2006). They may consult in an interrogation as long as it is being conducted according to the principle that allows no harm to the person being interrogated. A psychologist may not consult for the interrogation of a person for whom the psychologist has mental health responsibilities (Behnke, 2006), nor may information from a health record be used to plan or implement an interrogation strategy.

A psychologist is obliged to report an interrogation that is unethical, and indeed, is obliged to stop it if at all possible. Behnke (2006) contends that psychologists have a unique responsibility specific to their profession. This is to observe and intervene when an interrogation begins to drift away from ethical behavior. Recently psychologists affirmed their ethics position by approving the APA Resolution Against Torture and Other Cruel, Inhuman, or Degrading Punishment (American Psychological Association, 2006).

In conclusion, psychologists are forbidden to engage directly in interrogations, and they are not allowed to have indirect involvement in coercive or harm producing interrogations or interrogations that compromise the psychologist/client relationship.

Selected Psychological Explanations for Detainee Abuse

Soldiers, contractors, and psychologists are for the most part ordinary people, not sadists or psychopaths. There are multiple, additive factors that may result in detainee abuse. Some of these factors are presented here. They are not comprehensive, nor are they presented in a hierarchy of importance. Individual detention and interrogation centers have unique circumstances and group dynamics that create an interplay of these psychological factors and others.

About two months ago I stopped at a recruiters table outside the college dining area. I asked the recruiter what he thought about the government's admissions that there was no link between the Iraq war and the terrorist attacks in our country. He said he didn't care, he respected his leaders and would obey them no matter what. When asked about his response more recently, the officer said of course he would not break the law for a superior.

This example illustrates the Milgram phenomenon, named after a researcher who showed that individuals will obey authority to the extreme of inflicting grave injury unto death to another individual (Milgram, 1974). It is one of two well known psychological principles that play a powerful role in mistreatment of detainees. The tendency to obey authority is valued and reinforced in the military. Obeying orders makes a good soldier. The second principle is the tendency for persons in a guard role quickly to begin to mistreat prisoners. This was demonstrated by the Stanford prison experiments (Zimbardo, 2004). Well meaning college students quickly transformed into cruel guards as other well meaning college students became their defiant or abject prisoners. To this laboratory experiment add the real life stress of American guards under fire on enemy ground, with friends being killed by people who look like the prisoners, and this tendency toward cruelty of the imprisoned can explode.

Documents obtained by Public Broadcasting System Frontline investigators (2005) show top authorities in the Justice Department compromising human values by endorsing illegal maltreatment of detainees in Guantanamo Bay and Iraq. (Program transcript, interviews, and supportive documents are available at http://pbs.org/wbgh/pages/frontline/torture/paper.) Attorney General John Ashcroft (2002) ruled against applying the Geneva Convention to imprisoned detainees, whether they were known to be enemy combatants or innocents rounded up in the chaos of war. When useful intelligence was not forthcoming from the Guantanamo Bay detainees, Defense Secretary Donald Rumsfeld ordered the use of increasingly coercive techniques. The officers who protested or refused to obey were replaced with others who followed orders.

The orders from the Administration wended their way down the hierarchy to guards, interrogators, and psychologists. In cognitive psychology GIGO is an acronym meaning "Garbage in, garbage out." In the case of Abu Ghraib, initially the prison system was chaotic and not organized for detainees. There existed different lists of instructions with conflicting information on how to treat and interrogate detainees (Public Broadcasting System, 2005). Supervision was ineffectual, and confused guards and interrogators were left to make their own interpretations. Group dynamics led to abuse.

While an authority may not have directly ordered severe abuse at the prisons, the words and intent from the Attorney General and Secretary Rumsfeld set a tone of the acceptability of crossing former boundaries. A combination of active encouragement of coercive interrogations, silence from authority and peers (which is interpreted as permission) in response to torture, and chaotic ambiguity of directions contributed to expanding the boundaries of acceptability.

Not getting good intelligence from the detainees is unsurprising. It has been estimated that at least one-half of the Guantanamo detainees were not actually enemy combatants, but were innocents plucked out of vehicles or homes or off the street, and turned over to Americans for bounty money (Public Broadcasting System, 2005). Among those who are now thought to be terrorist combatants, most are from the rank and file who have no knowledge of higher level organization or planned attacks. Kassin's (2005) extensive research on interrogations and confessions suggests that when suspects are truly innocent and deny involvement in a crime, their denial is often interpreted as deceit. Innocent suspects actually undergo harsher interrogating than guilty suspects. Under coercion they are then especially vulnerable to making false confessions.

Social research suggests that the nature of individual behavior quickly becomes subordinate to the group (Fiske, Harris, and Cuddy, 2004; Staub, 2003) and within specific contexts, one group (the in-group) becomes abusive toward another group (the out-group or the Others). Staub (2003) describes the evolution of violence, in which perpetrators are influenced by difficult conditions, and view Others as less than human, deserving of blame and punishment, and enemies. The business of war is the business of killing enemies. When soldiers are trained to kill enemies of their country, the training overcomes the natural reluctance of humans to harm other humans. Then when the soldiers are out of combat, the training must be left behind (Grossman, 1995/1996). Changing the perception of dehumanized enemies to humans deserving of decent treatment is often hard to accomplish after successful training.

Each time a guard or interrogator participates in abuse, even as a bystander, a higher level of abuse becomes easier for group members. A single bystander who actively intervenes can be a powerful deterrent to harm against others (Staub, 2003). But military personnel are trained to conform and obey, and the intense survival bonding in combat deployment leads individuals to be less likely to defy the group and also less likely to develop a sense of individual accountability for actions (Grossman, 1995/1996).

Given dynamics of identification with the close knit group, the behavioral training to obey authority and kill the enemy, the difficult, violent and dangerous contexts in which soldiers struggle to survive, soldiers will often be vulnerable to compelling influences, internal and external, for engaging in unsanctioned violence.

This paper briefly covered two related topics. The first was the ethics of psychologists involved in military detainee interrogations. The second concerned psychological explanations of why detainees were mistreated and shall always be at high risk for being mistreated. Concluding this paper is a discussion of actions that might minimize this risk.

Psychology has much to offer society in the sharing of information and skills. First, more communication can lower risks of abuse. Evil acts occur in secret, and bringing them into the light, bringing them beyond the small group whose dynamics have led the group to sanction and engage in harm, brings acts to the critical scrutiny of the larger group of humanity (Fiske et al, 2004). Second, comprehensive, ongoing training can be provided on acceptable and unacceptable treatment of detainees. Our own personnel can be taught to recognize the stress and other factors that will influence their attitudes and behavior, so they may acknowledge and counteract these tendencies to demean and then to harm Others. They can also be taught to become active bystanders and to intervene early with peers when behavior becomes harmful (Staub, 2003). It would be useful to have an individual and group accountability system with oversight from outside the groups so that behavior in the field closely resembles intention of the ethical rules in the manuals. Finally, more training can be provided on what to do when superiors call for or engage in unethical behavior.

References

American Psychological Association, Executive Committee for the Study of Peace, Conflict, and Violence: Peace Psychology. (2005, August). Coercive Interrogation. Retrieved

February 24 from http://www.webster.edu/peacepsychology/CIResponse.html.

American Psychological Association. (2006, August) Resolution Against Torture and Other Cruel, Inhuman, or Degrading Treatment or Punishment: Justification Statement. Retrieved February 24, 2007 from http://www.webster.edu/peacepsychology/ResolJustification Statement.html.)

Ashcroft, J. (2002, February 1). Letter to President George W. Bush. Retrieved January 22, 2007, from http://news.findlaw.com/wp/docs/torture/jash20102ltr.html.

Behnke, S. (2006).Ethics and interrogation: Comparing and contrasting the American Psychological, American Medical and American Psychiatric Association positions. *Monitor on Psychology*, 66-67.

Fiske, S.T., Harris, L.T., and Cuddy, A.J.C. (2004). Why ordinary people torture enemy prisoners. Science, 306 (5701), 1482-1483. Retrieved from http://web.ebscohost.com.exproxy.uvsc.edu.ehost/detail.

Grossman, D. (1995/1996). *On killing: The psychological cost of learning to kill in war and society*. New York: Back Bay.

Kassin, S. M. (2005). On the psychology of confessions: Does innocence put innocents at risk? *American Psychologist*, 60 (3), 215-228.

Leoning, C. D. (2006, December 14).Pentagon report cited detention concerns.

Washington Post. Retrieved December 14, 2006, from http://www.washingtonpost.com/wp-dyn/content/article/2006/12/13/

Milgram, S. (1974). *Obedience to authority*. New York: Harper and Row.

Okie, S. (2005). Glimpses of Guantanamo---Medical ethics and the war on terror. *The New England Journal of Medicine*, 353, 2529-2534. Retrieved January 23, 2007 from http://www.content.nejm.org/egi/content/full/353/24/2529.

Public Broadcasting System (2005). *FRONTLINE*: The Torture Question. Retrieved February 24, 2007, from http://pbs.org/wgbh/pages/frontline/torture/paper.

Savage, C. (2005, March 31). Split seen on interrogation technique: Navy official says many back stance against coercion. *Boston Globe*. Retrieved February 24, 2007, from http://www.boston.com/news/world/latinamerica/articles/2005/03/31.

Schmitt, E., & Marshall, C. (2006, March 19). In secret unit's "Black Room," a grim portrait of U.S. abuse. *The New York Times*. Retrieved March 20, 2006, from http://www.nytimes.com/03/19/international/mideast/19abuse.html.

Staub, E. (2003). *The psychology of good and evil: Why children, adults and groups help and harm others*. Cambridge,UK: Cambridge.

White, J. (2005, September 24) New reports surface about detainee abuse: Mistreatment was routine, soldiers say. *Washington Post*. Retrieved September 26, 2006, from http//www.washingotnpost.com.

Zimbardo, P. (2004). A situationist perspective on the psychology of evil: Understanding how good people are transformed into perpetrators. In A.G. Miller (Ed.), *The social psychology of good and evil* (pp. 21-50). New York: Guilford.

Military Ethics of Detainee Interrogation

By
Lieutenant Colonel Ronald E. Fischer

The purpose of US intelligence is to enhance national security and foreign relations through accurate and timely information. It is clear from many of the events starting with Watergate in the 1970's through the events surrounding September 11, 2001 that intelligence shortfalls can be devastating. In particular the collection of HUMINT data, the one-on-one interrogation scenario, has been insufficient.

There is the false notion that the military uses torture in their interrogations of detainees and that that is one of the main tools used in the collection of HUMINT data. The military does not use torture in the interrogation process for many reasons. The prime reason is that it is illegal. A service member using torture can be prosecuted and punished under the Uniform Code of Military Justice (UCMJ). In addition, it has been learned that torture may bring about unreliable results and damage subsequent collection efforts.

Interrogation is defined in the Army Field Manual 2-22.3, paragraph 1-20 as "the systemic effort to procure information to answer specific collection requirements by direct and indirect questioning techniques of a person who is in the custody of the forces conducting the questioning." There is a simple two step test to determine if the interrogations are humane. First, if the proposed approach technique were used by the enemy against one of your fellow soldiers, would you believe the soldier had been abused? Second, could your conduct in carrying out the proposed technique violate a law or regulation? If the interrogator answers yes to either or both of these questions, the actions contemplated should not be conducted.

Currently the pneumonic device "THINK" is used to determine if action to be taken would be legal and appropriate. T stands for treat all detainees with the same standard. H stands for humane treatment. I stands for interrogators interrogate. N stands for the need to report abuses. K stands for know the approved techniques.

Per current Department of Defense directives all personnel in this department will "comply with the law of war during all armed conflicts," and "all detainees shall be treated humanely and in accordance with U. S. Law, the law of war, and applicable U.S. policy."

Humane treatment requires that all detainees be treated like humans. This includes the filling of basic life needs to include adequate food, drinking water, shelter, clothing, and medical treatment. It encompasses basic human needs to include free exercise of religion (within detention requirements), respect as human beings, and protection from threats or acts of violence. All actions which are inconsistent with humane treatment are prohibited. The test of these criteria is, again, if the proposed approach technique were used against your fellow soldier, would you believe the soldier had been abused?

Only interrogators will interrogate. Non-interrogators may provide information about the detainees based on observations from passively-collected information, such as leaders, habits, groups, and action in the camp, but they will not attempt to extract information through interrogation.

There is a need to report any abuses. If a soldier becomes aware of any torture, abuse, or mistreatment, it must be reported immediately. Knowledge should be documented and, where possible, the abuse must be stopped immediately. This report may go to the chain of command, the Provost Marshal, the Chaplain, the Staff Judge Advocate, or the Inspector General. If the soldier fails to report abuse, this is in violation of the Uniform Code of Military Justice. Retribution for reporting offenses will not be tolerated. Anyone involved in retribution for reporting must be reported also. There is no excuse for abuse. The soldier can never be authorized nor ordered to violate the UCMJ. Detainee abuse is never justified for military necessity, defense of the nation, saving others, or following orders.

There are sufficient legal interrogation techniques that neither abuse nor torture the detainee. The soldier must know the approved techniques that include the direct approach, the incentive approach, emotional love, emotional hate, fear-up, fear-down, pride and ego-up, pride and ego-down, emotional futility, we know all, file and dossier, establish your identity, repetition, rapid fire, silence, and change of scenery. Special approval is required for the use of the good cop/bad cop (Mutt and Jeff), false flag, and separation.

On the other hand there are also illegal interrogation techniques which must be avoided and for which the violator may be prosecuted under the UCMJ. These include violence or harm of any kind (actual or threatened), bodily injury, threatened removal of any Geneva Convention Right, degrading behavior, sexual attack, rape, forced prostitution, indecent assault, stress positions, public curiosity, reprisals of any kind, coercion, nakedness, hostage taking, use of dogs, punishment, sleep deprivation, and illegal forms of incentive. Anything that is not listed as legal in the Field Manual is illegal.

Another aspect of proper interrogation is that promises are kept. The interrogator will not use conditional promises nor will promises of asylum, amnesty especially for crimes, change in status, or early release be used; however, the interrogator can offer to provide positive input to investigators, prosecutors, State Department, etc.

The elephant in the living room here is the widely-publicized atrocities which occurred at Abu Ghraib during the end of 2003 and the beginning of 2004. Those who committed the crimes related to detainee interrogation have been prosecuted under the UCMJ and sentenced under this code. Those who were on the periphery who may have not been directly involved have received the proper military punishment which may have included relief of command or letters of reprimand.

There is no excuse for violation of the Uniform Code of Military Justice (UCMJ) as was observed world-wide in the Abu Ghraib incident; however, it must be noted that there were many factors which contributed to the sad violations which occurred. It is difficult to understand how those in power would take advantage of detainees; however, there have been extensive studies to indicate that this behavior may occur if individuals are put in a position of power over a detainee. A Stanford prison experiment conducted in the 70's bore this out clearly.

By the 6th day of this experiment it had to be stopped due to the abuses that were occurring.

Some unique factors contributed to the gross violations observed world-wide at Abu Ghraib. In no particular order, some of these factors include but are not limited to:

- Placing soldiers in the position to inflict some retribution on those who had killed their fellow soldiers
- Unit cohesion was lost by cross leveling of reservists into a new unit where they neither knew the leaders nor did the leaders know them.
- Untrained military police (MP) were doing interviews rather than trained interrogators. --Ratios of MPs to detainees were 5 times above the accepted standard.
- Detainees threw human excrement and rocks at MPs, MPs were working 24/7 and only sleeping 4 hours a night on the average.
- Iraqi police were smuggling in loaded weapons to the detainees which resulted in fire fights in the detention facility.
- MPs saw how effective dogs were in searching the Iraqi police for weapons which spurred the idea to use dogs illegally.
- Mortars were striking the compound.
- As reservists, these MPs were citizen soldiers who had been taken from their civilian jobs and ordered into the circumstances of Abu Ghraib. They did not receive requisite training prior to taking on their roll in Iraq.

It is hard to tell where a person's breaking point is, but I would ask all readers of this article to put themselves in the place of these citizen soldiers who were in an uncontrollable situation with fire fights, mortars, excrement flying, and little sleep to see if there may be some greater level of understanding why they may have gone over the edge and broken the law. They are obliged to keep the law in all circumstances regardless of the difficulty or face the consequences of their violation. We are a people of law and order regardless of the lack of law and order that may be surrounding us. There were much more appropriate courses of action these MPs could have employed; however, they chose to act out their prejudice against the detainees in a criminal manner and consequently deserved their punishment regardless of the difficult situation in which they found themselves. No one of them was greater than the law.

It is clear that detainee interrogation is a topic of great interest to all; however, it should be noted that when properly executed there should be no serious repercussions. The content of this short paper is attributed to information gathered from MAJ Sean M. Condron of the Staff Judge Advocate School Charlottesville, Virginia and Lieutenant Colonel David M. Price of the Utah National Guard who was assigned to Abu Ghraib at the time of the incidents; however, he was not involved in the abuses nor was he prosecuted for any violations.

Compassion Downrange: Ethical Concerns for Military Interrogations & Detainee Treatment

By
Heath Bell

In the past few years, the United States Military has been under scrutiny concerning its ethical behavior, especially regarding detainees and terrorist suspects (Johnston and Risen, 2004). Although there has been a black eye dealt to the military by a few individuals within the military, their behavior does not represent the military as a whole. It has been my direct experience from a soldiers' point of view, that the United States Military is in my opinion the best trained and equipped military, and that our training is directly reflected in our outstanding behavior and actions in areas of the world dominated by constant physical and emotional stress.

My background is military. My father was a Green Beret in the Vietnam War, and since he was my most influential role model growing up, I followed in his footsteps. He taught me at a young age the Special Forces Creed, De Oppreso Liber. It means to free the oppressed (FM 3-05, 2006). With that thought in mind I joined the military. I graduated Infantry School when I was nineteen, Airborne School when I was twenty, and then continued my military career in the Special Forces. As Gwynne Dyer wrote in his book War (1985), it is easier to make young men believe in what they are fighting for (Dyer, 1985). Well, I was young then, and at twenty seven years, I still believe.

In The Global War on Terror I was deployed to Southwest Asia, where I fought with the Command Joint Special Operation Task Force. We were primarily deployed to Afghanistan, but we managed to end up in various other countries along the way. I worked with Special Operations Soldiers on the battle front and there were times that our stress level was very high. Despite this I never saw anybody, even in the heat of battle, disrupt their military bearing and do anything that would embarrass themselves, their unit, or their country. Everybody kept their calm about them in a world of chaos.

The direct concern with ethical behavior in the military is reflected by the way that we treat detainees, and particularly how we interrogate them. As mentioned before, the military was dealt a black eye by the events in which a few individuals participated. Most notably was Abu Ghraib, a scandal that happened in Iraq during the time I was in Afghanistan (Shanker, 2004). Although the vast majority of soldiers did not have any direct involvement to what happened in Abu Ghraib, all soldiers felt the sting and backlash throughout the military. As professional soldiers we knew that what had happened was wrong, and we felt strongly that it should be corrected. It should also be noted that the individuals who were involved with the Abu Ghraib prison scandal were not interrogators, they were in fact military police. Their actions were individual and despicable, and they have received punishment.

The actions of a few soldiers have painted a horrible picture of the soldiers responsible for collecting human intelligence. It has produced the image that soldiers use methods of torture and abuse to gather information. That however is not the case, and the soldiers who are responsible for collecting this information are being trained to use very civil and humane techniques to gather human intelligence.

Ninety Seven Echo is the Military Operation Specialty that designates a soldier as a human intelligence collector, or better known as an interrogator. These are the soldiers who have been tasked to collect information from detainees, and transfer it down range as soon as possible to other soldiers requiring the information in the field (2007). Ninety Seven Echoes train at Fort Huachuca Arizona. They know exactly what is required of them, and the specific code of conduct used for dealing with human intelligence (FM 2-22.3, 2006). Any good interrogator will tell you that torture is not acceptable, it is not humane, and it has never been condoned as reliable. Also, as Colonel Grossman explains in is book On Killing (1996), people have the innate concern with not wanting to hurt other people. For these reasons, and many more, interrogators take a very personal approach to their jobs. This help to ensure that information is transferred down range as soon as possible with the most accurate and up to date intelligence. Good interrogators do not compromise themselves, and would not bring shame to themselves, their unit, or their country. Good soldiers hold themselves to the high standard set forth by The Soldier's Creed (STP 21-24, 2006).

Although Ninety Seven Echoes are the primary human intelligence collectors for the military, there are occasionally needs for a field interrogation (FM 3-05, 2006). It is during these interrogations that there is a margin for higher error, or so it would seem. It is no secret that during combat operations the military takes people into custody. Many times we capture detainees right after a firefight, an ambush, or in some cases ordinary patrols during which emotions run high. Very often it is imperative that we collect immediate information to protect ourselves and the indigenous Afghani soldiers who fight with us. In these cases we are given permission by our commanders to conduct field interviews and gather the required information (FM 3-05, 2006). Again, I have never participated in or seen anyone else participate in any behavior that would endanger a detainees' physical or psychological well being. The interrogations that we conducted were professional and accurate.

One such incident in which I was involved happened while I was pulling security at a Forward Operating Base near Baghram, Afghanistan. Because of the nature of Special Forces, we rely on the native Afghanis to help us succeed. One of the particular ways in which we help the local people is by giving them jobs on our posts, to help them support their families and their interests. No doubt, there is a large concern for security when letting civilians into our compound, and we combated this by conducting thorough searches on every local civilian who entered the compound. However, things frequently managed to be smuggled either in or out. On this particular day, I was at the front gate when a group of Afghanis came to work. I lined them up and my partner pulled security by watching over me while I searched everyone. The searches include checking their hats, waistbands, shoes, and then thoroughly patting down the rest of their body. Since this was not an unusual event, everyone knew what was expected. However, about the third person through the line started to act like he did not know what I was talking about. This was a common ploy used against us. If a person did not know what we were saying, then they thought they might not be held responsible. However, I was not going to let him slip by my security, so I took longer to do my search than I usually did. I made gestures for him to take off his hat and shoes, at which time he started acting very suspicious.

He removed his hat, but not his shoes, and when I physically had to touch him he tried to run. I immediately detained him, and my partner called for help. When help arrived I explained what had happened, and our watch commander agreed that he was acting far too suspicious, and gave us permission to finish searching him. When I removed his shoes, he had a battery and some wire hidden in one of them. Naturally there was no reason for him to have these items, so it alarmed us. We then received permission to interrogate him about these particular items, and through our process we learned that he was smuggling in a bomb, and had the intention to set it off later that night near one of our barracks.

Through the whole process I treated the individual with respect. I made thorough communication, and even signaled my intentions. Even after he tried to run, I used only the force necessary to detain him, and then treated him as fairly as possible while in my custody. I had my concern for safety, my partners' concern for safety, and the detainees' concern for safety all at the top of my mind. However, I also was concerned about how my actions would be perceived by my commander, my friends, and the person whom I had in custody. My military bearing was as important to me right then as it was when I had first learned it at Fort Benning. Furthermore, the interrogation process that we used was thorough. It was direct dialogue through an interpreter, and I believe that because I had treated him fairly, he was willing to work with us, and give us the information that we needed to save lives.

Although this story was unique to me, every Soldier, Marine, Sailor and Airman receives the same training. We all know what is expected of us, and we all know to keep our wits about us in a world of chaos. We are trained to take responsibility for our actions. We know what behavior is expected of us. We also are held under an obligation to follow orders, and that leads to another aspect of ethical behavior (STP 21-24, 2006). What about the orders that are given by command? Were we given orders to mistreat detainees? Were we expected to harm detainees in the act of national security? The answer is no, of course not.

The military is a type of loyal and secretive place. Young soldiers are taught that if a command is given, they follow it. There is very little room on the battlefield for second guessing orders, so obedience is a necessity in the chain of command. This obedience is preached over and over again through drill and ceremony, through firing line exercises, and through physical fitness. Every soldier knows that a command that is given is a command that is completed (FM 6-22, 2006). It is this type of Pavlovian conditioning that leads people to believe that an order coming from the top of the chain of command will come through unhindered to the lowest possible level. This, however, is not the case.

The military runs simultaneous missions at every level. A leader is expected to be able to disseminate the necessary information to the appropriate people at the appropriate time. Because of security restrictions, and pure mission interests, the information that is needed is the information that is passed down (FM 6-22, 2006). So my point is that at some high level of upper management, somebody did not pass down the message that John Ashcroft gave permission to use torture on terrorist suspects (Johnston, Risen, 2006). No one ever told me or anyone that I know that we should mistreat detainees. Nobody told us to try unethical tactics on people in our custody. I think that that shows that somewhere in the military there is an ethical concern for how we treat detainees.

I understand that there is certain unpopularity for the war in Iraq. I understand that there have been a very few accounts of soldiers doing the wrong thing at the wrong time. It is a disgrace, but in no way should the actions of a few misguided people overwrite the amazing things that our soldiers are doing in the face of impossible odds. War is hell, and nobody likes to be there, especially the soldiers faced with chaos everyday. I believe that soldiers have an ethical compassion for the people for whom they are fighting for and against. I believe that that compassion compels them to help the people of Iraq and Afghanistan, and I believe that soldiers will always act compassionately and ethically towards oppressed people. De Opresso Liber is the Special Forces Creed. It means to free the oppressed, and through our ethical concern and behavior to both detainees and civilians, we will free them (FM 3-05,2006). They will not remain oppressed.

Bibliography

(2007). Careers and Jobs. Retrieved February 22, 2007, from Go Army Web site: http://www. goarmy.com/JobDetail.do?id=152

Shanker, Thomas (2004, March 21). *The Struggle For Iraq: The Military; 6 G.I.'s in Iraq Are Charged With Abuse Of Prisoners*. New York Times, p. A1.

Dyer, G (1985). *War*. London: Guild.

FM 2-22.3 Human Intelligence Collector Operations. (2006). FM 2-22.3 (1st ed., Washington D.C.: Department of the Army.

FM 3-05 Special Operations Forces. (2006). (1st ed., Washington D.C.: Department of the Army.

FM 6-22 Army Leadership. (2006). FM 6-22 (1st ed., Washington D.C.: Department of the Army.

Grossman, D (1996). *On Killing*. New York, NY: Back Bay Books.

Johnston, & Risen, D, & J (2004, June 27). The Reach of War: The Interrogation; Aides Say Memo Backed Coercion Already in Use. *The New York Times*, p. 1.

STP 21-24 SMCT. (2006). (2nd ed., Washington D.C.: Department of the Army.

Ethical History:
A Contradiction in Terms?

By
Albert Winkler

It is curious that as many historians struggle to make their discipline meaningful to students, these instructors often rob the subject matter of its most fascinating and important aspects. History has long had the reputation of being among the most boring of all courses, and many young people look on their experience with the topic as a bunch of senseless and meaningless facts and dates. Some of this problem relates to the approach historians use which kills any interest their students might engender in the discipline. Among the biggest failings of the profession is a strong tendency to take humanity out of one of the most humane of all studies. In short, rather than giving students examples of moral accomplishments, history does the exact opposite. In many aspects, the historical profession is morally bankrupt by praising killers, by ignoring the peace makers, and by intimidating students rather than inspiring them. Rather than a vehicle for social change and moral action, sometimes history has degenerated to a profession of excuses and cover ups in which anything and everything is justified, forgiven, or praised.

In his book *Killing the Spirit*, which was an indictment of higher education in the United States, Page Smith has argued that when scholars refuse to use "value judgments" they present information that has no value. Smith also referred to questionnaires given to incoming freshmen at prominent American universities, which asked the students what they wanted to receive from their education. Many responded that they wanted the means of understanding humanity and getting information to help them make better decisions. Smith argued that these students were being short changed in the valueless instruction given to them.

Many historians have long been praising immorality and denigrating morality. They continually say that history does not teach lessons, clearly ignoring the ethical behavior of literally billions of human beings over several millennia as though their experience has nothing to teach us about proper conduct. Recently, I watched a program on C-SPAN in which several prominent historians were sitting in a panel in a bookstore. One of the participants was James McPherson, an important Civil War historian. These esteemed scholars took questions at the end of their presentations and an attendee at the session asked them if history teaches lessons. In every case, their responses were negative. One of them indicated that history might teach lessons, but we are unclear what they might be. In all fairness to these scholars, they answered the enquiry on a relatively minute level apparently assuming that the question referred to a partisan political interpretation of the past. Nonetheless, I was shocked because I believed very strongly that I could come up with a simple list of lessons almost off the top of my head. This would include much that is manifestly obvious such as peace is better than war, democracy is better than tyranny, freedom is better than slavery, toleration is better than bigotry, and life is better than murder. But despite my obviousness, I must freely admit that many historians have made reverse arguments to every supposition I just made. Rather than argue that history does not teach lessons, I assert that history is actually a gigantic morality play in which all kinds of human activities have been demonstrated in numerous cultural contexts. I also assert that the range of human experience has much to teach the modern world, and the importance of such knowledge is of some significant value to our students.

In the motion picture *Judgment at Nuremberg* about the travesty of the Holocaust, the screenwriter, Abby Mann, has one of his characters lament about the moral ambivalence of the German people to the Holocaust. The character, Ernst Janning, a convicted criminal with a conscience nonetheless, shouts in dismay, "What were we? deaf, dumb, blind" to the evil around us. I sadly admit that many historians are clearly "deaf, dumb, and blind" to evil.

One of the more insightful observers of the Nazi regime was Albert Speer, who served as Hitler's armaments minister and spent twenty years in prison for the crime of using forced labor. A criminal with a conscience, Speer was the only defendant at the Nuremberg trials who pled guilty to his crimes. After his release from prison, he wrote three books on his experiences and granted many interviews. In one of these, he kept referring to the lesson of the Nazi regime. Finally, the interviewer asked him what this lesson was. Without hesitation Speer responded, "You should never suppress public opinion." I have found this observation or value judgement on the past to be a very insightful, and it has stimulated my thinking on many historical topics in a very profound way. It has clearly helped me in understanding other historical issues better. And I believe strongly that if Speer said there was nothing to be learned from the Nazi experience, he would have been doing us all a grave disservice. Albert Speer also gave other reasons for his moral failure as a human being. As a trained architect, he claimed that his education had taught him the esthetics of buildings, but it failed to teach him anything about moral conduct. He clearly indicated that his ability to make immoral decisions was in part fed by an education system that failed to teach him to prize humanity. In a like manner, I fear that history teaching also robs our students of the ability to feel and to understand the human condition and moral conduct.

There have been numerous attempts to understand evil in society, and many theories have been argued. Among them is the idea that child abuse makes people more prone to violence and cruelty. In her book *For Your Own Good: Hidden Cruelty in Child Rearing and the Roots of Violence*, Alice Miller, a German psychiatrist, gave this theory a broad interpretation, including the historical framework. In her attempt to make the Nazi era in Germany more understandable, she took a hard look at what she considered to be the misuse of history. According to Miller:

> Would it be desirable to raise our children to be people who could hear about the gassing of a million children without ever giving way to feelings of outrage and pain? Of what use are historians to us if they are able to write books about it in which their only concern is to be historically and objectively accurate? What good is this ability to be coldly objective in the face of horror? Wouldn't our children then be in danger of submitting to every new Fascist regime that came along?"

The term "objective" is often used as the epitome of historical methodology. According to this idea, if we achieve the ability to look at every human act and condition without bias or emotion, then we have reached the height of our profession and can do truly good work. The important historian of Western Civilization, Will Durant, who has written 11 masterful volumes on the human cultural experience, made an interesting observation: "There is nothing in historical writing so irritating as objectivity." Of course, true objectivity does not exist because every scholar unavoidably brings his or her own biases to the subject matter, and the attempt to be objective is simply another case of partiality. I must say I believe strongly in the historical method. All competent historians need to examine the sources as carefully as possible and try to understand history from all different angles. But I also strongly believe that historians have the obligation to point out the faults and failings of historical characters. This is not to say that all history should be pejorative and presented to justify any and all preconceptions, but I am arguing that sometimes it is necessary to take some kind of moral stance to understand better.

One method by which historians dodge any moral responsibility for examining the human record is to state that we cannot judge the past. They assert that to do so is to place our own values on the activities of others, and this is simply distorting a proper view of history. I find this to be very amusing because historians judge the past continuously. After all, that is our job. I was very surprised when I was watching a program on television dealing the bombing of Hiroshima during the 50th anniversary of that event. A prominent military historian from Brigham Young University simply stated that we should not judge historical actions or the decision to drop the Atomic Bomb, which killed 50,000 human beings. Clearly, he believed we must not judge the moral activities of anyone in the past.

I recently read in a text book relating to Western Civilization the idea that we must not judge even the most egregious crimes. The text was referring to a slaughter of people and the enslavement of societies. I find this to be very curious. The text spent much space judging many civilizations' art, literature, architecture, philosophy, political ideologies, and technical advances just to name a few. But we must never judge their conduct! We need not place our values on another society to criticize what their citizens did, and we can clearly use the criteria of the civilizations themselves. We need only to take the perspective of the victim to criticize. No one has ever been able to answer the question as to why the injured party is irrelevant in a crime. In fact, this is absurd. After all, virtually every legal system in the world and every concept of justice demands that we examine crimes from the standpoint of those hurt by them. We can well imagine what the victims of murder were thinking when they were killed, and I seriously doubt any of them were using historical perspective to say that their deaths were justified or that their suffering did not matter. The great Renaissance scholar, Garrett Mattingly, once argued that the primary function of all history is to do justice no matter how belatedly. He clearly stated that justice should always matter, but many scholars are fleeing from that very concept by trying to excuse everything.

In their quest to understand, to be objective, and to forgive anything and everything, historical determinists believe that what happened in the past was destined to be and no other alternative was possible. According to this theory, people of the past had no choice but do what they did because of historical forces far beyond their control. This is ridiculous. I am completely convinced that I have choices. For example, when I leave my house, our neighbor's cat often comes to me and meows clearly asking for a hand out of cat food. Every day, I have the choice among other things to kick the cat or give it something to eat. No social, religious, or historical trends take away my ability to choose my conduct and make me give food to that cat, and I believe historical characters had choices as well. We often forget that no historical character ever lived in the past or the future for that matter. Without doubt, every person always lived in the present from his or her own perspective. Every moment of their lives they faced decisions and many alternate choices, just as I did when I gave the cat some food. Sometimes historical characters chose to act in a responsible and humane manner, but unfortunately they also chose to act in a brutal and harsh manner. But they always had a choice.

As a point of reference, let us briefly reexamine the issue of the Holocaust, and refer once again to the example as expressed by Alice Miller. In this case, I freely admit that I am being facetious, but I am being so to show the absurdity of historical determinists. As is well documented, the Nazis murdered about one million babies and small children. Many of these unfortunate victims were burned alive, and we know that these unfortunate and innocent children cried and writhed in their mortal agony as they died. If we take the perspective that historians must not judge, then the distress of the babies makes no sense. The little ones just failed to understand the proper historical perspective in their cries of anguish. After all, murdering babies is just what the Nazis did. We should not judge those mass murderers, and we should never put our values on them. If you think this is absurd please note how many times such actions have been justified by historians. When Hitler ordered prisoners of war to be murdered that is considered to be a crime, but when Napoleon did the same thing it is considered to be glorious. I sadly fear that the Nazis will eventually be excused much as Napoleon and many mass murders of the past. It is only a matter of time before the Holocaust will be understood as a historical event that we should never condemn but only seek to justify.

I think we could also ask a similar question of ourselves. If I were the whipped slave or the victim of prejudice and pain, I must wonder if I would look at my persecutors and believe that they just did what they had to and my agony does not matter. We must never forget that all humans in all ages have much in common. Just as is the case with all people, if you cut me, I bleed. If you hurt me, I cry.

Hitler is a case study in evil, but we often overlook some of the means by which he justified himself. In many respects, he used the historical record, or the common interpretation of the historical record to justify himself. As a young, impoverished man on the streets of Vienna, he often borrowed books from libraries at a nominal fee, and he often read about the significant figures of history. No doubt, he was aware of the "greats" of history such as Peter the Great, Frederick the Great, Catherine the Great, and Napoleon. One of the many features all of these persons had in common was the huge suffering and great loss of life caused by their policies, practices, and wars. But all this is forgotten in history's mad rush to praise killers and denigrate peace makers. In the same generation of most of these so-called greats, Joseph II ruled in Austria. He gave his people religious toleration, and he lowered the huge tax burden on the poor. He also freed the serfs, discontinued censorship, built hospitals, expanded education, and even allowed poor peasants to enter public parks. His policies were among the most enlightened and progressive of his age, but Joseph II is often forgotten not only because of the fact he conquered no one in war, but also because he simply failed to kill enough people and spread sufficient misery.

Hitler actually used the historical perspective, and how it is often interpreted, when ordering his men to be brutal in the attack on Poland in 1939. He even referred to Genghis Kahn, one of the most brutal men ever, by saying that his slaughters were forgotten, and he was only remembered as a founder of a state. In his own admonition to his troops, Hitler also referred to the Armenian Genocide, which was the butchery of one million Christians in Turkey in 1915, stating clearly that this brutal event is simply forgotten. Napoleon is another case in point. He took power illegally in a military coup, made up millions of votes to support his actions, destroyed freedom of expression in the theater and the press, tortured those who disagreed with him, enslaved peoples, subverted religion, denigrated women, murdered millions of men in insane and senseless wars, and destroyed hundreds of towns and thousands of villages while ravaging Europe from Lisbon to Moscow. His real legacy is rape, plunder, and ravages and the spread of his brand of military dictatorship everywhere he went. And still he remains one of the most praised and popular characters in all of history. Roughly 100,000 books have been written about him almost all of which find many reasons to praise him. I fully expect that those who applaud such mass murders are secretly in love with power and want to have lived such a life of dominance and butchery. In these cases, I believe that the weak want to forgive the strong in order to emulate them at least in their own minds.

There is an old saying that "to understand all is to forgive all." I wonder if we should, therefore, understand Ted Bundy, Klaus Barbie, or Joseph Mengele and forgive them. I would look at this statement and change it to something like "to understand all is to forgive nothing." Or "to understand all is to condemn more completely." Maybe we would actually be wise to shock and offend our students a bit more often to get the point across that many incorrect and immoral decisions have been made and have severe consequences.

The historical figures that have garnished the most attention tend to be power brokers. Truly admirable characters such as Black Kettle, a Cheyenne chief who worked tirelessly for peace until he was murdered by George Armstrong Custer's men, are simply forgotten. Needless to say that George Armstrong Custer is known to almost every American, and his most-famous legacy is murder. Henry Bergh who worked tirelessly to end child abuse in America is passed over without mention. Such characters are just thrown on the dung-heap of history ever to be ignored and forgotten. I recently asked a class of more than thirty students, mostly history majors, if they knew about Belgian relief during World War I and how Herbert Hoover and others saved the lives of millions of innocent people during and after the war. Even though this was one of the most admirable American accomplishments, the students met me with blank stares and frank admissions that they had never heard of it.

Many have argued that slavery is not a moral evil and that it had many positive features. Some have added that mass murder is excusable even when the cause is not admirable. I once had a conversation with a historian of the American West who argued that the theft of Indian lands, the degradation of Native Americans, the incarceration of many nations of peoples on hell-holes we call reservations, and the premature death of thousands of people were simply unavoidable, and he asked what else could have been done. My response was, "How long of a list do you want?"

In the historian's moral ambivalence, many of them have the attitude that what they say or write does not matter. I take the complete opposite approach. What we say matters a great deal. I am often reminded of Voltaire who took on every brutal cause in Europe for decades. In more than 100 cases, he fought any injustice and the use of torture. His pen was so powerful that torture was soon made illegal in many countries, and the judiciary systems of Europe began to be less brutal and more honest. In a like manner, what we say can truly make a difference. I often urge my history students, who will soon have the opportunity to speak and write on numerous historical issues, to attack immoral people and brutal actions with their words.

My first interest in the past was in the realm of military history. Later when I was attending college during the Vietnam War, my professors challenged my interest in the topic by accusing me of being in favor of war. I argued the exact opposite by stating that I studied war for the same reasons medical doctors study disease, to understand it in order to prevent it or even offer some cures. In a like manner, I think that historical areas should be examined to learn something of value from them, and to urge everyone to make better decisions.

When I published my first academic article many years ago, I addressed a massacre of about twenty Indians in Circleville, Utah. I did my level best to understand the event from the standpoint of all involved, but my conclusion was that these unfortunate victims were simply murdered. I believe that this conclusion was substantiated by the evidence, and I did not back off from this moral judgment. My most recent articles have dealt with the destruction of Jews in Germany at the approach of the Black Death in the Middle Ages. The scenes were horrible. On the basis of prejudice, improper court proceedings, and groundless rumor thousands of innocent people were burned alive. Once again, I have done my best to understand what happened and why, and I am as convinced as I can possibly be that the mass murder of Jews at that time was completely unjustified. In my opinion, to say anything else, such as we should not judge or these events did not matter, would be intellectually dishonest, historically inaccurate, and morally indefensible.

When I have told my students that I still feel sorry for my friends who suffered and died in Vietnam while fighting a brutal, senseless, and immoral war, I have been criticized for doing so. One student suggested that my fallen friends would not want me to feel so sorry for so long. No doubt, he thought there is no reason why I should bring up something so disturbing. Clearly, I have no idea what these dead men could possibly think of me now, but nothing excuses me from trying to look at their experiences and learning something from them. Also, I cannot image these men wanting me to forget them or disregard what happened to them. I firmly believe that my attempts to understand the events and crimes of the past has given me a broader perspective, and the effort has helped me greatly in my attempts to become a better human being. I am loath to admit what kind of bigot I was as a young man and how I used to denigrate minorities and think war was a grand adventure even as my friends were killed in Vietnam. But my reading of history books on the struggle of humanity and my attempts to understand war led me to reexamine my values, and I found them terribly misguided. I sincerely believe that the values I have learned from my study of history have made me a better human being, and I also strongly believe that the examination of human conduct from an ethical perspective may help our students as well.

One of the great burdens of history is the fact that nothing can change the past. This means that any injustice or needless suffering that has ever occurred cannot be altered, but I hope I will mourn for these errors for my entire life. But I also believe strongly that we ignore the human experience at grave peril to ourselves. It is my opinion that we can make progress in preventing the problems of the past by examining them carefully and condemning what needs to be condemned. But we must also praise that which is admirable. Rather than being value neutral, the past can enlighten us and give us examples of proper and improper behavior that can guide us to make better decisions. We should make it clear that improper or immoral decisions can lead to grave consequences. Only by this means can we historians hope to prepare any future generation in what they need to know to make human existence more tolerant and compassionate.

2300
and Still Counting

Choreographed by
Angela Banchero-Kelleher

(The following text describes a dance performance from the session on Ethics and The Arts)

A rt has long been recognized as a vehicle for social change, as a Modern Dancer I come from a long lineage of dancers and choreographers who saw it as their duty to expose the injustice that they saw around them. Starting with the New Dance Group in 1932, which was a response to the terrible deprivation of the depression and the oppression of Americans, dancers have often sought to identify themselves with those who lack a voice. Ethical considerations abound when one considers the role of art as a vehicle for social change. My piece, *2300 and Still Counting*, presents a viewpoint that may not be shared by all of the performers. The following comments seek to explain my viewpoint regarding the use of students in Faculty choreography.

2300 and Still Counting is my response to those who literally no longer have a voice. 2300 and Still Counting was choreographed in the spring of 2006. The American death toll in the Iraq war conflict is now well over 3000, a staggering increase in only a few short months. This administration has sought to manage this war through the selective release of information about the war. I believe that this is a deliberate effort on the part of the Government under the guise of national security to keep Americans from fully FEELING the consequences of our actions. Regardless of your beliefs about the legitimacy of this war, it is our American duty to bear witness to the American men and women who are giving their lives in this conflict.

This piece brings up many issues, one is central to the Educator/Student dialogue; what is the nature of the relationship between art and education? As a College professor I am aware of the delicate interplay between academic/artistic freedom and the responsibility as an educator that I have to students who may be chosen to perform in my work. There are several issues that arise from this area of concern. What is the nature of the responsibility that we as educators have to students? Do we automatically remove the opportunity for students to work with difficult material because of a perception of its controversial nature? How do we as faculty create a place for students to decline to participate given the power inequality inherent in the professor/student relationship? What is the ethical response to a situation like this?

I believe a solution to the issues that arise over controversial material can be found in a commitment to the idea that the possibility of artistry exists in all human endeavors and the nature of the questions that an artist asks is ultimately the same one "How do the choices I make reflect my ability to bring this idea forward". As educators we are able to be artists. If we hold to the idea that we are providing opportunities for learning for our students then the choice about how to proceed when there is conflict can be made more clearly. It is not always in the best interest of learning to seek to manage the difficult, the controversial, the challenging for our students. Students are able to opt out of the learning experience but they bear the consequences of their choices and that is an important learning moment as well.

As an educator I understand the sensitivity to material that is presumed to be controversial, but I believe that it is here that one can have the most opportunity for growth. By constantly removing the opportunity to deal with material that is perceived to be difficult, we manage our student's education in a way for them that, in my opinion, is akin to the way the Bush administration has managed our access to information about this war. Not all of the student performers agree with my take on the issue, many of them did not really have an opinion at all. As a human being who strives to behave in an ethical manner, I have to be upfront with my dancers about my viewpoint. I strive to maintain open channels of communication in order to allow for discussion of the issues. My art compels me to explore the more difficult issues, I look forward to the support of the department and college as I continue to develop as an artist educator and I also welcome the opportunity to explore the difficult moment with my student dancers.

UVSC Student Dancers: Performing "2300 and Still Counting"

The Tuskeegee Experiment

Choreographed by
Nicole Ortega
(The following text describes a dance performance from the session on Ethics and The Arts)

The Tuskegee Experiment is a piece I choreographed, in an attempt to heighten the awareness of the tragic experiment conducted between 1932 and 1972 in Alabama. Students were involved in the creative process as a means of increasing in their understanding of this event and enhancing the performance quality. In several sections of the choreography, students were asked to create their own movement given specific instructions. In one section, students were instructed to create movement based on what it would feel like to have the effects of a disease take over different parts of their bodies. Many sections of the piece were created by utilizing the names of the Tuskegee victims to inspire the choreography. Each student was given a victim's name and asked to create movement by writing the name in the air or on the floor using different body parts. This allowed the students to "become" a Tuskegee Experiment victim and to understand the severity of this incident. Most of the students involved in this piece had difficulty comprehending that this level of injustice took place in the United States. This piece was created to inform, remind, and inspire the dancers and the observers to take action.

UVSC Student Dancers: Performing "The Tuskegee Experiment"

About
the Contributors

DR. MARY ALLEN, PhD. University of Maryland, adjunct at UVSC since 1999 has taught at an embarrasing number of universities, treasuring them all.

ANGELA BANCHERO-KELLEHER is a Choreographer and an Assistant Professor of Modern Dance at Utah Valley State College.

HEATH BELL served in the Global War on Terror in Afghanistan with the Command Joint Special Operations Task Force where he was involved with combatant interrogations. Heath is a Student at Utah Valley State College.

KATHERINE BLACK, JD is an Associate Professor of Accounting at Utah Valley State College.

TED BUTTERFIELD was a student of Ruhul Kuddus at Utah Valley State College where he assisted professor Kuddus with this research.

ROB CARNEY, PHD. is the author of Weather Report (Somondoco P 2006), and Boasts, Toasts, and Ghosts (Pinyon P 2003). His poems and shorts have appeared in Flash Fiction Forward (Norton 2006) and many literary journals.

F. DENNIS FARNSWORTH, JR. is Professor of Political Science. His research interests include organizational theory, corporate cultures, American Foreign Policy, and Foreign Policy of the Peoples Republic of China.

LTC RONALD E. FISCHER, Assistant Professor of Military Science and Recruiting Operations Officer for UVSC. Earned BA and MA from BYU and MBA from Kansas University. Deployed to both Bosnia and Kosovo and worked for Balkans Task force at the Defense Intelligence Agency (DIA).

DR. KATHRYN FRENCH is Professor of Behavioral Science. Her research has been in early atypical development, and she is currently involved in an oral history of Utah peace and justice activists.

MARY ELLEN GREENWOOD earned her Masters degree from Utah State University and taught composition there before joining UVSC as an English instructor in the fall of 2004. Her research areas of interest are curriculum development, college composition, folklore, and memoir.

LARRY D. HARTMAN, PHD. is an associate professor of Business Management at Utah Valley State College

CAROLYN HOWARD-MORRIS is an Assistant Professor of Law and a practicing attorney in criminal defense and family law. She has conducted over 250 hours of mediation, primarily with juveniles in the victim-offender program. Carolyn is also the Paralegal Director for the Legal Studies Department. She is the author of "Conflict Resolution in Business and Personal Disputes." She has a husband and one son, named Matthew.

JILL O. JASPERSON, JD. is an associate professor of Legal Studies in the School of Business at Utah Valley State College. Her research interests include service learning, legal ethics, Chinese law and intellectual property.

DAVID CLARK KNOWLTON, PHD. is associate professor of anthropology. His research involves social change in the Andean region as well as transnational religion.

DR. OLGA R. KOPP is an Associate Professor of Biology. Her research area of interest is Plant Molecular Biology.

DR. RUHUL KUDDUS is a member of the Biology Department of UVSC. He served as the Scholar in Residence for the American Society for Microbiology (2006) and was selected the UVSC Faculty Scholar of the Year in 2007. Dr. Kuddus' research interests include social impacts of biotechnology.

DR. SUSAN R. MADSEN is an Associate Professor of Management and the Administrator and Chair of the Institutional Review Board at UVSC. Her research areas are leadership development, ethics in higher education, work-life issues, and faculty development.

DIANNE MCADAMS-JONES is an Assistant Professor of Nursing Science. Her research areas of interest are Music in Adult Learning, Human Nutrition and Obesity, The Right to Live vs. the Right to Die and Organ Tranplants.

JEFF MCCLELLAN is the Director of Advisor Training at Utah Valley State College.

RICK MCDONALD, PHD. is an Associate Professor of English and the Associate Director of the Ethics Center. His research areas of interest are Medieval and Renaissance Literature, Medieval Mysticism, and College Pedagogy.

DR. TROY NIELSON is an Associate Professor of Management and the Business Management Department Chair. His research areas of interest are mentoring, human resource management, and leadership.

NICOLE ORTEGA is a Choreographer and an Assistant Professor of Modern Dance at Utah Valley State College.

DR. ANDREA ROZTIEN, received her Ph.D. in Clinical Psychology from Texas A & M. She is an Assistant Professor of Psychology at Grand Valley State University, specializing in Clinical Child Psychology and Psychology and Law, particularly in areas related to expert witnesses and jury decision-making.

LYNN R. SMITH is a Lecturer in the Accounting Education Department, and has worked in public accounting and public school finance/administration as well as teaching at various institutions.

SHELDON SMITH, PH.D is Professor of Accounting at Utah Valley State College.

J.P. SPAGNOLO is the coordinator of Student Activities for Student Leadership & Activities at Utah Valley State College.

DR. ANTON TOLMAN is a clinical and forensic psychologist and Associate Professor in the Department of Behavioral Sciences. His research areas of interest include the assessment of violence risk, expert testimony, the practice of forensic psychology., and the application of learner centered teaching approaches in college.

OVILLA TURNBULL is currently a graduate student in communications at the University of Utah and graduated in 2004 with a integrated studies bachelor's degree with foci in communications and business management/human resources.

JANS WAGER, PHD. is an associate professor of English at Utah Valley State College and a former Associate Dean of the School of Humanities Arts and Social Sciences. Her research interests include Cinema Studies, Gender Studies, and Race & Gender in Film.

DR. ALBERT WINKLER is the history librarian at Brigham Young University. He has published in the areas of Utah history, the Indian wars, and Medieval history.

DAVID YELLS, PHD. is Associate Professor of Psychology and Chair of the Behavioral Science Department. His research interests include human memory and psychopharmacology.